Lipsticks

&

Bullets

ISIS, Crisis, and the Cost of Revolution

Fairouz Abdalla

Copyright

© Fairouz Abdalla 2017

سنصير شعباً، إن أردنا، حين نعلم أننا لسنا ملائكةً، وأنّ الشرَّ ليس من اختصاص الآخرينْ

سنصير شعباً حين لا نتلو صلاة الشكر للوطن المقدَّس، كلما وجد الفقيرُ عشاءَهُ...

سنصير شعباً حين نشتم حاجب السلطان والسلطان، دون محاكمةْ

سنصير شعباً حين ننسى ما تقول لنا القبيلة ... حين يُعلي الفرد من شأن التفاصيل الصغيرةُ

سنصير شعباً حين تحمي شرطة الآداب غانيةً وزانيةً من الضرب المبرّح في الشوارعْ!

سنصير شعباً، إن أردنا، حين يؤذَن للمغنّي أن يرتّل آية من <سورة الرحمن> في حفل الزواج المُختَلطْ

سنصير شعباً حين نحترم الصواب، وحين نحترم الغلطْ!

محمود درويش

We will be a nation, if we want to, when we learn that we are not angels, and that evil is not the prerogative of others

We will be a nation when we no longer say a thanksgiving prayer to the sacred homeland, every single time a poor man finds something to eat for dinner

We will be a nation when we can badmouth the Sultan's doorman and badmouth the Sultan himself, and walk away . . .

We will be a nation when we forget what the tribe tells us, when the individual recognizes the importance of small details

When the morality police protect the whore and the adulteress from being beaten up on the streets.

We will be a nation, if we want to, when we can celebrate a mixed marriage singing verses from Surat al-Rahman

We will be a nation when we respect the right to be right and the right to be wrong.

— **Mahmoud Darwish**

To Syria, the land of sultans, scholars and doves.

Prologue

When the noon raids began, Mother was in the outhouse, kissing an ISIS fighter.

Between one shell and another, the ginger jihadi groaned in her ear and demanded to know why she was resisting. Wasn't she supposed to obey the law and fulfil her duty in jihad?

A new shell fell and killed the answer.

The jihadi had not made it out in time – but Mother did, carrying his Kalashnikov. Her crisp white blouse stained red with blood, she staggered back to the house then sat numbly on the edge of the bed.

'Fairouz, go check on your grandmother,' she said, her voice shaking.

Another series of explosions began from up above. Carpet bombing. 'It's the Russians!' a neighbour yelled from his window.

Our house shook, cement dust filled my nose and lungs, and as debris and ash floated down from the sky, eight were killed and twenty were wounded in just two minutes. Meanwhile, a wave of sharp cries rose as people rushed out into the street only to find the road had been blown into a shallow crater by the bomb.

'Go down to the shelter!' My grandmother pushed me in the direction of the bunker, desperation etched on her face.

Only the bold stayed above ground to search for trapped bodies; bombings usually occur in twos – the second is meant for the rescuers. Panic dominated everything. Women wailed chapters from the Quran and parents tried to console shell-shocked babies as we took refuge in a dark bunker that held more of us then it was designed to accommodate. Although well accustomed to the sounds and images of war, every time the cellar vibrated madly, we huddled closer together on thin mattresses, bodies covered with splinters, wild eyes glazed with fear, wondering which neighbours were perishing outside.

There we were: Syrians sandwiched between brutal dictatorships and extremist groups – one destroying our souls from up in the sky, and the latter setting its dark presence in our lives on the ground.

'Dear God, the jets have gone,' Abu Talha called out as he unbolted the bunker door.

We crawled back into the rubble-filled street beneath the cover of darkness, hurrying to salvage what we could, inspecting the devastation caused by the latest attacks before loading bodies into pick-up trucks.

I squeezed Mother tight and put my other arm around my grandmother, and for a moment we all remained silent, still afraid of what could have happened – and tremendously relieved that nothing did.

This morning, our house still stands, albeit the windows are completely blown out. The sweeping window views of emerald-green hills, quilted with olive groves and citrus trees, are now replaced by a shoreline of human remains – fossils of normal lives. A teddy bear in the arms of a headless toddler lying on piled-up bricks and a hole through young Mohamed's Lionel Messi shirt. As the fog of dust and cordite settles, more bloodied body parts; more rubble. A lamp, a broken headboard, a torso of a woman in lingerie. Poor Syria. Different predators are treading on her exhausted body.

I squeeze my eyes shut and picture a Syria with no roadside car bombs, no Assad-Iranian snipers and no extremist forces patrolling the streets. Instead, a Syria whose air is perfumed with the subtle smell of camphor, apple-flavoured *nargileh* and jasmine flowers.

I think of summertime and my friends. When we freely held cigarettes and glasses of tea to our lips. I remember strolling miles down the souk, and succulent smells of lamb, beef, and chicken shawarma that seemed to settle my soul immediately. The women at the local fruit shop with their barrels of cumin; the hipsters at university with their skinny jeans; the old men playing backgammon all day; the neighbourhood children chasing a ball along with the stray dogs, all of them being chased by a mother brandishing a slipper.

And my beautiful boy.

I look outside the huge hole in the wall again and can see ISIS fighters jump out of an SUV to scour the wreckage. They're looking for their missing fighter. A jihadist with an Australian accent points his old Soviet machine gun to one of the rescuers. 'Your socks.' He jabs his gun in their direction. 'That is haram. We bought Islam to the people of Shaam so that they can live according to God, not foreign infidels!'

The apologetic young man nimbly bends down to remove his Homer Simpson socks. In just a manner of minutes, the stern jihadi is sure to make his way to our home – and perhaps one day to a home near you too.

'Marhaba!'

'Marhabtain, Ya Fairouz! We were waiting for you! We were just about to order.'

It was late yesterday evening when I entered the striking, beautifully lit restaurant overlooking the waterwheels on the Al-Asi River. And in Hama—perhaps only Hama – there was the most beautiful intermingling of a myriad colours; the sun at the horizon was a deep orange-red, and the sky was a riot of colours, ranging from blue to magenta to what can only be described as a golden pink. Glittering neon-green lights from the mosque minarets illuminated the cityscape, and the old-style lighting reflected against the moving waters.

Chilled-out Sabah Fakhri music blended in the air with the sweet smell of hookah smoke, and the grassy slope of a nearby park was full of families enjoying their Friday picnic. In Syria, live music and lit-up public parks call visitors to celebrate the weekend, celebrate the evening – celebrate being alive.

Inside, we watched the evening sky turn to pure blue bordering on purple as the moonlight made its way into the dining area through the vast and seemingly endless windows.

My friends had secured the table with the best view before the social butterflies started flitting in, and the consumption of *arak* had started early, giving the restaurant an air of joviality. For the night, my university friends and I abandoned all forms of schedule, assignments, and itineraries to relax a little.

Late into the night, Bassam asked sombrely, '*Ya jamaa'h*, guys, did you see the news today?'

'Do you mean about Libya? Tunisia? Egypt?' replied Reem as she dipped one hand into the baba ganoush and the other into her pocket to take out her iPhone. 'You have *got* to see how fast the Arab Spring is progressing– I'm green with envy.'

'Oh the idea of revolution – how romantic,' Firas remarked sarcastically, his words carrying a touch of malice. He had pursued Reem when we'd all first met at school, but she'd never taken to him in the same way. While he's now moved on — engaged to his cousin–sister in an arranged marriage — he remains sour, and timid Reem seems an easy target. He lashes out at her whenever the opportunity arises.

'A revolution won't happen in Syria because the Assads will just pull out their machine guns and mow people down, or are you hoping for Ahdath al-Thamaninat round two?'

Sarcasm dripped from his words. He was referring to the events of the 1980s – a dark period in Syria that reached a deadly climax in 1982 when forty thousand protesters and activists were killed in Hama. The then rulers made an example of Hama by leaving it in ruins.

Reem glanced at Firas and then down at her phone again, her cheeks slightly pink. There was an awkward silence. No one likes to talk about that time, especially the older generation, who only ever mention it in hushed terms. The thought of a repeat is unfathomable, and perhaps that is why the Syrian blogosphere has been the shyest in comparison to the rest of the Middle East. But deep inside, something tells me that the passion of the Tunisians is infectious and that sooner or later, Syrians too will be brave enough to demand political reform.

'*Shu rai'yak?* What do you think?' Reem interrupted my thoughts and the uncomfortable silence.

'*Shu biya'reefni*? Who knows?' I replied. 'But surely Bashar al-Assad has to bring in *some* kind of new tax system. If he doesn't find a way to redistribute wealth, the poor could rise up.'

Bassam half-laughed loudly and shook his head.

'Assad is an ass. Take off your rose-tinted spectacles!' snarled Madmour, who was quite drunk by then. 'All that talk of reform he is promising now is bullshit. The entire country hates him, and people just tolerate him because they have to. But his time is coming, because everyone knows his talk is cheap.'

'Shut up, all of you!' Reem glanced around the room anxiously and lowered her voice. 'Or you'll get us all in trouble.'

In Syria, we have a saying – *even the walls are informers with ears*. Paranoia has now morphed into crippling fear. As the Arab Spring unfolds in other countries, Syrian generals are wary of a Tunisia-style challenge and as a result, agents have begun to patrol every street thrice daily. At our university, it's much worse. Agents and Ba'ath spies are everywhere. Who is a student? Who is an agent? Nobody knows, any more. Nobody knows anything, any more.

12 March, 2011

I am sitting at my late grandfather's desk, a nineteenth-century exotic writing table with Syrian marquetry inlaid with mother-of-pearl. It features various-sized compartments and a secret drawer that can be released with a pin mechanism. I've admired it since I was tall enough to peer over and watch my Jido, as I called him, pen letters and write his poetry and political essays, but it is only today that I have conjured up the courage to come up to his room.

I hold up his purple ink bottle and wipe the dust from his sentimental clutter – mementos that no doubt invoked memories which inspired his writing. Suddenly, rays of sunlight hit the open window and the room is filled with warm air. As the birds chirp in the neighbour's cypress tree, I come to a realisation that writing might just be the loveliest thing in the world.

With small political protests springing up around Syria, our family have been remembering Jido a lot lately. Unlike them, I've never hailed him as a hero – or even had a chance to get to properly know about him. I've always thought that he retreated to his writing desk to escape the melancholia and the pain he held within. The savagery he faced at the hands of Hafez al-Assad's regime thirty-odd years ago, and his subsequent torture in prison, made him almost mute and a recluse. He had no words and showed little emotion. He had moved into our large family home in a village on the outskirts of Hama on his release from prison ten years ago, and I'd often felt bitter and sad . . . More so for my grandmother, who constantly reminded me to be patient with his coldness.

'Hell is better than Assad's prisons,' she'd repeat when Jido became unresponsive or angry. 'He does love you.'

The traumatic repression, Jido's struggle to translate his emotions, and the physical pain from his long-term injuries were familiar challenges for families that had men dragged away to Syria's torture dungeons during the Hama massacre. I shudder at the thought of Jido spending nearly ten years of his life in such a place . . . it's the first time I have given it deep thought.

In Syria, these events remain part of the Syrian collective memory despite being banned from public discussion, but we are the internet-savvy generation, living in an increasingly digitalised and transnational world, and I can't remain quiet about what the Syrian military units did to our family.

The grandfather that I had never known properly, the one that everyone had described as compassionate and selfless, the one who wanted to better the lives of Syrians and free them from tyranny, was a stranger to me. The grandfather I knew was someone whose hands shook so badly, he couldn't tie shoelaces or hold heavy items and had night terrors so vivid he would fall out of bed. As a child, I would yell at him to speak to me; there was no response, no acknowledgement, just a blank face . . . no words.

I begin to tidy up his desk. Pulling out the secret compartment, I find lots of old documents, a small notebook filled with his controversial poetry – the controversial poetry that landed him in prison – a faded identity card, old money, photographs – there's one photograph of him cradling and kissing the forehead of a baby girl that looks exactly like me as a newborn, taken just days after he was released by the regime. His only female grandchild at the time.

'Speak to me!' I used to shriek at him. 'In any way you choose!'

My beloved Jido, your actions always spoke louder than your words.

15 March, 2011

Time passed slowly for me as I waited in the university for Dina. All the other English language students had already left class and I was beginning to get impatient. A knock sounded at the door and Dina peeked around the corner.

'Thank God you waited for me,' she gasped, and then caught her breath again when a teacher entered to ask why we were staying behind.

'Make sure you don't stay around for long,' the teacher said in a cutting voice.

Never has the university been so tense. There were several small demonstrations earlier today around Syria, and security forces were keeping a watchful eye on students. The organisers on Facebook, who had called for Syrians to break the pervasive fear among themselves, had failed to attract large numbers, but everyone is now calling this first step the *sharara* – or spark – that will ignite the fire soon. Ground networking and grouping is taking place in Homs and Daraa, with spontaneous demonstrations expected.

'Each small demonstration will make us more hardened, bold, and experienced,' Dina whispered to me as she logged on to a computer to prepare flyers. Flyer distribution has always been the standard method of announcing events and sharing ideologies among activists – a very risqué underground activity. 'It will give others courage to follow our lead.' She grinned.

My best friend, Dina, of Armenian origin from Syria's second largest ethnic minority, had just returned from a small demonstration at the busy intersection next to Hama's clock tower. She is full of passion and energy. An outspoken student known for her strong views, she is an outstanding mistress of words. Though she is quite boyish by nature, masses of silky brown curls fall over her shoulders and she has naturally pouting heart-shaped reddish lips that tempt all the boys.

That said, anyone dismissing her as just a pretty face would be a fool. Government officials targeted her in 2009 along with other influential Syrian internet activists who were consequently detained on charges 'of inciting anti-government feelings' and 'terrorism'. While many were sentenced to long prison terms, Dina got away because of her *wasta*.

In Syria, if you know the right people you can just about get anything done. The magic W is a lubricant that smooths the way to everything – from jobs to promotions, from university places to the best bed for your sick relative in hospital.

It's all about that *wasta* (or as we call it, vitamin W), which sadly I have a deficiency of. Dina, on the other hand . . . Her uncle had an influential position at the time – I remember his huge house, surrounded by armed security guards, and his blacked-out Land Rover – the telltale sign that he was a Soviet advisor, and so, even though she equated nepotism with corruption, it worked for Dina. However, the newsletter she had created and distributed to the general public was banned, despite not being really radical. In it, she had called for minor changes – things such as the elimination of the Emergency Law, release of political prisoners, freedom of speech, freedom of press, fair elections, and the creation of a strong, independent judiciary. This time, if the regime responds with more massive force – as I suspect it will, since it is the only way they know how to respond – it is going to blow up in their face.

What I wish for is an orderly evolution of the Syrian government rather than a messy revolution. Unlike Dina and some of my other friends, I am not prepared to see the blood of Syrians spilled onto the streets.

'You should focus on a few bullet points and not get carried away printing out an entire detailed manifesto,' I told her as she typed away furiously on the keyboard.

'I'm just an average girl voicing her anger, making sure that my irrelevant voice is heard, but think about it, Fairouz – my voice next to that of another and another mounts to more than just a mere whisper.'

Dina is right. Maybe if more people were to voice their opinions and air their grievances, then we might just be able to cause a ripple. It takes just one person to push over the first domino piece, which could cause this reign of terror to come crumbling to the ground.

The weather is changeable here, the days warm and sunny, but the evenings are still cool and there is nothing more comforting than my grandmother's heart-warming *shakriya* – lamb in a delicious, creamy, tangy yoghurt sauce, piping hot and aromatic. As usual, my mother left it to her mother-in-law to make her son's favourite food. There is always competition between a daughter-in-law and mother-in-law, and the dominance of the mother-in-law is normal in every Middle Eastern family, irrespective of whether they are Muslim, Jewish, or Christian.

'*Teslam edak ya*, Mama. God bless your hand,' my father said as he smacked his lips. He is careful not to show this complete admiration when it is my mother who cooks because even though she follows the same recipes and methods, according to my father, Grandmother's food just comes out infinitely better.

'You didn't eat enough, here, let me dish you some more,' my grandmother fussed.

'Teta, please no more . . .' I pleaded. But as in any Levantine household, when offered food, no means yes, yes means double.

We ate with gusto. Not only was the food so warm and filling, but it being rather late in the day, we were all quite hungry. Syria is known for its warm yoghurt dishes, and *shakriya* is a prime example of a staple local dish. After the meat and yoghurt sauce was generously ladled over rice and served with a plate of fresh, flavourful vegetables, everyone scooped it up with their hands from the communal dish.

The calm was only disturbed by the undercurrent of television noise – Al Jazeera's breaking news showed live shots of simultaneous demonstrations taking place in Syria. A doctor was on the phone from Daraa. He was so distraught that the anchorman in Doha could hardly get in his questions as he continued to speak.

'The killing of demonstrators in Daraa today is a turning point for Syria!' the doctor yelled.

Both he and the anchorman were speaking very loudly. Images of plain-clothed Syrian police brandishing batons at protesters filled the side of the screen, and live news updates from other revolutions were running across the bottom in red lettering, like warnings from another world – a world descending into pandemonium.

The Arab world is in crisis. Anyone watching Al Jazeera at that moment could understand that fact immediately. And a lot of people here watch Al Jazeera. It has become more than just background noise since the Arab Spring began, especially among the elders, who don't have the same level of access to modern gadgets and social media. A large animated banner appeared on the screen, backed by dramatic music. The banner read: 'Online activists in Syria are calling today "Friday of Dignity".'

'Dignity? Dignity wasn't a birthright given to Syrians,' said my father, blithely ignoring my alarmed mother who had rushed to draw the shutters, fearing neighbours and passers-by would hear. Father had never demonstrated such passion against the system before, and I could see my mother's lips quiver as he continued to rant loudly, the scenes on the television making him even more furious.

My mother, Layla – a Christian – was born in the mountainous town of Maaloula, located thirty-five miles to the north-west of Damascus. Brown doe-like eyes sat underneath thin blonde eyebrows and with her striking facial features, soft blonde hair, and small waist, it is no wonder my father – a Muslim – was instantly smitten with her. Despite criticisms from naysayers at the time, Layla and Rami – or Layla and Majnoon, as they fondly called one another – ignored all concerns that their marriage would not work and got married anyway. They had recently celebrated another anniversary and had achieved three children, two cats, and happiness. Today was the first day I began to see cracks appearing in their seemingly idyllic life. Enjoying a merciful breeze at my window, I am watching the day end. I look out at our handsome open courtyard, with the rest of our indoor rooms centred around it, bordered by the *liwan*, a semi-open outdoor space that connects the interior to the exterior. It is where we socialise, eat, and spend our days. Fragrant with lemon trees and jasmine, and featuring an ornate fountain in the centre of it all, one might mistake it for a scene from Arabian Nights.

However, three other households now share the once elaborate courtyard, which belonged to my ancestors. The tenants moved in after Father was fired. He lost his job as a maths professor at the local university and has been struggling to find a new one ever since. One of his students was related to a military commander, and the student had pressured my father to award him a higher grade. My father, being my father, refused the student's well-connected family, who had not only insisted on some corrections to the exam papers, but had threatened him with severe consequences if he didn't comply.

Blacklisted for life, he now spends his days smoking, looking for work, and making bad oil paintings. Unemployment didn't only leave him devastated, it has changed the course of our lives; our middle-class abode turned into a house full of strangers.

I gaze at the gritty mother-of-pearl seats that line the wall, at the fraying red cushions, at the blue and white ornate fountain that no longer flows, and at the greying walls. Our home with its red, white and blue and grey – like the grey difficulties that my family now face in our once colourfully vibrant and comfortable world.

Today I woke up with Dina sleeping in my bedroom. She had slept over after we had marched through Hama, doing the once unthinkable: protesting.

We always walk through the sun-speckled, tree-lined Al-Asi Square with its happy dogs and men frying falafel to feed passers-by. Yesterday morning, we weren't weaving between newlyweds strolling arm in arm, nor mothers pushing carriages. Instead, people had congregated in large groups, waving banners and chanting, erecting tents and roasting marshmallows over fires. It's clear they were relishing in the thought that soon they may no longer have to play the role of docile, pliant, submissive sheep to the elite. Labourers, teachers, students, doctors, truck drivers, merchants, seculars, religious clerics, grandparents with grandchildren, people from all walks of life marched without supervision. It was a peaceful, jovial place, and we met up with Reem, Madmour, and Bassam too.

As the night on the 'Friday of Glory' darkened, I saw a jeep arrive with young, serious-faced, armed policemen who jumped off and positioned themselves behind trees and took selfies with protesters.

Hama, it seemed, was as weird and contradictory as ever.

Last weekend was eventful. Residents could be seen tearing down posters of the president – posters that are slathered on billboards and buildings on every prominent road. In fact, most Syrian households have photos of the president framed on their wall, just like the Germans who once had Hitler framed on theirs. Our mantelpiece, however, has never held any such memorabilia. This isn't because we aren't patriotic; it is because of our greater loyalty to my grandfather. Neighbours who wanted brownie points would kiss up to the regime and plaster their house and car windows with current politicians as well as dinosaurs of the regime. Today, even *they* could be seen tearing pictures down with triumphant smiles. Grocery stores dragged out barrels of ice and chilled drinks to give to the protesters. There was a not a police officer in sight. 'Are we free yet?' I asked Dina. Relieved that the streets were calm, if not fully at peace, I went home.

Fast-forward to Friday and those happy little gatherings were no more. Instead, the streets were replaced with columns of police boots and batons and pistols along with helicopters circling above. The atmosphere was eerie and suddenly I found myself in a rush of people who were scurrying down the street.

'Fairouz, come this way!' I heard Madmour's voice call.

I puffed a sigh of relief and flung myself into the cafe, where we crouched with Reem and a dozen others taking refuge inside.

'They're clearing the streets, stay inside until it's safe.' The shopkeeper pushed down his grill shutters.

Inside the cafe, blonde journalists with crocs on their feet were glued to MacBooks, typing furiously. Waves of panic filled the air as shots were fired outside. Bassam had escaped in his car. Where was Dina? Apparently last seen right at the front near the burning bins, according to Madmour. Unlike defiant Dina with her placards, our friend Firas refused to take part in demonstrations but came to rescue us anyway.

Finally safe at home, but still invariably horrified at witnessing the intensity of the anger that the regime manifested, I decided to join my grandmother in the kitchen – the one person who could always calm my fears.

'*Shu fi? Fi shi?* What's going on? Why do you look so troubled?' She handed me the chopping board with a bunch of washed parsley on it. Parsley is always washed in lukewarm, well-salted water because, according to Teta, the salt cleanses the parsley and the warmer water perks up even partially wilted leaves.

It's the perfect time to talk; the tabbouleh salad is always the first and longest preparation.

'*Mafi shi*. Nothing. It's just all this talk of the revolution.'

She handed me the curved chopping knife; Grandma strongly disapproves of food processors.

'I fear Syria might be on a dangerous path.' My eyes clouded with tears as I spoke.

'Listen, *habeebti*, there may or may not be violence, but as long as you have breath, you have to fight to survive.'

'But Teta, why can't we just have a peaceful uprising? One that leads to a change in government without any blood being shed?' I asked.

I drained the bitter excess juice from the parsley in a strainer. Some families like to add raw bulgur to their tabbouleh, but we add bulgur to the chopped tomato to soak in their juices first.

'*Ya* Fairouz, it will take time to adjust to the dramatic changes.' Her soothing voice reassured me.

'But I'm afraid, Teta. I don't want this to be another Libya.' I finished dicing the onions.

'Listen to me – we Syrians have developed a kind of defence mechanism that has helped us survive. It's easier to cope with the humiliation of living as slaves by pretending that we are well-kept slaves, after all.'

I nodded my head. I mixed the chopped-up parsley along with the bulgur and tomatoes. In went the onions and a handful of chopped mint.

'Not too much, please, it gets bitter,' grandmother reminded me. I added a swirl of olive oil, a dusting of sea salt, and also a little ground chilli pepper to give it some zing, then stirred it all before scooping it all into another large wooden bowl lined with fresh lettuce leaves.

Grandmother's face was filled with a raw look of determination as she kneaded her bread. 'The first step towards freedom is recognising that we are living in prison.'

Obviously sensing my doubts, she began to give me my first real, uncensored history lesson.

I learned that Jido had been challenging the ruling elite for the same reasons as the thousands that filled the streets today – for equal access to economic opportunities, for social justice, for freedoms of thought and expression. For a democratisation which didn't require religious mobilisation, foreign invasion, or meetings in Washington.

In a country where surveillance is a normal fact of life, where it is forbidden to reminisce over dark times gone by, and where children in schools are taught an alternate and fabricated history syllabus, I was now learning the truth.

I had no idea how gruelling it must have been for my grandmother. She is almost eighty years of age and has lost Jido for a second time. She has lived her life sacrificing herself for others. She has raised her sons and daughters with the little money she made selling bakery and preserved foods. She stood behind my grandfather, stood her ground, and remained strong in the face of adversity. She resisted the regime's threats and the secret police's terrifying visits, and she rose above the tyranny. *She* is the real hero and resistance fighter here.

She kept repeating the line '*Alf kilmet Allah yarhamu, wa la yaqoolu as-suri jabaan,*' meaning 'It is better to say rest in peace a thousand times, than to say that the Syrian is a coward.'

I watched her with new-found adoration as she slapped bread onto the side of the *tanoor* – the bread oven – the palms of her henna-coloured hands undeterred by the flames rising from the pebbles in the ground.

22 April, 2011 - Good Friday

Our rural home is always a vision during springtime, and this Easter seems like any other to start: sunshine and spring breezes and the fields overflowing with tulips. There have been memorable family moments by the intoxicating glow of candlelight, traditional sweets in silver trays, mint tea in porcelain teacups, and pretty, pleated pink skirts paired with delicate silk blouses. Having my mother's family come over to visit us has been a treat. All sat around our large dining table once again, passing food around in Mother's best china . . . There are comfortable silences and conversations that last long into the night, and it seems that, just for a little while, the diaspora outside is non-existent.

However, major elements of our usual Easter traditions are missing. Our church has cancelled some of the elaborate festivities, along with hundreds of other churches in honour and respect of those martyred in recent weeks. The only processions on the streets are those by the military. State television is broadcasting recitals of pro-Bashar poetry while wishing everyone a happy Easter. Seriously?

Ever since the trouble on the streets began, Syrian media has been trying to cling to normalcy by painting the rest of the world's media as liars, distracting the public with conspiracy theories and branding protesters and activists as Israeli agents. At one point today, my uncles expressed their dismay when a high-ranking priest appeared in front of the cameras in support of Assad's regime – most likely by coercion.

Despite our Syriac orthodox church not participating in any political activities until now, there is word that many Christians are preparing to march. Syrian Christians have long suffered under the regime, but in my opinion we've been used as a PR tool whenever the regime wanted to look good in the eyes of the West.

Despite being a Muslim married to a Christian, my father allowed his offspring to choose their faith freely. My youngest brother, Yahya, chose Islam, I chose Christianity, and the middle child, Adam, chose trouble. In a liberal household, religion wasn't taken so seriously, but for the first time, I felt myself calling desperately to God to rescue his children.

'I'd like to say a blessing,' my mother's eldest brother, Ammo Antoun, announced at the dining table. Everyone's heads were bowed down, and I closed my eyes.

'*Abana Lazi Fi Samawat*, Our Father, who art in heaven,' he began. 'We thank you for bringing us all around this table together, and for providing us with nourishment. Please continue to bless us and keep us safe. Amen.'

Lord bless the holy land of Syria, Lord have mercy on us. Amen, Muslim and Christian, we all whispered in unison.

29 May, 2011

'Now listen, Fairouz. What's said in this house stays in this house, and you can't bring attention to yourself at university or they will come to our home and rake through our lives with a fine-tooth comb.'

Mother had begun to give me such warnings every day as I kissed her goodbye. Ever since the tragic capture of fourteen-year-old Hamza al-Khatib, who was tortured and killed after scribbling anti-regime slogans on a wall with his friends, every parent worried for the fate of their child. Children are being used to scaremonger; to somehow prove the elite are so merciless as to sever children's testicles and burn them alive.

Our so-called leaders have gone on a slaughtering spree in other parts of the country. There is a heavy presence of soldiers with arms, and reminders of state security on every road we pass. Today, I felt nervous on the minibus ride to my university, which is around an hour's journey from home. Upon arrival, I found armed *Mukhabarat*, secret agents, guarding the campus entrance, and armed guards checking student identifications outside our lecture halls. They are apparently here to stay.

At our overcrowded university, students who until now have been living vicariously through the Arab Spring in neighbouring countries, are gaining momentum, and support for anti-Assad groups, both on the ground and on the internet, is growing. All eyes are on anti-government protesters in the southern city of Daraa, near the border with Jordan, who have had deadly confrontations with security forces in recent days. Deep emotions ebb and flow with every turn of event.

The news that a bloody military campaign in the cities of Rastan and Talbiseh resulted in a hundred martyrs travelled rapidly on Post-It notes throughout classrooms, carrying universal sorrow and tension.

After lessons, I met up with my friends to go to our weekly poetry reading session – my best friend Dina and I are active in the university's poetry club, serving as head co-ordinators. Even former pupils come to the university to sit in and absorb the selections of poetry.

Arab poetry is filled with themes of hardship, liberation, and emancipation, and addresses social and economic conditions, struggles between tradition and modernity, secularism and religion, materialism and spiritualism and love. However, including sensitive topics such as political and social injustice publicly in your works is not a great idea unless you want to spend your life in exile, and that's only if you're as profoundly influential as the likes of Adunis and Darwish.

'These verses were written on a table napkin in a small coffee shop near Qasr Ibn Wardan,' I told the group of students that had gathered.

Fire your bullets all you want, for our hearts are already on fire

In this land, rivers are made with tears

Fire your bullets all you want, you bloodthirsty vultures

For I won't put my pen down

My blood fertilises and pollinates this land

And plants a gifted generation that is fully alert

Limbs grow from seeds of shrapnel

Breasts are formed and our women's wombs produce more soldiers

Our ancestors are buried in this holy ground

Wherever I am, I belong here

I don't care if there are bombs

I don't mind the sound of thunder

For rain brings rainbows and flowers

When penning the poem, the Arab Spring permeated my thinking, and as I read it aloud, it's all I could think about. The audience seemed spellbound. Filled with passion, I lifted my head and recited it in classical Arabic in my best voice – copying al-Mutanabbi's lyrical style – completely forgetting everything my mother had reminded of me that morning.

30 May, 2011

Four or five in the morning is the perfect time to forcefully break into a residence with a heavy metal cylinder object and catch everyone off guard. That is what happened today . . . to us. Utter chaos, screams, and my family running in panic is the last thing I remember from this morning before Syrian plain-clothed policemen knocked me down and whipped my back so hard that I only regained consciousness at 5 p.m.

'Your daughter's skin is beautiful,' they had said, leering at my mother, their faces twisted with viciousness.

With a sore body and my mother next to me holding my hand while clutching her cross for comfort, I try to remember the events of yesterday. The delightful moment when the students at my university cheered and shouted *'Allahu akbar!'* – God is great – after my poetry recital.

The beauty of that memory is now distorted with wounds that fill my back and still hurt when I roll on the bed. The most important thing to me, however, is knowing that I have broken the silence and maybe even eliminated the fear of expressing free thoughts and ideas. I could not simply be the girl that was forced to remain silent when I knew that the stories from my grandmother I possessed could make a difference in the life and minds of others.

I was no longer the girl that didn't side with the regime nor the revolution, or the al-Samitah – the silent majority who lacked courage. If someone were to ask me if I would do it all over again, my response would be an unequivocal Yes – and in a heartbeat.

'Don't you run off to the internet cafe this morning, we have guests coming,' my mother yelled. 'Fairouz, will you *please* come downstairs and set the table?'

I couldn't refuse. Mother was exasperated.

'Fairouz!' she shouted again.

'Coming, Mama,' I replied. I had never been so pleased to hear we'd be hosting guests as I was today. The table had been laid out with cheese, olives, yoghurt, bread, and a variety of fruits and sweet treats, and we were each served chicken – a rare delicacy that we could ill afford these days. However, behind this façade, the depressive last few months had meant that the littlest luxuries in life have become scarce in our home. Father is even more reluctant to use our savings on expensive groceries and only buys what is essential to keep the household fed and warm. Grandmother says it is because he is scared a civil war will break out at any time and we need every coin we'd ever had to survive.

Today was a seldom treat, and I began to appreciate and cherish every bite of chicken and *kenafa* and take as many grapes as I could eat. I was interrupted only once by father's friend, who asked me how my university studies were going. I was too embarrassed to tell him I had been expelled. My poetry reading had been the last straw, and I had been unceremoniously escorted from the building when I had turned up for lectures a few days after. There was an uneasy silence as my mother fussed and filled up everyone's plate.

Father's long-time friend, a prominent surgeon from Damascus, is such a stunning man, both physically and intellectually. You can't look at Ammo Saleh's face and not feel a rush of warm, genuine love; he is the most authentic and perfect person we'd had in our lives and has supported Father through life's troubles. However, love for the sake of love is his most worthy talent and curse – his Lattakian wife, also exquisitely beautiful but a truly horrid woman, had left him for a younger man. He was that one person I thought our family would always have timeless contact with – Father's many years of friendship with him had made him a godfather figure to me.

After lunch, Ammo Saleh's two daughters and my mother retreated to the lounge to watch their favourite Turkish soap while his cute son, Elyas, and I followed our fathers outdoors. Grandmother had freshly polished the marble surfaces in our courtyard after morning prayers so as the afternoon sun shone brightly from above, the marble sent back the light in iridescence. Our cats Um Ali and Haleeb could be seen devouring the remnants of our meal in the corner.

'So Fairouz, *shu fi ma fi?* What's new?' Elyas asked.

I told him about some new books I've been reading and how I've just been spending the summer with friends. I'm very careful not to mention activism with Elyas since it's a sensitive topic. He has always teased me since he first heard about my interest in this revolution.

'How can you expect these religious zealots to give you your freedom?' he'd said. I had tried to defend my writings and actions, but Elyas would have none of it.

'This is just another campaign by the Muslim Brotherhood trying to retaliate for government campaigns against their members. Are you going to convert and start wearing a veil now too?'

I was uncomfortable with him likening me to Islamists, and I told him the movement was actually focused on straightforward, practical demands for everyone, whether they were religiously observant or lax, or whether they were Christian or Muslim, Sunni or Shia. But he'd read his American conspiracies and didn't want to be placed in the revolutionary camp. As I saw no polite way out of it, today I just shut up and let Elyas go on. And on. As my brothers were at a basketball tournament in Homs, I was left to entertain him by myself.

'Hey, have you seen this new movie?' He suddenly handed me a small case.

'Oh, it's the movie I've been wanting to see!' I exclaimed.

'Well, I downloaded it for you as I know it's only on in the Damascus cinemas,' he said with a grin.

I giggled. Elyas's mischievous grin was infectious, making his eyes sparkle all the more, and at that very moment I wondered if my eyes were as bewitching to him.

This new Damascene film is of particular interest to me because it highlights problems faced by minority Arab communities. Elyas, a Christian like me, understands how hard it is to uphold a Christian identity in a predominantly Muslim society. Unlike me, though, he is less bound by cultural shackles living in Damascus. He was born into the nouveau riche of the capital city, where his father has done well. He has recently purchased a second home and the children were all sent to American universities.

I looked over at our fathers lounging in the heat . . . Elyas's father doesn't practise Christianity any more than my father practises Islam. Syrians by nature are traders and practise only business. Money and business is the prominent Syrian religion. However, it was my grandparents' influence that has definitely made me identify with my Christian faith.

Later that evening, my mother deliberately switched her seat so that I could be next to Elyas at the dinner table. In fact, there has always been a distinct you-should-marry-Ammo-Saleh's-son, he-is-a-good-looking-well-off-family-friend-and-you-would-make-the-perfect-trophy-wife kind of vibe from all of the adults, who have hinted that he was more than a suitable prospect for marriage. And yet, I found myself losing all respect for him as he started spewing religious hatred towards Muslim protesters.

Interestingly, the Druze and the Christians in Syria have continued to remain, for the most part, silent – because they have been keeping to themselves. But the likes of Elyas are spreading religious-driven hate among the youth. I brought the topic up at dinner and Elyas almost choked on his food.

'I am ashamed of knowing an extremist. You cocktail Christian . . . you stupid, immature girl. Stop with your fantasies. But why should I be surprised? You have Muslim blood in you, after all.' He stood up, pushing his chair back violently, and stormed off.

Such a vehement reaction from a once sweet boy. If uniting with Christians means embracing fanatical ideologies and turning back on my Muslim counterparts, then no thanks, I'm all for division.

I sat waiting in the elegant colonial-style lobby of the Apamee Cham Palace Hotel in the centre of town. As it does anywhere in the world, conflict and disaster generate a virtual stampede of aid workers, journalists, and diplomats from around the globe to places they've never visited before. Suddenly, as history is being made, Hama is hot on the map. It was hard to find a place to sit as the place was crawling with reporters.

The hotel sits across from the water wheels – it's a modern building with a traditional neo-Oriental structure adorned with delicately sculpted pink marble columns, which hold up the marble arches. There is a fountain located in the middle of the lobby and giant portraits of the president hang on the walls.

As I waited for the journalist I was scheduled to meet – and for the cup of coffee I'd ordered – I scrolled through the March 2011 'Power' issue of *Vogue,* which featured an article titled 'A Rose in the Desert' about the first lady of Syria, Asma al-Assad. It left me with a sick feeling in my stomach. Asma always comes across as a vibrant, smart advocate of the Syrian people, but she is far from that.

Luckily, the waiter returned quickly with a steaming copper *rakweh* and a small cup on a tray, and then poured the thick liquid slowly into the cup.

'*Sahtayn*, two healths.' He offered the usual pleasantry.

'*Ala qalbak*, on your heart,' I replied before he retreated.

When the Western journalist – Robert – finally arrived, we headed upstairs for the interview. Robert had contacted me because he, like so many others, was using Twitter and Skype to communicate with activists and civilians on the ground. A battery of television cameras had been set up on the rooftop so that correspondents could film their segments with dramatic pictures of the hazy mountains in the distance. What an illusion: the footage looked remote and rugged even though filmed from the roof of a comfortable international hotel.

'How charmless and dated . . . this place needs investment to bring it back to the beauty it once was in the eighties,' Robert said as we headed on the other side of the roof where his camera crew were sitting.

A camera with a wide shot of the cityscape with its minarets, domes of Ottoman hammams, and a cluster of residential houses and markets interwoven with narrow, bustling streets was being continuously recorded so should there be a barrel-bombing or a missile strike, the world would be able to watch us all die on instant replay.

He was tall, dreamy, well-built, and had a sort of noble look about him. He was looking right at me. '*Marhaba*! I hope you don't mind some company,' he said with homegrown politeness as he took a seat.

'*Ahlayn*!' I replied.

'What brings you here?' he asked.

'I'm here to meet my friends who are coming here from a large demonstration march from Al-Masood mosque towards the city centre.'

'*La wallah*? What, really? I am here for the same reason!'

I was at the local bustling restaurant the other afternoon, hoping to hang out with Madmour, Reem, and the rest, but instead ran into what turned out to be one of Reem's cousins, Emad. We discovered our mutual association when he said he recognised me, and further probing revealed the Reem connection.

The restaurant was set in an attractively converted courtyard house in the newly pedestrianised Artists' Quarter; we sat near the entrance of the former *bayt 'arabi*, a traditional Arab courtyard home. Emad insisted on buying me a tea while we waited for the rest of our friends.

The restaurant grew busier and as people arrived for *al-ghada* – the afternoon meal and traditionally Syria's heaviest, usually served at about one in the afternoon – the ambience in the lofty courtyard became pleasant.

The low brass tables and brocade-upholstered chairs were arranged around a central marble fountain. Large goldfish inhabited the bubbling fountain in the centre and portraits of fine Arabian horses adorned the stone walls.

'How did you recognise me?' I asked him suspiciously. The waiter came to take our order.

'I've seen you before.'

'Really?' I tried to recall where we had met.

'Remember your poem recital at the night demo in Jarajmeh neighbourhood last week?'

'Aha.' My face flushed with embarrassment.

'Would you like to whet your appetite?' He glanced at his watch again. 'I'm ordering some *muqabbilat*.' He pointed to the hot and cold starters on the menu.

'The tea will do it for me, thank you. Besides, I can't help wondering what is taking the others so long.'

We talked about a recent exhibit in Aleppo, about our family, politics, life in general, the latest Lady Gaga music video – you know, the usual. He talked about his travels to Europe and how he'd taken a break from studies at Tishreen University in Latakia City.

Like his father, Emad had excelled in engineering and was also involved in the Arab student movement. His father hailed from the prominent al-Atassi family – his ancestors were heads of state in the 1960s. His family members included magistrates, governors, ambassadors, heads of political parties, military officers, and other public officials. He was born and bred in Homs but his mother is a Palestinian from Safed. His mother's family had been wealthy merchants in the tailoring trade but then came the *Nakba* – the Catastrophe – and the bloody days of the 1948 Palestine war resulted in his family fleeing to Syria.

'What about your family?' He leaned forward to give me more attention.

'Well nothing interesting, I was born to a Muslim father and a Christian mother,' I replied.

'Just like Obama then,' Emad teased. His smile was radiant.

The waiter bought over the mezze platter.

'I spent my childhood in between the majestic landscapes of Maaloula and back here on the outskirts of Hama at my grandfather's ancestral home. I'm from a middle-class family, nothing as exciting as you.'

He was silent for a moment and then shrugged his shoulders. 'The revolution has changed all of that, but it's okay. *Hayk id-dunya*, that's just the way things are, and besides, it's given me time to re-evaluate my life and realise my greater goals. I just really want to help my nation and make a difference.' His eyes were warm and sincere.

'*Hayya*, here she is!' He suddenly motioned at Reem, who had just walked in carrying a fistful of leaflets. I was relieved to see the others, who arrived behind her.

'*Ahlan, Fairouz*! I'm guessing you've already met my cousin Emad,' Reem said, bubbling with enthusiasm. Then, turning to Emad, she said '*Kaifak?*'

'*Mineeh*, I'm fine,' he replied with a nervous smile as Reem collapsed on the chair next to him.

After a couple of hours of discussion and consumption of fabulous *frareej meshweeyeh* – chargrilled butterflied chicken – in the musty warmth of the restaurant, the blast of cold, crisp evening air awakened us.

'Let's order some *nargilehs* and play backgammon.' Firas rose and gestured towards the waiters.

A few moments later, a young boy in traditional clothing glided between the maze of tables and arrived lugging a few pipes under his arms, followed by a ash-smeared man whose job it is to walk around and service pipes with the help of his portable brazier of glowing charcoal. As the waiter with his steel tongs fired the coal beside him, Emad sat backwards and leaned in closer next to me to give the man more room. His warm cheek gently caressed my bare shoulder as we moved closer. A tingle of excitement shot through my body. Alarmed, I felt my body jitter, and suddenly our thighs were touching. Emad swallowed and tried to move his leg away, but there was no room. His gaze was fixed firmly straight ahead and his face grew red with nervous heat.

Our accidental movements were unmistakable, even in the dark. Reem scrolled down on her smartphone, giving no indication of having seen anything. But as she continued scrolling, I noticed her mischievous smile and then her wink at Madmour. She'd most definitely had a hand in setting up the whole thing. It wasn't by coincidence that I'd encountered her cousin; Reem had conspired with Madmour and the others to match-make.

As much as I wanted to throttle her at that point for trying – yet again – to find me a match, I let it go. The waiter took the metal hose, sucked on to it to get the airflow going and the water bubbling, then attached the plastic clip on the end of it, and within minutes, the mound of charcoal was glowing red and Emad was releasing a curling wisp of sweetly scented smoke from the corners of his mouth.

He dragged on his hookah for a few moments then turned around to me with a boyish grin. *Oh, those provocative pastel eyes.* 'Want to smoke mine?' I felt his warm breath on my face.

Bassam, Reem, Madmour, and even Firas – who always saw Bashar al-Assad as a cosmopolitan reformer – turned up to our pre-protest meeting today.

'*Shu sar ma'ak*? What happened with you?' Reem asked Firas as he scrambled into King Food – our favourite Western fast food place – near Hama bus station.

He seemed a little shaken but insisted nothing was wrong. He had just been running from soldiers who had chased him after he failed to hand over his ID card at one of their many sandbagged army encampments. We were taking a break from the scorching heat with our sandwich meals and Pepsis as since the early hours, we'd been distributing information in the suburbs about staging points, marching routes, and alternative gatherings for those who couldn't make it to Al-Asi Square in the centre of the city.

Freedom Callers had named today the Friday of Saleh Al-Ali in honour of the old Alawite Syrian leader who fought the French occupation in 1920 and who had refused to have an independent Alawi state.

'I really hope that present-day Alawites will help topple the Syrian dictatorship,' I said absentmindedly.

'They've always been happy to be led by the Assad ruling clique. Are you out of your mind?' Madmour snapped.

'I agree, I watched leaked footage of Alawite officers insulting and actually killing protesters,' Bassam said.

'No, the government leaked that footage on purpose,' Reem insisted.

I agreed with her; I'd been speaking to secular Shiite-Alawite activists in Tartous who had been complaining about how their towns had been emptied of their youth, who had been forced to join the military to quash the uprising. The regime had been 'leaking' footage on both sides, showing rebels burning Alawites in order to scare Alawites and bring them closer.

'Look at the Alawite youth in Latakia and Banias – they've been outspoken against the regime since the start of the uprising.' I was getting angry that my friends could have such narrow views on a whole community.

'Enough of this arguing! *Wa jaa dilhum billati hiya ahsan*,' Firas ordered, referencing a verse in the Quran that translated to 'And argue with them in ways that are best and most gracious'.

Growing up with Muslims of all sects, there had been no distinction among Sunnis or Shiites. At school, we didn't say 'he's Shiite and she's Sunni'. Only now that the Mullahs from Iran are sending weaponry to the al-Assad regime has this new sectarianism been encouraged. This isn't in the nature of Syrians; this is Iran and Assad trying to divide us all. I hope to God we don't focus our energies on hurting and mistrusting each other, but focus on overpowering our regime as it continues to kill masses and masses of protesters.

More than a thousand people dead in just two months and tonight, tanks are arriving into Hama. Helicopter gunships have been seen coming in too . . . and children are being hidden away in their homes as Hama turns into a city of fear and ghosts. Our phones show the 'no service' sign. Internet access has been blocked, and foreign media have been kicked out. It's scary to think what they'll do to us without the world even knowing.

Oh, three flickers; there goes the electricity too. Gunfire and explosions are now as common in the city of Hama as streetlights are in the capital cities of Europe.

'Not Iran, not Hezbollah, we want a president who is afraid of Allah!' were the chants I heard yesterday in the centre of town.

For the past few weeks, people have seen Iranian combatants and members of the militant group Hezbollah patrolling and firing alongside the Syrian army – who are said to be even more ruthless than the army in their attacks. Until now, there has never been such enmity towards Hezbollah and Iran – but people are finally opening their eyes to the hypocrites who pretend to be the saviours of Palestine.

Night has fallen once again on our quiet Hama suburb; a desert wind from the south splashes us with sand, and no matter how hard I try to sleep, I know torment will stay with me until daybreak. Staying awake is a nightmare, and yet my sleep is filled with bad dreams; much like the dreams of freedom by the Syrian people, who live in misery or exile – or both. Dreams of freedom have come and flashed past us like the lightning in the night sky, leaving it even darker than before.

Everyone had thought that with President Assad disappearing off the scene in mid-April, he must have been withering away, and just like Egypt's Mubarak, would soon step down from power. To everyone's surprise and dismay, Assad came back laughing and joking – quite literally. To our surprise, he was *still* in Damascus, holding meetings with delegations, continuing his 'duties' as normal, and, of course, greeting his loyal fans. He was alive, healthy, and looked really well.

The fact that his own people had been killed in cold blood, and the carnage that followed the attacks on cities and villages by Assad's Shabiha gangs, and Hezbollah and Syrian soldiers, did not seem to have any effect on his mood. But his false promises of 'national dialogue' and 'reforms' are falling on deaf ears. He discredited himself the moment he called the protesters 'extremists, vandals, and outlaws' and blamed the protests on a foreign plot to sabotage Syria. Making it seem like a whole conspiracy has only angered Syrians more. According to him, the protests were all filmed in a studio set of Al Jazeera in Qatar.

After enduring his seventy-minute speech, my entire neighbourhood could be seen raging out of their homes and shops – the men who had gathered outside the internet cafe where I, too, had gone to watch the speech started yelling and throwing slippers at the television; the owners didn't even dare try to stop them.

Bashar al-Assad's speech had turned a dusty and humid Monday into a Friday as the streets filled up in large numbers with protests calling for revenge for the dead. In his speech, al-Assad had called the Syrian 'conspirators' – aka the protesters – 'germs'. On the streets, people were yelling, 'The germs want the regime to fall!'

My friends joined in, yelling, 'Pack your bags, and go to Tehran!'

Al-Assad's speech and appearance has been a bitter pill to swallow. The fallen Tunisian president, Ben Ali, had given three speeches and then stepped down; Egypt's Mubarak had given three speeches then fled; we Syrians want this to be al-Assad's third and final speech. There is no going back.

23 June, 2011

'Let those fuckers kill each other,' Firas murmured as he passed the tray of *arak* around.

I needed alcohol, so I pulled the tray to me. Another flurry of automatic gunfire echoed and a long trail of it rumbled back behind some apartment blocks in the distance. This time it was answered with more intensity and didn't stop.

The movie had just started. We weren't planning on ending our night just yet. Emad had arrived and sitting beside him were Dina, looking so pretty with her new hair extensions, and the others, huddled together in Firas's apartment.

It had just gone past eleven o'clock, and Firas and Madmour were camped on the floor mattress. Firas was insistent on turning the computer screen off.

'I've still got videos from today's protest loading on YouTube,' Madmour complained.

Despite Firas being occasionally disgruntled with his best friend's involvement in the revolution, he and Madmour remain as inseparable as ever. Madmour – twenty-eight years old, Syrian-Sufi, skinny, and bookish, with an undergraduate degree in anthropology, which doesn't take you very far in Syria. Firas, on the other hand, red-headed and blue-eyed, is from a wealthy landowning family, and landed a position as an apprentice technician with a foreign firm with a salary of three hundred dollars a month. He has a MacBook, a Suzuki, and is engaged to his cousin–sister – although we think he is marrying her Canadian citizenship instead of her. Madmour has no girlfriend, no job, and lives with his father, a prominent figure among the Naqshbandi Sufi order, who publicly denounce the Iranian and Syrian regimes as 'sectarian' and call for reform.

Haki fadi – nonsense – is how Firas describes Madmour's weekly *dhikr* sessions at the *zawiya*. While Madmour has encouraged Firas to attend some of their *halaqaat* – informal circles – the only gatherings he attends are ones where joints of hashish are plenty and whisky flows. So he leaves it at that. But Firas and Madmour always have each other's backs and bond over console games.

'If the revolution fails, the alcohol, the food, the car, the clothes, broadband – you can kiss it all goodbye.' Madmour stubbornly kept his laptop switched on.

Firas tossed the bowl of pistachio shells over him and laughed. 'Okay, saviour of Syria, do what you gotta do, just turn the volume down.'

We reach the world from our keyboards. Correspondents from the likes of the *Guardian*, *Le Monde*, and *Huffington Post* acknowledge us – and even rely on us. It's a serious task.

The most vital work is describing the plight of Syrians to human rights organisations, who then confront and inform the international community. This task is daunting because we have to be so careful not to misinform or exaggerate the number of deaths. The last thing we want is to be labelled fabricators – some online activists have, in their desperation, fabricated many stories and videos; however, this has only harmed our cause and cast doubt on all our other work.

As we sat on the comfortable couches that night, we had no idea that after the bombing had ended, a manhunt, street by street, had begun. Assad's dogs, the Shabiha, were looking for influential rebels. One by one.

At around midnight, Madmour received a text message and his face lost all colour as he read it. 'Oh my god! He's dead!' he cried, and started sobbing loudly. We all gasped for breath; we instantly knew who he meant. Madmour's father was extremely passionate about the *thawra* – revolution – and had called others to join peaceful resistance – and he had been targeted for it. He was one of dozens of martyrs gunned down that night.

Madmour's sobs turned to silent whimpers before he passed out in Firas's arms. The news was a shock to us all and even today, two days later as the disciples, his *sufi mureed*, are about to go to wash the corpse and prepare his shroud and dress him one last time in a white cloth, poor Madmour is finding it hard to process it.

The womenfolk, including my mother and grandmother, are preparing garlands and wreathes of flowers to adorn the body at today's funeral procession. I don't think I will be able to handle the customary loud and public funerary lamentation. The women will wail noisily and chant laments and verses of the Quran. His wife will no doubt be displaying her sorrow and female relatives, neighbours, and friends will no doubt augment her grief.

There is no time to mourn and no, I am not being disrespectful. Rather, it is in the hands of those of us who have been left behind, and in the hands of the younger generation, to continue the struggle for justice and freedom. The martyrs who have died in the fight have handed us the torch that will be passed on so that equal rights, human rights, and equality will one day be a standard part of all societies throughout the world.

Prayers and blessings to all who have gone, but my tribute to the deceased is to continue the mission they left behind. As the saying goes: shit just got serious.

It is after 10 p.m. A steady stream of red tracer fire from helicopters is arcing back and forth, penetrating the Hama countryside. A defection is taking place, according to my uncle. Soldiers could be seen earlier fleeing away from their base, dodging shots from those remaining behind and returning fire as they ran from their posts. About ten men who previously fought for Assad bolted towards our neighbourhood and arrived exhausted but ecstatic – the newest recruits to the Free Syrian Army. People rushed out of their homes to embrace them. Their palms were scraped and bleeding. They'd refused orders to shoot at civilians.

Things have escalated so fast here. Makeshift checkpoints made of burnt-out cars and dustbins protect Hama's neighbourhoods. Isn't it so strange how one's life can turn around just by a single life choice or a single event? How in an instant you can lose your entire way of life, daily routine and those things that you love and cherish the most? That one life-changing event can take you on to another path, long away from home with little chance of going back to how it was. Often that path may not be so much in the miles that you've walked from home, but rather in the things you've lost on that path, like your childhood innocence, friends, and trust and faith in the goodness of other human beings.

For me, the ultimate loss of trust was the realisation that my own grandparents – on my mother's side – would not even acknowledge the protesters, let alone mourn those who had spilled their blood for freedom and for a worthy cause, just as Christ had done.

I broke down one afternoon to Dina. 'These are the same grandparents who have raised me, who I went to church with, who taught me how to behave, and who showed me the light in the world.'

I know this is to be my hardest decision yet. My grandparents strongly sympathise with the government and would never accept my choice to stand up and fight for a cause I truly believe in. I remind myself that my focus is on God. He's shown me this new beginning and my every decision is based on Him. To live as a Christian is all I know, for I've not lived any other way.

My grandparents, being solid Christians, have given me a strong foundation, but now my faith has become my own instead of theirs. I won't be made to feel guilty for supporting a cause that so many Christians are staying clear of. That will make me as ignorant as some of the Alawites or Shiites who blindly support Assad because of a common religion or ideology. I can't fathom how Christian love and communion can stand side by side with supporting a tyrant that murders innocent women and children.

While many Christian clergymen have even risked their lives – just as many imams have done – to denounce the regime's violence, some Christians remain paranoid about the alternative options. The regime are partly to blame for this paranoia, though, as their desperation has led them to sow seeds of doubt in the minds of minorities and convince them that the protesters are all extreme Salafists and Muslim Brotherhood fanatics who plan to eliminate all other Syrian ethnic groups.

If the Sunni majority do overthrow the Baathists, where will that leave the Christians? Would this revolution be like the Iranian revolution that bought Islamic extremists into power? According to the regime, after Islamisation, Arab nationalism would not matter and Christian Arabs would have to live under severe persecution and/or be driven out of their homeland.

It isn't just Christian minorities or the Alawites that have turned their backs on their fallen brothers and sisters; the major cities of Aleppo and Damascus have remained motionless. Their quietness is a stab in the back to the rest of the towns and villages, who have sacrificed time, energy, and loved ones. Class and geography divide even Sunni Muslims. The Sunni upper and middle classes of Damascus and Aleppo have too much to lose in terms of material wealth and status. God forbid their comfortable lives might be hindered. God forbid they'd lose their higher status.

On the other hand, Syria's third largest city, Homs, has been at the frontline – and also lost the most lives. There, seven hundred and sixty civilians have been killed thus far. Here in Hama, official human rights organisations have counted three hundred and fifty dead. In contrast, Damascus has lost ninety lives and Aleppo has counted forty-four martyrs. I do not glorify death, but state the number of martyrs simply to show comparison between the bigger and smaller cities and how disproportionate the figures are.

Unclaimed bodies lie in the road after clashes at the Friday protest, and people pass by, lift the sheet slightly to make sure it's not a sibling, a cousin, or a neighbour, and move on. Blood in the streets, bits of limbs, brains, and guts – you see a protester's eyes open wide when they're struck by a bullet and then go dull as death darkens them.

Today's Friday protest was named the 'Friday of Departure.' Once again, Hama topped protester numbers all around Syria – we have been the most passionate, most persistent, and most peaceful. More than half a million were out demonstrating on the streets of Hama. Also, for the first time, protests were held in Damascus, and albeit small in number, they were immediately shot at and shut down. Last week, about fifteen thousand protesters joined to march on the highway linking Damascus to Aleppo – a major breakthrough. Many other towns that have not been keen to come out to demos have debuted too. As always, it was Hama, Homs, Daraa, Lattakia, Qamishli Al-Kisweh, Al-Qusayr who were out in huge force – and also subsequently suffered the most losses.

I sensed a major change in atmosphere from the previous Fridays. Not only were there scores more people, the atmosphere was no longer reminiscent of the atmosphere of an Eid festival or street celebration. The chants and songs have become more anger-filled and most of all, tear-filled. Today, families also came out to bury the fallen heroes, and as bodies were paraded out in their shrouds on the streets, I felt the rawness of death. Unable to contain my emotions, I decided to leave the protests and told my friends Bassam and Reem that I'd be leaving early.

Before I left, I was hoping to find a cheerful shawarma place to eat. I had been running around taking photos, manning a barricade, and helping the co-ordinators to keep the protesters marching at a quicker pace to avoid crushing, and in the excitement and urgency of it all, I had forgotten to eat. But looking in my bag, I found that I had little money left. It was a difficult decision to make: food or a full taxi journey home? Exhausted, but even more hungry, I decided to go to eat; however, as the area was new to me, I took a wrong turn. Instead of turning right towards a main road, I turned left into a dark and narrow street.

I hadn't realised my mistake until I was halfway down in the middle, where some of the military had set up a roadblock. My legs began to shake at the realisation that I was not only in unknown territory, but also surrounded by soldiers who were out to stop people like me. I still had my face paint on, and still had my flag and banner in my hands, as well as a bag full of items that would get me into a lot of trouble. Fears flashed in my head, but I knew this was no time to stop and think about the worst. I had to get away from the roadblock without drawing too much attention to myself – but how?

I could see men fully covered with face protectors and huge body costumes, giving them the appearance of huge cartoon-like figures, coming towards me, guns and batons in hand. I hid behind a tree and then sprinted through another alleyway as fast as my legs could take me. I ran for about fifteen minutes, my chest ready to burst, until I reached a busy road where I saw pro-revolution protesters ushering everyone to stay to one side of town.

'They're coming to fire at us!' someone screamed.

'They're coming from the west, go take cover!' another yelled.

People were panicking, and as the crowds were the largest they'd ever been, in the confusion children had lost mothers, husbands had been misplaced from wives, and in the heat and dust of summer, everyone was dehydrated and fatigued.

Just a few minutes later, the men who I had seen earlier were now standing shoulder to shoulder, coming towards me at full force, and unlike other days, these men – we later found out – were elite soldiers of Assad's army units combined with Iranian soldiers. As the huge crowds stared, transfixed and afraid, I quickly raised my camera to capture what I knew would be ground-breaking footage.

But before anyone even had time to figure out what was going on, the covered men fired volleys of tear gas at the protesters right in the front of the crowd. I was in the front too.

A bang. A gas canister had hit a man standing next to me, seriously damaging his hands. Another bang. This time the gas dropped in front of me – and exploded into my face.

I felt my lungs freeze. Luckily, I had the presence of mind to remember what we had been warned to do, so I took quick, short breaths. I could, however, see nothing. I was blinded, and my eyes felt like they were on fire. I tried to scream but I couldn't. I wasn't deaf, though, and could hear someone telling me not to touch my eyes.

People were screaming as more tear gas canisters landed. I stumbled on what felt like a child and in the scramble to run away, there was a stampede. I struggled to keep my balance as I was shoved and pushed from side to side. I was coughing frantically, and the sensation in my lungs was the most painful thing I had ever felt, but I ran, blinded and eyes streaming with tears, from the advancing soldiers. The strenuous activity forced me to breathe more deeply, my lungs still burning. I struggled but picked up speed until I felt a strong arm grab me.

'Are you okay?' a man's voice asked firmly.

'No . . . my lungs are going to burst!' I started crying.

The man was from a group of medics who had arrived at the scene to help the civilians. 'Open your eyes wide,' he commanded.

Despite the burning, I tried my best to open my eyes as he poured milk into them. Within a minute, I could just about see again.

'Now go there to the left.' The medic pointed towards a street.

My vision was still blurry and I had been separated from my friends. I looked around to see medics carrying an old man in a stretcher, blood flowing from his head and arms. A lady could be seen scurrying away, blood draining her headscarf and *abaya*. A protester was begging for water and help loudly as he vomited all over the sidewalk. Another young protester could be seen slumped on the side of the road, medics attending to his bullet wounds. While it felt like we had escaped the danger zone, we could hear shots fired somewhere nearby and tanks rumbling in the distance. I knew I had to find my way home; this was definitely not the Friday of Departure for Assad and his men.

Marhaba, ya bintee! *Ya hala*! *Ya hala*! Hello, my daughter, welcome, welcome!' Dina's father exclaimed as we finally entered their home in Rastan.

'*Waynik ya, Fairouz? Ishtaktilik ya hilwa . . . kteer kteer*! Where have you been, Fairouz? I've missed you sweetheart, lots and lots!' Her mother ran to the door, arms open, throwing her kitchen towel in the air behind her.

'I'm waiting to hear about this new boy,' Amti Diana teased good-naturedly. I shook my head. Suddenly, she was distraught. 'I really fear this activism will hinder marriage prospects for you girls.'

She pushed trays of nuts in front of me. It was pistachio season, so we munched gratefully.

I had not been to visit Dina's family in Rastan for a while, ever since the complete siege on the area had prevented anyone, even ambulances, from entering. It was heart-warming to see her mother express her mock anger towards me for not visiting as though things were still normal. I often sit back and ruminate on the simple pleasures that I've neglected, the petty arguments that I never got round to resolving, and the moments that I didn't take time to enjoy before this revolution.

'Dina, don't take her straight to your computer.' Dina's mother's shoulders slumped as she saw her daughter's determined face.

'No, Mother, we went to the field clinics today and documented everything so we need to go through it,' Dina replied.

'I've started preparing some *kefta* for you girls but *ala hawaak*, as you wish,' she said with sadness.

'*Wa la yhimmik*, don't worry, we have time to eat first.' I ushered my reluctant friend to join her mother and father at the dinner table, where mouth-watering sweet and sour *kousa mahshi* – stuffed squash – was served hot as a main course with rice, salad, and pita bread, together with glasses of tea with fresh mint. We discussed the current situation and expressed disgust and anger towards certain regime officials, as well as our fear and uncertainty about the future.

After dinner, everyone else headed out in the courtyard while I followed Dina's mother, Amti Diana, into the kitchen to prepare another round of tea and finish those *keftas*. I was nostalgic for the times I spent learning cooking techniques and bonding over her secret recipes around a table full of mysterious spices and kitchenware. As she placed the herbs and ground lamb – lamb and goats are plentiful in Syria – in a mortar and pestle and began to pulverize them together with her secret spices, she told me to wet my hands and start forming the *kefta* into little logs.

'You see this? This is what the regime will do to you if they catch you. They'll turn you into *kefta*,' Amti Diana said as she added garlic cloves, fresh coriander, and salt to the pestle and hammered it away until it was completely crushed.

'I worry about the safety of you girls. You're so involved in this revolution that you leave no time to take care of yourselves, or make the most of your childhood.'

Our mothers and grandmothers, bless their hearts, continue on with their exquisite cooking, despite the fact that supplies of food are running low, especially where the regime has been using food as a weapon by starving areas like Rastan that are under siege. In between all of it, they keep their aprons on and nourish their families. Keeping our kitchens alive, and eating and cooking hearty family meals, brings back some degree of normalcy.

A little after ten o'clock, as we were sat smoking *nargileh* on the rooftop to help digest the food, our chatter was disturbed by heart-piercing screeches of incoming artillery crashing down on a nearby field. Even louder shelling followed it, causing us to run down to the basement. Emboldened with our drinking of *arak*, we went up again after a little while to watch the fire in the sky.

'*Zeeh al-borday shwayy*. Draw the curtain a little.' Dina's father pointed to the window. Everyone in the neighbourhood could be seen peeking through their windows in their darkened rooms, mesmerised by the spectacle.

It was the heaviest crackdown on activists in around a month. Now we are awake in Dina's bedroom, adding subtitles to yet more footage of civilians being killed in cold blood – like eighteen-year-old Muhammad Taha, a senior in high school who passed his exams with tremendous marks to gain entry in medicine, only to be shot dead by security forces this morning.

The sound of sporadic shooting and bombing is constant, and the house occasionally shakes. The Syrian army is particularly angry today because a colonel from Deir Ezzor has announced he has defected to the opposition, taking hundreds of soldiers with him. They're calling themselves the Free Syrian Army and are seeking new recruits. I am sceptical – and scared. Nevertheless, we know of many people who are preparing to take up arms and fight back at the brutal Syrian army; no doubt many of them are young men with nothing else to do, as youth employment in Syria was over sixty percent before the revolution and is increasing even more now.

And that gives me no pleasure. As children, we all heard the stories of our neighbour, Lebanon. My parents and grandparents always drilled into our heads when we were growing up: *Arabs killing Arabs is more wrong and absurd than foreigners killing us.* Killings of all sorts were condemned, of course, but more than thirty years of sectarian strife in neighbouring Lebanon between the Arabs and we always thought we'd never become that way, until now . . .

I finally have a smartphone! What a remarkable combination of a phone, computer, camera, and television, which is not quite like any of them, and yet more than all four together. After getting help from Dina, I have set up my email, connected to Facebook, and chosen a custom ringtone. We had also browsed through Facebook and found Reem's page – and then, giggling mischievously, Dina had seized the phone and found Emad's profile, scrolling through it and reading parts aloud as I tried in vain to get the phone back from her. She must have noticed the expression on my face as she stopped scrolling and looked at me questioningly.

'He doesn't notice me,' I said, sadly.

'He has more important things to think of!' Dina tapped out of his photo gallery and directs me to a page filled with photos of *thuwaar*, revolutionaries. I am happy because I can now access social media platforms and update them without having to be a slave of the internet cafe. I can easily shoot footage from the street, take photos, and instantly funnel out videos underground via phone.

However, I still have to be careful as Syrian intelligence is using technology to track down activists and arrest them. On the streets, I am no longer in unfamiliar territory; the more I attend protests and meetings, the more real connections I am making.

Brave Dina has helped found a local network to organise and attend demonstrations, document abuses, and relay the story of the uprising, and our group now has more than one hundred and sixty members, with numbers increasing daily. We mainly use Paltalk to hold online meetings with other groups and Skype to stay in touch with each other. Whether online or on the street, none of us will spare a moment but to serve our cause – especially more since the past few weeks. It's so essential we stay organised and keep our online presence active, because people speaking to international press via video calls are being arrested and tortured. There is already a media blackout, and the regime's PR team is calling for pro-Assad supporters to line the streets. They have the resources – the fancy flags, professional banners, and slogans – while we manage with cards, fabric, chalk, marker pens, and anything we can find. Our team is trying to work with printers to come up with larger signs and other protest gear, but it is difficult to focus on smaller things like that when our casualties are rising every day.

All the while, our television screens are awash with images of tens of thousands of pro-regime demonstrators attending pro-Assad rallies, who chant their love for their country and their allegiance to their president. I don't understand what they are supporting, though. Are they supporting the spilling of blood, or the death of their fellow countrymen and women? It is another bitter thing to accept, but unfortunately there does exist a minority who genuinely adore and worship President Assad. We can't deny that, and the truth of the matter is, it would be wrong to.

Throughout it all, there is barely any time to sit back and write in my diary. There is no time to absorb the immensity of what is happening. Everything is moving so fast that in between documenting the battles, the endless bombardment, the shelling, and injuries, I don't even know what day it is. My days are dedicated to Syria.

Dina and I update the Facebook revolution page in English, which now has more than two hundred thousand followers, but we use little emotion any more. There are dead bodies to count and factual stories to relay. A little while ago, Aleppo activists informed us that police have carried out a raid at an Aleppo University campus and arrested dozens. So, we prepare to take hold of our weapons again: our smartphones.

The dogs that they have hired out to do their dirty work – otherwise known as the Shabiha – know no boundaries. Nothing is holy or sacred to them. Not innocent children, not women, not the elderly and sick, not Ramadan.

On the eve of Ramadan, our town was stormed and more than two hundred and fifty people were butchered in the ten days that followed. Animals are slaughtered better then Syrians are. Civilians were so scared to bury their dead loved ones during the siege of Hama that they took them home and dug holes in their gardens and buried them there instead. We didn't leave our house for days – not even for food. When the electricity went out, we lived in darkness, almost waiting for the army to come and raid and kill us all because of our participation in the protests.

After the tanks and Shabiha thugs arrived, they arrested hundreds, shot at people randomly, and as the heavy gunfire erupted, my grandmother said, 'It feels like 1982 all over again.'

Hama is still shaking with anger and protests continue daily. Tonight is the night that Muslims call the night of *Laylatul Qadr* (Night of Destiny), the holiest night of the month, and in our predominantly Muslim city, the roads are filled with prayer mats as mosques overflowing with worshippers can't accommodate them all.

As I often like to do, I stop and sit outside and observe the prayers, losing myself in the musical voices of the reciters. As beautiful as the mesmerising recitations are, there is so much insanity in this country. We hug our friends and family each day, not knowing if it will be our last embraces; every dinner feels like the last, and the killing of babies and children makes me sick. The Syrian army stoops to the lowest levels.

A tank ran over and killed a sweet neighbourhood child; we've since barricaded the entrance to roads to prevent the army from entering. Social media on my phone is telling me that security have arrested masses of people around Syria because they expected them to protest massively after the strong and soaring Ramadan prayers taking place at the mosques. My heart is broken for the eighty-year-old imam in Damascus who was dragged away and murdered.

Despite my not being a Muslim, I hope God accepts my only wish on this holy night, which is for Syria to become a free nation free of Assad's thugs and for it to thrive and shine once again.

I look at the starry sky, which is shining particularly radiantly on this blessed night. It illuminates the palm trees and the tall graceful minarets with its light. I look down at all the lively children of the worshippers, playing in the mosques' courtyards under the watchful eyes of their mothers, who occasionally scold the kids for disturbing the prayers of the other women.

Oh, those playful children. Their fate is so unknown, and it's sad to think they may not have a stable childhood ahead of them. While Libya's revolt seems to be moving forward, Syria's uprising is moving backwards. On this holy 'Night of Destiny', may our regime's actions return to haunt them a thousand fold and be their own destiny.

5 September, 2011

'Look here, you donkey . . . You wanted to break away from the army, did you?'

Syrian soldiers marched into the restaurant at sunset, and my friends and I crumbled to our knees in fear. They grabbed the man's head back by his hair and as he squirmed to free himself, a knife was held to his throat.

'No, I swear I didn't!' he cried.

They slapped him repeatedly. One of Assad's soldiers hit his knees with a baton.

'Who is your god?'

'Bashar is my god.'

'Who created you?' they yelled.

'Bashar!'

'Allah is who?'

'Bashar!'

'Muhammad is who?'

'Bashar!'

'Allah or Bashar? Who is better?

'Mercy, please!' The man began crying

'Answer the question.' One of the soldiers spat on his face.

'Bashar is better, sir.'

'Better than who?' They began rubbing the knife on his throat again.

'Bashar is better than Allah, sir.'

The soldiers mocked him as he shivered and shook, his life in their hands.

In between the ear-splitting music from Rotana Channel on the nearby television, and the clinking of glasses and crockery as the chef set down a mezze platter (filled with a selection of appetisers including hummus, tabbouleh, baba ghanoush, mttabel, dolmas, and falafels all served up with warm pita bread) nobody dared to breath.

'*La illaha Bashar al-Assad*. There is no god but Bashar al-Assad. Say it!' they demanded.

The man repeated their words. They were his final words because as soon as he finished them, they finished him using the blunt knife to cut his throat. A gurgling sound made the children in the restaurant whimper, and the blood that flowed from his neck was enough for the women to start crying.

They purposefully used a blunt knife to decapitate him so that he'd suffer more. This afternoon, we found the army defector's remains dumped near the river. We saw stray dogs digging into his corpse; one was seen carrying his skull in its jaws.

It is still hot here in Hama in the middle of the day but cool in the evenings and at night. We are still optimistic that this insane revolution and crisis will finish before the end of the year. I plan to add a lot of manure to the garden here before the winter so it will be great next year.

It is a beautiful time of year – temperatures are ideal – and so we receive wedding invitations daily. I will be attending my cousin Nesreen's wedding soon. I love September and October celebrations; it is just so serene here – you get to enjoy the weather and the late summer goods and stay out all day without burning in the heat or getting dusty and dry. Eid came and went. My brother moved to Damascus, where he plays basketball, and Father is still trying to make ends meet in our struggling home. The rest of the family just live day to day, hoping and praying for stability.

The pro-freedom movement is growing, and there are many people who are doing a great job supporting the backlines and who are as important as the ones in the front of the battle. I am on the backlines, but by no means am I special – there are dozens who contribute to the news as reporters struggle to come into Syria to gather information. Each day, the videos become more and more disturbing – videos taken by the Syrian army, which have become available via the black market, show regime thugs torturing innocent protesters, humiliating and degrading them. These videos, and the ones shot on the streets by citizen journalists, are hard to watch, but we've almost become immune to it.

The Syrian regime seems more afraid of online activists than the ones on the streets – they've rounded up social media activists and taken them to torture cellars where they've forced them to reveal passwords and details of other bloggers. I try to keep my activism hidden from my family, who hear horror stories about Facebook and Twitter accounts being compromised and account owners being detained and worry about me.

More than ten thousand social media users have been arrested for their illegal anti-regime content, and those who are at the forefront have a huge bounty on their heads. It is getting increasingly hard to smuggle footage out to news media outlets as we face huge technical issues, among other constraints. The regime continuously cuts power and electricity and blocks telephone and mobile lines in cities like ours where protesters are active. We've found ways to resist this too by using satellite phones and using generators when necessary to broadcast and spread our videos and breaking news around the world. Foreign activists then take the content and spread it further.

It is the snake that is Iran that has given the Syrian regime this technology to block signals, and so we've reached out to activists in Iran, who have experience on how to get around this system, as, of course, the Iranian regime used the very same techniques to squash the 2009 uprising there.

They say five thousand Iranian and Hezbollah operatives are helping Assad now, and yet it is still 'armed anti-government gangs' who are blamed for all the deaths and injuries that happen.

The other night, Al Alam, an Iranian state media channel, ludicrously claimed that it was Saudi snipers sent by Saudi prince Bandar Bin Sultan to kill the Syrians.

'Iran is a poisonous snake in the Arab world!' my father shouted at the screen. 'They've turned Iraq into an Iranian colony and now they want to meddle in Syria.'

He explained to me what happened in the eight-year war between Iran and Iraq and how the power of Arab unity was then tested and proven to be potent because it resulted in the defeat of Iran at the hands of Arabs and their American allies.

I wanted to know this enemy of ours as much as possible. This enemy that claimed to love Palestine – but never did – and who thought of themselves as the saviours of the Muslims and Arabs but only harmed them. I was naïve to think Iran's nemesis was Israel when all along it had only been part of their show-acting to gain trust from the Arabs.

What was far more alarming was how quickly they'd arrived into Syria to destroy anyone that defied their beloved ally – the Syrian regime. My father's pessimistic speculations, like those of millions of others, are justified. Today, more than four million Iranians are settled in Iraq with high positions in the government, and even the parliament. Arabs are ethnically and religiously cleansed regularly.

I do not want them meddling in our affairs. I do not want our efforts to be in vain, and we all want our political future to be in our own hands. Despite many Gulf leaders criticising Iran's illegitimate interests, and outrage on social media, nobody seems to be physically stopping them.

Last night, I spent an hour removing the semen of Syrian–Alawite soldiers from the prayer carpets at the mosque. I poured liquid detergent over the *mussalah* and brushed them over and over, rinsing them in hot water each time, until no stains were evident, then I hung them out over the railings of the mosque and brought out the fans from the storage rooms until they dried. Reem and her sister scrubbed at the walls, removing the splatters of sticky liquid that coated the highly stylised and floriated Islamic calligraphy known as Kufic script running all around the wall.

We couldn't, however, remove the graffiti they'd left behind: *No god but Bashar al-Assad, no prophet but the Baa'th party.*

We had been marching along a dusty footpath; afternoon crowds were chanting with olive branches in their hands, and some of the men took off their shirts to show they were peaceful and unarmed. But we soon discovered that not only were all the troops at the front of the demo shooting with live bullets, they were also preparing to 'clear' the street once and for all.

Just down the road, we could see black acrid smoke billowing out of the crowds and the familiar smell of blood. My friends and I ran to take shelter in a mosque nearby, but the mosque was closed so we climbed into the storage room at the side instead and shut ourselves in.

The two young girls looked like birds of paradise in their outfits. A silky blouse and chiffon skirt on one while the younger one had a pastel-patterned dress. Eyebrows drawn, cheekbones sculpted, they were dressed up for the demonstration. They had been kidnapped for protesting and brought into the mosque, where they had both been laid down and had their clothes ripped apart. Then, when their naked chests were on display, the men attacked them like rabid hyenas to prey.

'Wahhabbi whores!' they yelled. 'Sunni slaves of Zionists. Bitches of Qatar.'

Once they had tasted the sweet nectar of the Muslim women, they tossed them outside like unwanted carcasses. Blood flowed from their milky thighs. They landed facedown, their heads buried in the mud, but they were still alive and in pain. Semi-naked, they lay there in the middle of the road. The soldiers fired at their chests, not with semen but with gunshots this time. After a few minutes, the imam who lived inside the mosque ran out to rescue them, but it was a trap. They shot him dead too.

'Stay down!' Reem held me back from where we were crouched down.

Five minutes later, some neighbours came to try to rescue all three, but they, too, were shot dead.

We were consumed by intense pain through the cleaning process, knowing that the victims in here could have been us.

The Alawite soldiers' ejected sperm had fallen onto Islamic books. The hate they had for the Sunnis was on full display. This was once the land of Moses, Muhammad, and Jesus. We were taught as children to be Syrian first. Religion wasn't our thing. We were told that good Syrians equalled good people. And that was it.

The more you know, the more you realise there is a lot more you do *not* know – a simple truth, and a confusing one too. Choosing to follow my mother's religion strengthened my devotion to Christianity; however, it limited my ability to see the bigger picture.

For a long time, I had wondered what the difference between Sunni and Shiites were and thought the differences were insignificant, but now it has become apparent. The relationship between the Alawi-dominated government and the majority Sunni was – and is – a difficult one. It is only now that the regime has begun to demolish mosques and kill Sunni scholars that I've seen our nation become divided.

The regime is to blame. They are sparking sectarian battles in an attempt to justify their crackdowns and to lure more men to fight with the Shabiha (who consist mainly of Alawi and Shiite men). Last week, one of Syria's famous Sunni scholars had been killed for giving a sermon for calling for the bloodshed to end. Even the middle and upper classes of Damascus and the commercial city of Aleppo are getting caught in the trap of this dangerous sectarian schism.

'We have got to stop meeting like this, Fairouz.' His breath tickled the back of my neck, and I spun round to see Emad, smartly dressed and smiling at me.

'Emad! What are you doing here?'

'Same as you,' he said, nodding towards Nesreen and her new husband as they revolved slowly on the spot to the slow music. 'They are old friends of the family,' Emad added, as if reading the questions that were flitting through my mind.

We stood in silence for a moment. I was very aware of how close he was to me – not too close as to be improper, but closer than two people would usually stand.

'Would you like to dance?' he asked, extending his hand to me and lifting his eyebrow slightly. I took his hand and he led me onto the dancefloor, putting one of his arms gently around my waist, drawing me in to him slightly.

The George Wassouf song swelled up around us and as we glided around the dancefloor, I could almost forget everything that was going on and lose myself in Emad's arms.

'I haven't seen you in a while,' he said and as I looked up at him, he used one hand to brush a lock of hair from my face.

I swallowed and lowered my eyes again, feeling heat rush into my cheeks. 'I've been busy,' I said. 'You know, with. . .' I didn't want to say the words aloud, almost as if inviting the horrors into this safe place would ruin this moment.

Emad nodded. 'I know. It' s important work you're doing.'

My heart swelled to hear him say it, and as we danced in comfortable silence for the rest of the song, I felt myself relaxing more and more into his arms. I was just about to tilt my face up, idly wondering if his lips might find mine, when the song ended and the spell was broken.

I dropped his hand and stepped back and he smiled, slightly sadly.

'I hope to see you again soon, Fairouz,' he said, touching my arm lightly.

'Be safe, Emad,' I said, and returned to my seat to collect my diary before heading outside for fresh air and some space.

Now I sit writing in this beautiful spot, which is a profoundly meaningful and breathtaking place. It is on the banks of River Orontes, and the perfect location for Nesreen's wedding. The wedding venue overlooks the majestic wooden waterwheels of Hama. As the guests continue to dance inside – like I was doing just a few minutes ago – I gaze at the waterwheels and listen to their wailing noise as they turn around, as they have been doing for hundreds of years. This place has great power and this spot, where the trees grow and where the water falls, is a place that can sum up many of my happiest days – and my saddest . . .

The sun is setting beautifully and I can't help but appreciate Syria's untouched and pristine natural beauty. How sad would it be if places like these were no more? If things become worse for us and we would never enjoy days and memories like this again? Attractive women dressed in their shimmery, sequinned silk and French lace gowns, and the bride in her sweeping, ivory, silk chiffon dress embellished with floral motifs and delicate crystals, hand-beaded and tailored by a local dressmaker.

I have just read updates about the twenty girls from Damascus who were kidnapped by Assad forces. They've been returned to their families but have been raped and tortured brutally and have had their heads shaved.

My phone beeps constantly with updates. The constant shelling in Rastan, Dina's town, by government tanks to kill the one thousand army defectors hidden there is problematic for us all. I think of Dina's mother, dear Amti Diana, and her last long, warm kiss on my forehead when she was bidding me farewell.

'*Allah yiwafik, albi.* May God aid you, my dear.' She'd said it as though knowing she would be absent from my future. Dina hadn't turned up today and her timestamp on WhatsApp showed she hadn't appeared online since yesterday afternoon – a sure sign that something was not good at all.

God forbid anything happens to my loved ones. Where is the Arab League? Where are the influential politicians of the world? Why aren't the sheikhs of Syria and the world supporting their people? The Damascene patriarch of the Greek Orthodox Church, Ignace IV, has warned everyone not to rise against the regime because of the disorder it will cause and has warned there will be no Western help if we do.

We wonder about the West and their interests in Syria. Are they really interested? We don't have as much oil as Libya, so why would they come here? What is there to gain for them? It is very well known that certain 'Arabs' offered to pay the West to do their dirty work. Look at Libya right now – how successful they're becoming with Western intervention in return for oil.

Jasem, one of the group's admin on Paltalk, gave an impassioned lecture to Arabs around the world, telling them to get together and bomb Assad's regime. But the truth is, I believe they don't owe us anything – ordering other Arabs to fight our war would make us the same as the Alawite Syrians asking Iran to help them because they shared a same religious ideology or ethnicity.

'*Fairouz, shu sar ma'ik*? What happened to you? Why are you sitting down there tapping away on your phone – *yallah*, the bride and groom are about to have their first *dabke* dance with us,' the bride's sister Tasneem yells from the veranda.

The heavy beat of the tabla drum announces a shift towards a more dance rhythm and the girls in their fancy dresses stand in a line, ready to step to the incongruous beat of the tabla.

Dance? While people lie dead?

Suddenly, my dance earlier with Emad seems like a thousand years ago.

2 October, 2011

As I write this, I can hear Al Jazeera blaring in the lounge. It seems surreal that we are preparing for war and watching it at the same time on television. Nobody feels safe. Things were calmer yesterday, but today that changed, and we all know how quickly things can escalate without warning.

A few hours ago, I ran away from gunfire from heavy weapons used to disperse a demonstration in the neighbourhood. Some of my university friends are at a demonstration on Aleppo road and have reported the same. Thankfully, there are no casualties. Yet. This is daily routine now.

Also today, many of my relatives who live in the Hama villages of Kafar, Naboudeh, and Karnaz have fled after regime forces invaded, shooting randomly with heavy machine-gun fire. There are a lot of children injured. Most worryingly for me, there has been no news from Dina, and it is impossible to get to Rastan to find out.

The regime is taking revenge for huge losses while fighting against the brave Free Syrian Army rebels and are targeting villages where the families of army defectors live. Nearby in the countryside, there is dense gunfire at the army checkpoint in Sahl Alghab, and we know it will hit us soon.

It's good to know that while we prepare for the war that is on our doorstep, millions of people around the world are following events too, and whether they support us or not, it's a privilege to know they are still interested. The regime are well aware of this too. The Mufti of Syria, Ahmad Hassoun, and Sunni puppet of Assad issued a warning to the world and vowed to send suicide bombers to Europe and the USA if there was any foreign intervention. Ha! Even more reason for such a regime to be finished.

There are many, of course, who are still sceptical or blankly refuse the idea of foreign intervention for fear of repercussions or infiltration. I understand their view, because I, too, had this simplified and unrealistic outlook before. I really do hope the opposition unite; we can leave the hot debates for when Assad and his army finally go. After all, whether or not you agree with foreign intervention is entirely each Syrian's right; however, the choice in the matter must be made by those who are risking their lives at the frontlines. I don't want this to become another string to the regime's bow by allowing it to divide us. It's vital to remember the common goals we share, which are freedom, dignity, and the right for Syrian people to choose their next leader.

How the slaughter is stopped may be something we may not share the same opinions on, but it doesn't mean we have to waste our time arguing with each other about it. I wish everyone were trying to focus on doing something that will be useful to those suffering rather than feeding the egos of people that aren't really doing very much anyway. A personal opinion is just that – personal. There's a whole bigger picture out there, and there are vulnerable people that need our help urgently. How these tears sting, birds fly from our eyes, and poppies grow in our hearts.

Oh God, I have only slept for four hours after being awake for well over forty-eight. Now I remember: it was all the commotion in our neighbourhood along with my father and youngest brother getting armed and preparing to head out into battle that threw me in fresh agony, and which kept me awake till the early hours of the morning. It was not until the morning call to prayer I had some measure again and fell asleep.

There are now about ten thousand Syrian army defectors – most of them lower level officers. And then there are small units and independent groups of people who are getting organised, mostly in suburbs, like my father and his friends. I am hoping that this 'war' – as I don't like to call it – doesn't seriously injure my loved ones, and I pray it doesn't last too long. But who am I kidding? It's obvious from the word on the street and from the men's conversations that the Syrian military is extremely cohesive and it will be extremely difficult, even impossible, to penetrate their system any time soon.

The military take organisation so seriously. For example, when they realised that Hama was getting just a little out of control, they didn't care that it was Ramadan and immediately regained some sort of control over us. The risk of losing Hama was too high, and this territory would be so hard to gain back if lost completely. The same applies to Daraa and Rastan, which have felt the full force of the army to ensure they don't lose them completely. They know they have lost the hearts of the citizens, but losing land is one thing they cannot afford to do.

They certainly do not want Hama, Homs, and the other seriously rebellious cities to turn into Libya's Benghazi. Despite the efforts of the Free Syrian Army, along with all the other ethnic groups of fighters and independent fighters, the army is much better equipped. Very few of the rebels have had military experience; actually, I doubt most people have ever even handled guns before this. It's just like it was last night: take the guns and throw them over the Suzuki trucks and drive off. It would need a miracle to defeat the regime while being so outnumbered, especially with little resources or experience. For many, this miracle would be help from NATO.

'After seven months of this, there aren't exactly many options left,' Reem said over the cloud of cigarette smoke hanging over our heads as we chilled out in our tent at Al-Asi Square under the moonlight yesterday. 'This war could be ended quickly, though, if NATO imposed a No Fly Zone.'

'*Aywah ya,* Reem! Yes!' Madmour nodded as he lit another cigarette. 'Embargos and stopping oil being imported from Syria is not enough. We need foreign help now more than ever.'

This was enough to get the argument started. Everyone, everywhere is discussing it. Why aren't the West intervening like they did in Libya? Should they even do so? Basically, Gaddafi had nobody on his side, except for some business associates – just oil buyers. Assad, on the other hand, has powerful Russia and

Iran backing him. And most crucial to the West, he hardly has any oil. Everyone has an opinion.

'*Ya Shabab, kelna bil hawa sawa.* Guys, we're in this together.' I spun round at the familiar voice to see Emad, carrying a fistful of leaflets and brochures in his hand. I could barely hear him speak over the noise of my heartbeat.

Chubby Bassam, who was leaning back in his plastic chair, took a drag on his cigarette and grumbled as Emad flashed me a quick smile and then invited us to see the fresh new camera footage he had taken – a bloodied male corpse with a piece of masking tape across its chest that had scribbled on it 'Corpse no. 8'.

To our right, the fireworks that explode after *eisha* prayers each night to signal the start of protests erupted as men streaming out of the mosque were called to another nightly round of protesting. On the left, businesses ushered the protesters in for shawarmas and strawberry-filled chocolate crepes. Men, women, and children began to cluster in the square from all sides.

When we got up to march, we naturally followed Emad, who was not only a protest leader but also a leader in every sense. We chanted, '*Al-mawt wa la al-mazalleh*' – 'We would rather die than be humiliated.' The crowd roared as always, their infectious energy bettering the mood of even those that had lost hope or loved ones.

At one point, the intense crowds began to get hysterical, which caused people to surge around us. I began to get squashed in the middle of it all and nearly tumbled over when Emad, who was standing nearby, perfectly calm, wrestled a few of the men out of the way and pulled me free. We were still squashed up and squeezed closer together as the protesters chanted around us 'One, one, one. The Syrian people are one!' and called for unity and an end to sectarianism.

'Well, how are we going to get out now?' I looked up at tall, lean Emad.

He laughed as he said, 'I am not sure, but you'll have to just hold on.'

He didn't manage to stop the pushing and shoving, but I will never forget that spark I saw in his twinkling blue-green eyes as I held on to his body tightly. And we continued chanting.

18 October, 2011

The sharp clack of a woman's heels on concrete is enough to alert a sniper. We'd been returning from demonstrations late yesterday and upon nearing home, we saw that the main street was completely deserted apart from a bunch of burning bins.

Reem and I were quickly dragged into an alleyway and offered water and told to look up at the building opposite us. A hand from the hole in the wall moved a pair of night-vision binoculars to survey the area and focus down below. The FSA fighters who had pulled us to safety told us that we were safe here and out of sight of the Syrian Arab army sniper up there.

My heart was beating fast. It all happened so quickly that I wondered if it happened at all. A young lady dressed in a black *abaya* walked up the street. One hand lifted her long, black garment as she picked her way carefully through crushed glass in high heels, and her little child held her other hand. The sniper was an expert marksman – being a sniper in Syria is the job most in demand and best paid because of its difficulty.

The lady turned her head to cross the road. From the tenth floor, a single silent bullet from a hole in the wall shattered the right side of her skull. It tore her jaw from her dainty face, leaving it dangling by a thin piece of flesh. In a split second, her delicate features became a muzzle of spewing blood, broken exposed teeth, and her tongue and eyeballs fell on the floor. His mother's blood covered the little boy, whose clothes were splattered with parts of her brain, most of which now lay in the middle of the road.

He had escaped death, and one of the FSA rebels among us had managed to pull him to safety. Little Harith was four years old and didn't understand that his mother had died.

'So when will Mama wake up?' the little boy asked me an hour later, when we had managed to calm him down.

'Soon,' I replied, knowing that I was lying. I knelt down and took his tiny face in my hands. 'I don't know when, but she'll be with you later.'

I saw a gleam of delight in his timid brown eyes, similar to the look in a child's eyes on the morning of Eid. 'She's going to come home today?' he asked.

I kissed his forehead goodbye and lied again. 'Yes, *InshaAllah*, God willing.'

Once there were reports of sniper activity from the tall buildings in our area, we took no time in getting down to building barricades. Over the next few days, barrels, sanitation pipes, and sandbags were stacked up high to form makeshift barricades for protection against sniper fire.

The Free Syrian Army's weaponry is nothing in comparison to the high-performance Russian sniper rifles used by Assad's army.

19 October, 2011

The split between the regime loyalists and Syrian revolutionaries is heavy with consequences, and a civil war has become inevitable. Assad Jr has not delivered reforms and refuses to step down. Instead, his gangs have increased their killing, making it justifiable to fire on them back. There is no other option.

As my father said, 'We all went into this battle unarmed. We didn't have weapons, but they still shot at us.'

Regardless of our ideologies, the Free Syrian rebels want to overthrow Assad. They've moved into entire neighbourhoods all over Syria and have bases and units in residential areas, forcing people to leave their homes. There are teachers, carpenters, judges, scholars, intellectuals, farmers, policemen, and men from all walks of life fighting to keep the murderers away from their families.

Syrians are displaced in their own country. For those in the frontline of the fighting, there's no hope, because the regime targets any building that it suspects is a rebel base.

When there are short truces in fighting, we come out of our homes to inspect the damage and try to live a normal life, even though the local primary school now serves as a rebel base and snipers use the university rooftop.

The political and ethnic mosaic of Syria is so very fragile. Despite fears that Syria is on the verge of destruction and heading for a full-blown civil war, there is hope, as Syria's opposition have started to unite. The revolutionary groups have started coordinating and created a union called the Syrian National Council, led by an exiled Syrian academic in France. The SNC have somehow eased the tensions between the myriad ethnicities and faiths that make Syria's twenty-three million populace so diverse. They've chosen two hundred and thirty representatives, all with different political ideologies from different tribes and ethnic groups.

Many of my friends are optimistic, describing this as a slap in the face to Assad's illegal regime, which constantly tries to fracture us. My social media feed erupted with enthusiasm the day the council met in Istanbul to announce this coalition. And this social media buzz has reignited the youth on the streets. For the past few weeks, activists have not been as engaged in protests, and things have quietened in some areas.

The belief that this 'council' is a step closer to getting rid of the murderous regime seems still too far-fetched for me. The efforts of the now seemingly-united opposition are one thing, but the situation on the streets here in Hama is still a completely different story. This is our parents' and grandparents' second war, and despite progressive youth, many of the elders are staying bitter. It seems they want to live their youth through their children.

I witness this daily in our own household. My father, once a Syrian patriot, is allowing sectarian tensions to determine his views. He instils these ideologies in my young and impressionable brother. It's like he is reliving his childhood and making up for missed opportunities through Yahya.

'We need democratic, not religious, alternatives to Assad,' I argued one night while Father sat smoking and talking with his new-found rebel friends, a brand-new M-16 they'd stolen from Assad's men propped up in the corner.

'*Majnoona inti*? Are you crazy? And what is the alternative, young girl? I have to let your mother and you get raped and be killed while we search for peaceful alternatives?' he replied, sarcastically.

His fighter friends looked at me disapprovingly.

'Christians are allowed to wave crosses, but when we wave the banner of Shahadah or other Islamic slogans, we are labelled extremists?' Abu Yaman said.

Almost all of Father's new friends are from our twin city, Homs – the city that everyone calls the 'capital of the uprising'. The men seem very religious, very Sunni, and very passionate. I like having them around, despite some of their extreme views. But I am worried about my father, the once proud secularist. I have seen sweeping changes in him, and I hope he doesn't let this revolution change his moral compass and his liberal ideas.

I look at his growing scruffy beard and imagine many of Father's university classmates who are now sitting behind desks in far more luxurious offices in California or affluent areas in Europe. I imagine they are no more capable than Baba, but have had better fortune, and so my secularist, liberal, and educated father, who spent years waiting for his phone to ring for job opportunities, now carries an AK-47 and wears a religious headband.

20 October, 2011

'Al Mourabet Street,' I said.

'Okay, get inside, quickly,' the taxi driver said hastily.

I climbed into his rusty 1948 Chevrolet canary-yellow car and we sped away. Thank God this taxi driver was a familiar face – and a real gentleman. Dressed in a white *thawb*, his head was covered with a black and white *kuffiyeh* with a braided *agal* on top.

'*Tikrami ya binti.* You're welcome.' Abu Ali smiled. 'Did you hear about what happened here the other day?' he asked as we approached Al-Mazareb Bridge.

I looked into his emerald eyes, about to answer, but the elderly man rambled on without waiting for me to reply.

'Look from the rear window. You see that grey building near the roundabout? There are a lot of experienced snipers stationed there.'

I took a quick glance at the tall, graffiti-adorned building.

'I was dropping off some passengers here next to the bridge, but when they stepped out, the man, his wife, and their young child were all shot dead.'

He described how, when passers-by approached to rescue the wounded, the regime targeted them.

'The snipers shot at every single person on the street with a hail of bullets all at once. My whole car was covered in blood.'

I could tell he was trying to shake off the horrific memory.

'God saved me, the blood splattered all over the windows and the snipers could not see that I was still inside, alive.' The old man's voice trembled as he fixed his *masbaha*, rosary beads, hanging from the car mirror.

It took us a whole hour to reach Reem's house, but luckily I had fallen asleep throughout the ten checkpoints.

'*Yallah*, we're here,' Abu Ali turned down Sheikh Sudais on the stereo. I thanked him and asked him to send regards to his wife, a distant cousin and friend of my grandmother.

'See you soon, Ammo, please take care of yourself,' I said, and then hurried up the stairs to Reem's apartment.

'*Allah ma'ak*, God be with you,' he said with a gentle laugh.

The helicopters that regularly hovered over Reem's building were absent, so we gathered on the large open-air terrace to celebrate her birthday. Colourful and aromatic flowering plants hung from the railings, and the buffet table held a luminous bowl of pistachios, a platter of sweets, and a homemade chocolate cake.

'Happy birthday, *habibty, akbel el myeh*. Hope we get to celebrate your hundredth too,' I said, kissing her cheek.

'What does one have to do to get one of those *bousaat*?' I heard Reem's mother ask from behind. Aunt Amani ran over, her big brown eyes twinkling. 'I've missed you!'

As I lifted my head to kiss her forehead, I noticed an unfamiliar girl standing in the kitchen, watching us. Each fold on her hijab was draped immaculately and held together with a diamond clip. I drank in her profile: the delicate up-tilt of her nose; the long black lashes that swept her extremely and mysteriously black eyes; eyebrows arched perfectly on her porcelain skin; her dark blue gown featuring cross-stitch embroidery specific to her region. She was definitely Palestinian.

As I wondered who she could be, Aunt Amani quickly pulled me close.

'This is a relative of ours visiting from Nablus. Her name is Manal.'

Remembering my manners, I reached out to shake her hand.

'She's Emad's fiancée,' Aunt Amani gushed, her eyes filled with pride.

My heart came to a shuddering halt. Completely stunned, I tried not to express my shock or let my face betray my true emotions. I slowly turned my focus back to Reem and smiled faintly. There was nothing to say.

What had I been thinking anyway? It was *mustaheel*. Impossible. Emad is a Muslim, and one from a very religiously observant family. He's obviously bound to marry a good, decent

Muslim girl, and one from his own tribe. And at any rate, my mother's family would never approve of it. Even if my father is a Muslim and grandmother a practising one, it was all too far-fetched.

And why was I even thinking these things in the first place? Marriage? I barely knew him. And what would Emad see in me anyway?

'*Khalas*, enough, Fairouz. Stop thinking so much,' Reem whispered. 'It was all arranged last year, but his mother only announced it to the relatives last night. Just forget about it. *Wala shi*. It's nothing.'

But I can't bring myself to forget. *Fi shi*. There's something there.

If hotheaded Dina hadn't left us and gone into hiding with her family, she would have shaken her head in disbelief and told me to slap him and move on.

By the light of the full moon, we dipped crispy *markook* bread into the communal bowl of *kibbeh nayyeh*. To my right, on bamboo mats on the floor, Reem ate with gusto. On the other side, the menfolk chatted and filled their stomachs.

I could see Emad's face burning with nervous heat when I looked over. Manal caught us making eye contact and gave me a hostile stare. I turned my face away. She gave me a brutal examination, making it very clear that she resented my interest in Emad. I wondered if she knew we'd been exchanging sweet nothings over text messages. It was nothing serious, of course, but I still felt the pangs of rejection.

When did he get so important that he owned every bit of my heart? The way he brought me to my knees and made me paralyzed, then when he made me feel alive, it was like a rush of fire through my body that warmed me for days. The chemistry was undeniable. I could not deny the feelings that raged within me.

I excused myself and went to the kitchen with pathetic tears rolling down my face, slightly annoyed that nobody even seemed to notice I wasn't my usual chirpy self. Inside, Myriam Faris crooned 'Men Oyouni' on the radio as some of the young children lay flat on the sofa, nodding off to sleep. Just as I was about to open the refrigerator, there was a terrifying burst of noise.

The force of the bomb blast jerked my body back and forth, and I felt my body hurl through the air and land next to a whimpering baby. I was dazed and confused as I lay there, motionless. A rocket falling from the sky onto the building jolted me back into consciousness. Luckily, it landed on the empty apartment next door. I had to get up. I had to check on everybody. Over the multitude of shouting and crying and confusion in the dark, it appeared only someone on the ground floor had been seriously injured. Everyone huddled together tightly under the table that held the birthday cake until the deafening sound of military aircraft grew faint as they moved on to carry out a bombing raid on a different area.

A short while later, Emad cornered me as I went into a bedroom to tend to my bruises. 'Let me take a look at your injury.'

'It's nothing major, it doesn't hurt,' I said, trying to downplay his concern.

'It's not minor to me, I want to see,' he insisted.

'*La*, no! Leave me alone, I don't talk to liars!' I yelled, wringing back my hands.

'*Laysh intee za'lana?*' He looked crushed.

'How can you ask me why I am sad?' I fumed back. 'I'm pissed off because of your bullshit. Couldn't you just be honest with me?'

I didn't expect to see him start sobbing like he did. I could see the hurt, the open sores in his heart, the fear of breaking family tradition. I felt his sorrow even though my own heart was pinched with pain. It had been an emotional night, and we'd both thought we'd lost one another.

I turned to look at him; his heart was heavy, and his face sincere. I gave him a motherly embrace.

'If only things had been different. If only I had more time to get to know you,' he said as his eyes began to sparkle again.

I nodded silently.

He paused for a moment before he walked out of the door. 'Are we good?' he asked with a deep tender voice.

I smiled at him. '*Tab'aan*, of course,' I replied, feeling the first sparks of true love.

After the ambulances had left, carrying the injured and dead from the neighbourhood, the remainder of the night passed quietly, and when dawn finally came, we were awakened to news about last night's shelling.

A nest of Shabiha spies stationed in the area had notified the Syrian army of a large number of armed rebels hiding in the Al-Mazareb bridge area. They'd targeted a car filled with several of the rebel soldiers.

All seven rebels riding inside and the elderly driver of the yellow taxi – my friend Abu Ali – were killed instantly.

Bodies running, then falling, dropping down dead – just like in the movies. The views I see from up above are perhaps best appreciated from a distance rather than close up, though the scant remains of human body parts are hardly impressive from whatever angle you view them. Most of the thirty-six people that were killed today were in Hama.

Our group of media activists have decided to wear orange outfits that closely resemble the overalls of Syria's waste collectors. As a result, the general public, who smile at us with appreciation, now often jokingly refer to us as the neighbourhood's garbage men.

Today, I was responsible for the live stream of anti-regime demonstrations in Hama's al-Qusour neighbourhood, near al-Hadeed Bridge. Activists named today as the 'Friday of No Fly Zone'. Despite new and increased threats from Assad and his boys, around one hundred and seventy protests took place around Syria. Demonstrations were heating up in all neighbourhoods south of Mal'ab, Aleppo Road, Ein el-Lowzeh, and west of Mashtal until the army finally stormed and shelled them and scared everyone away by shooting from heavy machine guns.

One of the reasons I am kept awake at night is the apathy of so many. All one has to do is to look at the faces of the young and old in Al-Asi Square, beaming with pride and commitment, to feel the desperation emanating from the chanting crowds in Syria. I am so happy with this type of grassroots response to our plight – we need our voices to be heard loud and clear and show the world and especially the regime that we mean it. Tell them how it is. Enough of this madness. We have had enough.

What kind of rhetoric is 'the Assad regime or Islamic extremists'? Since when do we have to choose from the two delusional devils? It is nonsense and I will be honest – I grappled more than I ever had over my decision to rebel and take part in this revolution, and for a very long few nights after seeing my father and his religious-looking friends . . . but I simply cannot, *cannot*, ever concede that giving up and giving in to the lesser of the two evils is the answer. *No.* It is simply not in me. This battle for freedom must go on.

I have just received the news that a very dear family friend of ours, and the man who baptised me, died today. Having been in ministry for more than forty years, Father Joseph was not only renowned for his personal holiness, but also for being an exemplary human being. He was vivacious, intelligent, and brilliant and kind beyond measure. He truly had a heart of gold. He was loved by every Muslim and non-Muslim in our town and his church. Bless his soul. I will miss him, as we all will.

I do not know the details of his death, but he had been increasingly worried about Christian–Muslim relations in Syria recently. While most of the sectarian divisions haven't affected Christians as much, he inspired us all to come together as one.

My mother said she had last seen him two weeks ago, at a meeting that was held to discuss ways of preventing the Shabiha regime thugs from stealing Red Crescent ambulances to shoot protesters from. He was also greatly appalled by the way pharmacists and doctors are being hunted down and arrested because they are volunteering to give medical treatment to the injured at demonstrations.

He would visit private homes where people had set up makeshift clinics and give words of hope and prayers to medics and patients. Here, everyone is scared of going to the hospital. We would rather stay badly wounded at home instead of have the army collect us, as they do, from a hospital bed. They scour hospitals to look for dissidents to take away to question and torture.

No human can imagine the harrowing things Syrians are seeing on a regular basis. Dead Syrians lie where they fall, their pockets turned out by thieves, their watches removed, their wallets emptied, and their photos taken.

The kindness, compassion, and love that beings like Father Joseph gave to this world are rare commodities now; even more reasons to commemorate his death. May his soul rest in eternal peace. *Amen.*

The greatest sacrifice during the Eid festival of sacrifice – which, by the way, Syrians didn't even celebrate properly – has been by the noble people of Homs. For the past six days of tank shelling, searching for AWOL soldiers, shelling for the sake of shelling, bombarding residential properties, and arresting masses of people, Homs is a bloody disaster. It is the most brutal siege on Syria's bravest city, and the Syrian National Council is calling on the United Nations and its humanitarian organisations, the Organisation of Islamic Cooperation, the League of Arab States, and all international bodies concerned with human rights to wake up and recognise the suffering.

If the Homs siege doesn't awaken the world, I don't think much else will. There are more than two million people under siege, unable to get out. Dead bodies are lying on the street because there's no chance of burying them. The bombardment on heavily populated residential areas is constant, and medics say they've never seen such a humanitarian disaster before. The area of Bab Amr is of particular interest to the regime, and as they scramble to clear out Baba Amr from rebels, it seems that they have sent all of their warplanes to bomb the central region.

Now that international focus is on Homs, the regime has increased attacks in other cities, which is going unnoticed. I am so proud of my activist friends who are documenting everything to show the world. The world takes them for granted, but they are to be admired for keeping aloft the banner of truth, justice, and humanity in the face of lies, falsehood, and fabrications.

Journalists are banned from entering Homs and so, right now more than ever, the resolve and courage of those street journalists is appreciated. The most endearing of all is the Twitter Campaign by activists encouraging people to #CallHoms. The idea is that people from around the world and elsewhere in Syria dial random telephone numbers in Homs and reassure the people at the other end of the telephone line that the world is in solidarity with them; that they're not forgotten. This is so inspiring, and once again reminds me of the power and beauty of words.

The temperature is dropping here; it is getting into the low fifties, I think, and the expected low tonight is forty-six. So what do Arab women do? Make soup, of course. Ahhh, the smell of *shorabet al-adus* is so soothing, as is the familiar kitchen buzz of female voices. Mother and her sisters-in-law, my eldest cousin–sister, Nora, and my grandmother, all cutting onions, washing and drying the red lentils, and adding cumin, coriander seed, and Aleppo pepper among other beautiful, warming, and rich ingredients to the huge bubbling pot. What a hearty and nourishing soup, which will provide us with the nutrition to get us through this cold winter's day.

Father is on the couch, and the weight of the past few weeks has been too much for him. I'm watching him nod off, his head slumped on a cushion. He is mentally exhausted and just wants to rest.

The past couple of weeks have been draining. After the siege on Homs ended, tanks began arriving in the city centre of Hama. Snipers came and surrounded key protest spots, and explosions and gunfire were constant during the day. Electricity and internet services have been – and still continue to go – on and off.

Father is still nervous about being raided and sleeps a few streets away at an armed friend's house. Raids on residential homes have increased everywhere, particularly in Deir Ezzor, Hama, Daraa, and Homs.

'It's just a matter of time,' he constantly tells us. 'Try to destroy any evidence that proves we are dissidents.'

In Kafr Zeta, an area in Hama, army defectors killed eight soldiers and left many injured at a security checkpoint, and Father barely escaped. I always wonder, but dare not ask, if he has killed anyone yet. I don't want to picture him as a killer.

The FSA have rockets and RPGs, both of which I've seen photos of them handling on my brother's phone. This revolution is becoming more and more weaponised, and it's still hard to accept it. Weapons are being smuggled in, and money is being smuggled out.

Back in August, they blocked Visa and Mastercard in an attempt to prevent all transactions in Syria. Syrian businessmen who are fearful of the unstable economy are taking their assets to Lebanon. As our currency continues to drop lower in value, it is nearly impossible to exchange for dollars. When the city centre was quiet yesterday and some shops were trading as normal, Reem and I went to take some good still shots of the wreckage of a few buildings when we came across foreign businessmen entering the gold jewellery stores, eagerly filling their briefcases with all the jewellery on offer – no doubt for a pittance. Even businessmen are taking advantage of war, I guess. We waited around until they were gone and while the jewellery shop owner wouldn't disclose who they were, he did confirm that they'd all flown in from London to buy gold to take back to their native country.

'This is all your life's hard work. Don't give it away so cheaply.' Reem was furious.

'*Maa fii mishkile.* It's not a problem. I'm afraid this gold will be looted or taken away when the army raids the street,' he replied, smiling sadly.

He was just a man who, like the rest, now had to go about using savings for essential needs or to get away to a safer country. And for the rest of the world's savvy and money-hungry entrepreneurs, buying gold and other precious metals and resources while there was blood on the street was an opportunity not to be missed.

Silence. Meetings. Meetings. Discussions. Silence. Despite mediation efforts by the Arab League, despite people's hopes that there'd be a NATO intervention, despite all the other false hopes, everything is the same. And I think we are beginning to accept the bitter truth: Obama and the West won't be helping us like they did in Libya. There is nothing to gain here, and despite all the condemnations and lengthy discussions, we are on our own. Also, unlike Gaddafi, who didn't have much backing and support from other nations, our regime has China, Russia, Iraq's Muqtada al Sadr, Iran, and of course, Lebanon's Hezbollah. It's important to understand that in Libya it was Gaddafi, but here it's not Assad running the entire show . . . his father's minions are. The military have their own economy, for instance. If Assad is assassinated or steps down, this war won't end. Bashar was never destined for this throne; he may have been in line for the monarchy, true, but his father's crew are very much still alive.

The death toll has now surpassed four thousand, and as Russia delivers yet more missiles, more funerals are taking place in both Homs and Hama.

And me?

I am bored. Is it wrong to admit that? To even write or say that . . . when my people are dying for their country? It's true. I am struggling with boredom and emptiness. I miss summer days: fishing, swimming, strolling down Al-Mansour souk, eating out, partying, dancing, and enjoying the small pleasures of life, like love and friendships. Is this really just a temporary negative on the fabric of life? This is no way to live. I need to feel alive.

One of the pains of war is the isolation. It might be horrid to get injured when out there in the battlefield like the men, but at least there's adrenaline. It's exciting and interesting. It's tragic sitting and waiting at home, caged like a bird; the hours are slower, the days seem to be going nowhere, and there is nothing to look forward to.

When things are heated up, when surrounded with the buzz of people and passionate protesters, there are at least reasons to live – or reasons to die. My ever-comforting grandmother bought me my favourite drink earlier: ice cold rosewater with lemon juice, and made with fresh rose petals.

'Kick that feeling out! This is just a phase, it's not your fate.' She sat at the end of my bed.

I managed a meek smile and then grabbed my bag and headed out, not knowing where I wanted to go, but knowing I just wanted to leave, walk. Nothing mattered at that point more than the need to clear my mind. Not even the phone that kept on ringing.

With the setting sun, mosques around town produced sonorous recitations of the call to prayer, and as the competing calls emanated through loudspeakers from different directions, men and children on bicycles and donkey-drawn carts from nearby fields headed to the mosques. I headed in the opposite direction and walked a long distance until I reached al-Sayyad hill. There, I let the fresh evening breeze caress my face and smiled at the little bird that came to my feet. The hope that I needed; the sign that told me there's nothing to be afraid of, that I was still breathing, still alive and in touch with my senses, just a little lost.

I watched rebel fighters get up, from neat lines, and pray at the bottom of the hill. The phone vibrated in my pocket again. I took it out and smiled. It was him again. Just as the phone vibrations were about to end, I touched the answer button.

At last, I managed to say it to him.

'I miss you too.'

November's nine hundred and fifty death toll was the highest so far, and as winter sets in, the Arab Spring is well and truly over. This is now a full-blown war. Despite regular coverage from pan-Arab media, barbaric crimes against humanity occur constantly: a two-year-old child was shot dead in Latakia because the soldier didn't want her to grow into a protester. Women are being sexually abused, impregnated, and the vilest methods of torture are carried out on innocent human beings.

Soldiers who refuse to shoot at civilians are punished horrifically, children are being severely wounded with life-long injuries, and those trying to cross the borders are shot and killed. Not once has Syrian state television reported such crimes; perhaps they believe the word 'human' is exclusive to whoever is on their side. What is worse, the regime urged the necessity of attacking protesters, whom they call thugs, and so even locals who support the government – or are paid to – take part in the brutal massacres and harassment. The regime doesn't even pretend to be a benevolent defendant of human rights and democracy any more; they openly gun civilians down. Syrian security forces massacred the entire unarmed village of Kfar Oweid, near the Turkish border. They murdered a hundred in their homes after surrounding them completely.

Something else that has been on my mind is the marching orders given to one of our nation's revered fathers. Father Dall'oglio, who, of course, founded the community of Deir Mar Musa and welcomed people of all religions as sacred guests, like Abraham in both the Bible and the Quran, is a true, living human who took responsibility and shared his knowledge and opinions of the bloodshed with grace and care. If his expulsion won't open the eyes of my fellow Christians that the regime doesn't care for one of our legendary figures, let alone us, I don't know what will.

Our fathers belong in this land. This is the land of our ancestors, and the legacy of our great Christian fathers will most definitely outlive the forty years of Assad's. God bless his influence.

It is the day after Christmas; the first one that I've spent without my grandparents, my uncles and aunts, without my cousins, and without a Christmas tree or huge feast.

'Perhaps it's for the best that the road to Maaloula is dangerous,' my mother mumbled to my grandmother at breakfast.

However, everyone knows and can feel the growing tension between the families. My mother's side are extremely furious at my father and brother's involvement in the revolution, and they also know of my cyber and street activism. I have made it very clear to them that I am not interested in pleasing anybody, and as long as I believe in my convictions and feel my heart is on the right side – with the oppressed victims – I am virtuous. Admittedly, I do miss my now estranged family. I yearn for the little village with the rolling hills and all the glittery Christmas traditions.

My mother's attitude has been worsening, and her anxiety and depression is getting worse. Before this war, I used to think the hardest thing in life was burying loved ones, but watching them suffer, watching them cry and knowing I can do very little to change the things that make them so sad, is one of the hardest things ever. It hurts so badly to see my mother this way and to see her state of mind worsening. She does not deserve this, in any way.

My father is ignoring his wife's unhappiness and distancing himself from her and the family; the more involved he is in the revolution, the more he turns emotionally away from the family. This has resulted in Mother becoming so depressed, she is emotionally unavailable to her children and family.

It's not only this lack of cohesion in the family that is troubling me; the lack of political cohesion and lack of unity among the opposition groups mean the regime is cracking down on activists continuously and freely. And I specifically mean the opposition outside the country – the ones who continue to arm activists from the Free Syrian Army, especially in rural Syria, and encourage them to 'fight' like the rebels of Libya, despite no guaranteed protection from NATO or the world. Sitting at their desks in the West, it seems they don't actually feel the pain and loss we feel as our country destabilises and as our country drowns in blood. Actually, the heads of these groups are almost boastful of the numbers of the 'hero' martyrs.

I am more confused than sad. This is going to be a long winter.

I miss my father and I miss his stories, but today I miss his presence most painfully than ever, as today it is Baba's birthday. It has been more than two weeks since my father abruptly left. He disappeared on a protest Friday after a massive row with my mother. Tensions had become so hostile after all the door-slamming, the loud, late-night arguments about faith, ideologies, politics, commitment, and so forth, but we'd never ever thought he'd turn our back on us or leave without a word.

Mother is acting like nothing out of the ordinary has happened, while my poor grandmother sits dutifully for hours at a time, waiting at the window overlooking the door, watching out for his return. After the first few days of his absence, I was so sure that he would return home back any time, slinging his Kalashnikov over the garden bench and removing his grey boots. But as the days have gone by, we simply don't know where he has disappeared to – or even if he has disappeared at all. We only know that he has not been seen in the area. My younger brother, who normally accompanies him, also remains clueless.

At first, when the hours of his absence turned to days, we thought he would return and apologise for his selfish outburst, then when it turned to weeks, we realised that he was more than just upset.

I hear the sound of Mother coming through the front door. She has just returned from her doctor's appointment as she has a pretty bad case of flu. This is the last thing she needs. She is in a bad enough shape as it is – emotionally. Imagine what it feels like to be abandoned for the first time ever by your other half. Terrible, just terrible. But I know she, just like I and all the other women in this revolution, will heal.

I know I am strong, and I know how strong we Syrian women can be. But as 2011 has turned into 2012, strong as I feel, I am tired, so tired. I cannot find things to pass the days without electricity and without the freedom to go out with friends or relatives. I am trying to find joy in even the smallest of things, but my guard is not down, and the recent dramatic changes hurt like hell. The TV blares aimlessly in our house all day to make up for the lack of communication. When state TV news channels are on, we see how the world is supposed to be. When foreign news channels are switched on, we realise how the world really is.

So far, more than seven thousand Syrians have been killed in the quest for freedom, and the reluctance of the Arab League to make the repression and bombing end means Syria is now in a full-scale war. Syria is broken. She is bleeding – badly. Most people have been thinking of migrating as the chaos increases and as the regime shows no signs of negotiating, let alone stepping down. They don't care about the EU and Turkey imposing economic sanctions because they've got help from super-powers, namely Russia, China, and Iran.

The Arab League's laughable threats mean nothing to the regime. They recently blamed bomb attacks in Damascus on al-Qaeda terrorists when everyone knows they were staged. While the Syrian regime has just committed a gruesome massacre in Zabadani, with indiscriminate bombings on civilians and even more arrests, nearby in Homs, Syrians who once lived together are now cleansing people who don't follow their own ideology. People are being driven out of their homes.

According to an activist friend in Homs, people have been killed based on what's written on their ID card. The thing that sets Homs apart from other cities – even the pro-revolution ones – is that the Homsis are very much united; they don't differentiate between the lower and upper classes, the rich or the poor. Other cities, of course, *are* divided more with class, and so, for instance, rich Alawis and rich Sunnis will unite – even if they are of different ethnic groups – against the lower classes of society and against those calling for system reforms.

Not that it is an excuse of any kind, but the brutality of war has shattered some people's spirits and made them lose their respect and value for each other. Even in our home, I am so very sad that on his birthday, Baba has not even called to let us know how he is doing, even though his absence pains my grandmother, who has always lived with her eldest son. My dear, dear Teta; she sits on the prayer rug with her beads, praying out loud for him. She weeps, her tender eyes streaked with pain. It is a horrible thing for her to comprehend. And I do not need to repeat what hell that woman has been put through.

'Pray for him, pray for Mother too.' I pressed her feet. 'She is as lost as Father is and she is mad at the whole world.'

'May God guide her way. She is my daughter just as much as your father's sisters are, and may God keep my family safe from any more harm from the regime and heal us all,' she prayed.

I believe in the power of prayer and unity. I pray for healing. I know it can be done. Our whole, huge family knows that. Love is not unredeemable. There is no problem that cannot be solved; there is redemption, and Father just has to take that first step. God have mercy.

After what seems like forever, my father has finally come home. But my hopes of a perfect unison between him and my mother, and between them and her family, have been quashed. He has a scar in the middle of his forehead and looks even more rugged than before he left. When he first arrived today at dawn, things were tense, but when he approached my still-incoherent mother, he started to scream at her.

He scolded and berated her for a whole hour. Wasn't it supposed to be the other way around? *He* had been the one at fault. But no, the once intelligent, charming, and honourable husband brought back with him unbelievable discomfort and pain just by his presence in our home. He had been to Turkish territories in Iskenderun – or Alexandria as it's known in English. Apparently, Turkey was training opposition freedom fighters to fight in the increasingly violent civil war over there.

I have my qualms about why Turkey are getting so involved, and more so why freedom fighters from Syria are agreeing to be guided by them, but I think it's best to push those thoughts to the back of my mind because Syria is in crisis, and if I was a man trying to protect my loved ones and my land, I, too, would not be spending my time on analysis.

However, what is very clear is that my liberal, secular father, who by his own admission was a radical liberal, has now become increasingly sympathetic to religious leaders' messages. While he despises – and has always despised – fundamentalist perspectives like the ones imposed by the Taliban of Afghanistan or the Ayatollahs in Iran, he has begun to speak of the need for Islamically-based reform in Syria.

He has spent the day preaching about concepts that are entirely alien in our household. He has asked that I read commentary on the Quran, and that I observe the hijab.

'Mary wore the hijab too,' he argued.

I looked at him with wilful defiance but didn't dare argue back.

In the evening, after a tense supper consisting of grandmother's warm soup, bread, boiled eggs, and olives, he rudely asked me to switch off the television.

'I'll turn the volume low, if you like,' I replied. My mouth quivered with a nervous smile. 'My favourite show is on tonight – *Ayam Shamiyeh*.'

'You're still watching shows? Don't you know they want young people to distract themselves with nonsense TV programmes!' he said, his words dripping with hostility.

I take great joy in watching original and comical Syrian TV series, especially to lighten the day's load, and there he was forbidding my only source of entertainment. He was yelling at me about 'evil programming' that would ruin my mind and heart.

He became even more infuriated when an advert appeared on the flickery screen, featured a scantily clad Russian lady dancing while selling something behind the Arabic voiceover.

'Unacceptable in my household! Sexist and degrading to women.' He brandished his fist at the television. 'How can you sit and absorb this haram filth?'

It's hard for me to see him this impassioned about trivial issues, especially when there are lives being lost outside. I fully respect his dedication to the fight against the regime and his newly found faithfulness to his religion, but I know for the sake of my mental health, I must prepare to leave this toxic environment at home.

Revolution is a dirty, beautiful business, and certainly not for the faint of heart; it's most hard on them, and sometimes they don't recover. My grandfather was a living example of this. My grandmother said that the revolution of 1982 didn't end as he thought it would – peaceful and knowing. It ended with shrapnel and burnt buildings.

I hope Jido is now where everything is known and understood, and where he stands knowing how much he was adored by those who knew him through his youthful, sunny, and beautiful days – and appreciated by those who saw him on his dark days of struggles after he was released from prison. He was beautiful on both days.

Even today, thirty years later, the work and bravery of those martyrs inspires us. Despite what the regime plotted against us, the old heroes left behind their revolutionary work in the hands of the unborn. Today, the thirtieth anniversary of the 1982 Hama Massacre has befallen us, and on this day we remember and mourn our grandfather and our deceased and missing relatives more than any other day.

My iron-strong grandmother went to the graveyard. '*Ya Fairouz*, there are always tears left for the martyrs, and we can never stop crying,' she told me, before offering prayers throughout the evening.

Mother then told me how for years after the 1982 massacre, women, when embracing each other, would burst out crying before even greeting each other with *Salaam*. It was the most natural thing for people of Hama to do when they met or visited someone. This is because there were hardly any families here that had been spared. Every family had one hero at least.

This anniversary is like no other before it. This time, Syrians have openly mourned and openly shared their family's tales. The fear factor no longer exists. We are in the midst of another revolution in our homeland, and we have the help of international and social media. I have never seen Syrians so open about their family history. And for the youth like me, this has been our first proper opportunity to mourn our ancestors and, more importantly, find out what really happened.

A Facebook page has just been made specifically for this matter. The page contains first-hand accounts and narratives of those that lived through the 1982 tragedy. It includes photos of those who are still missing and biographies of the heroes, with some people openly admitting for the very first time that their fathers or grandfathers were killed. Activists who are working tirelessly to collect and sort the information have urged people not to be afraid and share the names of their deceased loved ones. This is because after the regime killed activists in the 80s, they'd made the families of the deceased sign documents which stated that their heroes were not killed by the regime, but murdered by the Muslim Brotherhood. They then kept the families quiet for all these years by offering them protection and other incentives.

The world may have not known – or had forgotten – about Hama's forty thousand murdered souls, the raped women, the injured children, and the brutal injuries carried out by the regime's thugs back then, but the stories aren't being suppressed any more. The adults have always been too petrified to discuss such a dangerous subject, but at the start of this revolution last year, it was Grandmother who began to tell me the true stories in detail and who inspired me to take up arms with my camera and choose to protest in the streets.

There were magnificent tributes at today's Friday protests around Syria, which were named 'Forgive Us, Hama'. The main message from the imam's public speech was that more than singing emotional songs and feeling bitter or sad, we had to take responsibility to keep those activists' legacies going. It would be the best way to pay tribute to such amazing brave souls.

Operating under my pseudonym as any sane Syrian activist does, I penned a tribute to my grandfather with the help of my grandmother and posted it on social media. I think it is more necessary than ever for all of us to document the true narratives of 1982, and despite the regime burying entire villages in mass graves, we cannot bury our elders' stories. Burying the truth would be betraying them.

It is in our hands to achieve what we are so capable of achieving. For me, people like my grandfather were our guide; now we must re-commit ourselves to their task. If it can be imagined, it can become reality

4 February, 2012

'Fairouz? Where are you? I need you!' Mother's voice was slurred and I could hear her stagger into the table in the kitchen.

'What is it, Mama?' I asked, following the sounds of the cupboards being banged open and shut. My heart broke a little when she spun round and I saw her wild eyes and dishevelled hair. She was drunk again.

'I need . . .' She broke off and then started weeping, fat tears rolling down her cheeks.

I took her by the elbow and led her into the bedroom, laying her down on the bed and smoothing my hand over her forehead, like I was the mother and she was the child. Gradually, her tears dried up and her breathing became deep and even.

I wonder who keeps bringing her the alcohol. I've gone round the house so many times to get rid of it, but she gets it from somewhere. I suspect it's one of the local Marlboro cigarette sellers that runs errands for her. She must have been drinking all day again to get in a state like this.

Yesterday, she started cursing at the womenfolk who were doing house chores in our shared courtyard. She got very belligerent, ugly, and foul, so they told her they would not sit there and listen to the insults. They locked themselves and their kids away. They don't do drunk – and neither do I.

I know she's been drinking to wash away her pain and anxiety, but I don't know how to handle it. My grandmother doesn't even tend to her or approach her. I know Father and Mother used to drink wine on occasion, and Father drinks socially, but this is new, and horrible. I know she's in pain and hurting but we all are. I can't agree with her decision to get drunk every day to solve the problems the whole family is trying to deal with.

Now I have retreated back to my safe place – my room – because you cannot help people who do not want to help themselves. As sad as it might be for her, her life is still okay and she can move on. But she will end up alienating good people who love her and are trying to help.

I haven't commented much on the current political situation of late. Largely because I have been unable to go outside much due to an increase in kidnappings, but also because my brain can't grasp all the layers of what's going on. But I believe I know enough.

My homeland is now thirsty, hungry, and bloodied. The Syrian regime is responsible for the lives of innocent people and for making my mother, brave as she is, lose the will to live.

5 𝓕ebruary, 2012

Today, I met up with a new online friend I had made via Facebook. Despite all the differences the Arab Spring has highlighted, it has also brought people together. A flood of original ideas, thoughts, and creative expression now replaces the previously stale narratives served up on the web from the Middle East. With the help of social media connections and the bonds made through our activism, I've made a whole new family. We share our hopes, pains, and our ups and downs. Love has also blossomed among many social activists.

I agreed to meet Ayah at a local coffeehouse. I am still new to activism, but Ayah is not only a long-time political and social activist, she is also a feminist, and through her, I have just discovered the Arab women's movement. She has alluring jet-black straight hair, olive skin, well-chiselled cheeks, and clear eyes behind thin spectacles, which give her an intellectual and chic air. And so it was easy telling her about my mother's issues and the way my father had physically assaulted her when he came home and found tens of beer bottles, most empty, and Mother in squalor. Ayah then shared with me her memories of violence at the hands of her abusive father.

'I got so used to Arab men being sexist, nasty, oppressive assholes, that I didn't know any different,' she explained over the bouncing beats of Arabic top forty music on the television. 'But we need to rise up against domestic abuse – and discrimination at work too.'

'But how?' I asked.

'Well, we need to make sure our revolutions aren't just focused on one issue. They need to tackle oppression and colonialism. And there needs to be some sort of understanding that patriarchy is oppressive!'

I had never before seen it this way. '*Mazboot*, you're right,' I replied. 'And the idea that we cannot talk about our families, and oppression, and abuse within the family. . . It's against what the revolution should stand for, and it holds us back.'

Ayah told me how she had horrible nightmares about living under her abuser's control and even as an adult, she suffered flashbacks and recurring nightmares of her abuse.

'I'm an adult in the dream, living under his control, and he is being violent and abusive and I can't get out.' She stared at her water pipe then looked up. 'These dreams unsettle me so much. I feel helpless, like when I was a child and had to witness my father attack my helpless Mama and me and my brothers and sisters, and there's nowhere to hide, no one to help us, and he has complete power over us.'

Abuse and violence in the family home of so many Syrians has led to very oppressive lives for Syrian women. For instance, I think of the lady who lives opposite us. Her husband is forever scolding her and demoralising her, making her do all the house chores and care for his children while he sits outside all day smoking cigars and hitting his depressed-looking donkey.

Not only are women like Ayah striving against the old misogynists and patriarchs, but also now, after the revolution began, one type of oppressive cultural behaviour is being replaced – or reaffirmed – with the rise of 'religious' oppression. What kind of revolution can we call this if women like myself are being bullied to cover up? My Father's comments about how I should wear the hijab swim to the front of my mind.

'The thing is,' said Ayah, sitting back in her chair, 'it's frustrating to see Eastern women complain about being oppressed but not doing anything about it. Look at Arab women in the West, for instance. They've taken their principles and their rights and combined them to what suits them. But here . . . Here, Arab women believe they are born just to marry and serve men. They don't strive for better.'

There was silence while I thought about this for a while. I always used to laugh when my grandmother would say, 'A women arrives at her husband's home wearing her white wedding dress and must remain until she leaves in her other white dress.'

'What dress is that?' I'd questioned her.

'Her *kafan*, her white burial cloth, of course,' she'd said, in a matter-of-fact way.

Ayah was looking at me, waiting for a response.

'I see what you're saying,' I said, slowly. 'But that kind of thinking has been taught to us since we were kids.'

Ayah banged her fist down on the table. 'Exactly! Enough is enough. It's time that democracy for men is also democracy for us. And not just democracy, human rights too.'

'And respect,' I said. 'Respect for our needs. We deserve to be educated, to be independent, employed, represented. We're all so worried about religious fundamentalists taking over that no one seems to be worried about the alternative – another government that seeks to keep us imprisoned in cultural changes. Over the last eleven months, women have contributed just as much as men to this revolt. We cannot let the revolution undo all that.'

Ayah nodded and smiled at me. 'You understand then, Fairouz? You understand why our group exists?'

'Yes, I do. Who started it?'

'A bunch of Egyptian women at first. Women who think the same way we do. They learned the hard way that women don't feature in plans for change.' Ayah laughed, drily. 'Can you ever imagine, God forbid, a woman leading Syria one day?'

As I walked home from our meeting, I felt so dispirited that we live in a country where domestic violence is seen as the norm. In fact, a man who has 'control' over his wife is heralded as a hero. This is a place where men can be abusive, both mentally and physically, without any accountability. Despite the importance of the pro-democracy protest movement outside, it is important to remember that the revolution starts at home.

6 February, 2012

Firas and Madmour, I suddenly realised, were now looking directly at one another, through holes in opposite buildings. This image will never leave my memory: the awkwardness between them – Madmour's coolness and composure, and Firas's love for him.

The strict media censorship by the Syrian regime, and the precarious conditions that journalists face, has thwarted the possibility of documenting fighters in combat. Due to our limited access to the frontlines, and because curiosity got the better of me, a few other activists and I have begun to follow fighters into action as they engage in fierce fire fights. My best friends were both pro-revolution and anti-revolution, and I didn't care, but for people to turn around and start shooting each other was unthinkable.

Friends try to stay in contact with each other since the war started but, understandably, we have all been distanced. It is incredible how little it takes for people who lived together, married among each other, did business together, and went to school together to become enemies – some by choice, others by force. Many a time, when men are engaged in fighting, just a few yards away, facing each other, they discover that the opponent is a relative or a friend of a friend, a neighbour, a former classmate.

'How is your brother doing these days, I heard he manages a company in Kuwait?' They sometimes even sit down, share cigarettes, and catch up on life. That's how it is in the Middle East – everyone's related somehow. People who come from outside to bomb Arabs are usually people who've been bought up to believe Arabs are terrorists. In Iraq and Afghanistan, it was invaders shooting down strangers. They had total detachment from the people they were shooting at. Here, guys who once kicked balls together and argued only over Real Madrid vs Barcelona now suddenly kick at each other's corpses.

If someone had asked me a year ago, before the civil war broke out, I'd never think this could happen. But the truth is, it can happen at any time and any place, in any part of the world. The divides were first political, and then ethnic, then religious. And then things just blew up.

We move back into a corner of the fifth-floor apartment to where the others are clustered.

'They've got us now, haven't they?' says Kirsten, the Austrian, softly.

Two interpreters, four photographers, two journalists, a stray dog, and seven rebel fighters all huddled together, wondering if Assad loyalists will pour fire inside.

'You get the redhead in the window, I'll take the guy on the roof,' a rebel tells Madmour. 'Now, go! Now!'

From where I'm crouched, I can see the red-headed guy silhouetted against the wall. His hand is on the trigger. The first guy on the roof is down. He was caught so off guard, he flipped over onto the elegant railings, and the rebel fighter shot at him again. Still screaming, his hands flailing wildly, clutching at the jasmine plants on a balcony on the top floor and crying for help, the dying man gasped his last breath, crumpled up, and fell forward. The body turned over and over in space until it hit the ground, mangled up in rubble. Two holes in the dead body stared up at us like eyes reddened with blood

Madmour's turn. He leaned out and fired a burst from his machine gun. The redhead was turning towards him when he pulled the trigger; their eyes met at the exact moment when he was hit.

I had the best view of it all. It was only for a second, but in that instant when their eyes locked, I saw Firas's lips twist in pain and then the look of surprise at seeing his best friend in the whole world pointing a gun at him – and at meeting death so suddenly.

A deathly hush fell after that. Madmour looked at his best friend falling dead through the hole and his body convulsed.

'Fuck, what did I do?' he cried out in anguish.

The other rebel fighters swiftly moved on, but Madmour stayed back and we went along with the photographers to see our friend, Firas. A flame of red hair falling over his face, he lay still. Madmour knelt down and felt his neck for a pulse, but got nothing. His AK47 had left gaping, bloody holes in Firas's chest, his body parts blown away by the sheer force of being shot at such close range.

He then pulled a blanket out from a nearby child's bunkbed and tenderly laid it on his corpse.

'I did this?' Madmour looked at me, crestfallen.

I reached my hand out to him, still shocked. Sweat beads fell from his forehead; I wondered how he could carry this in his heart and his memory. I looked into his eyes: the lust of war and revolution suddenly vanishing, his heart broken.

The menfolk are busy in our courtyard making explosives out of ammonium nitrate, plant fertiliser, batteries, electrical wiring, steel pipe, end caps, nails, and aluminium foil, and making catapults from street signposts.

Inside, Mother has placed a pot on the slow cooker: chicken, spices, onions, and olive oil. We have not eaten family-favourite *riz bi dijaj* – chicken with rice – for ages.

Hama is getting much too dangerous to go out even in the daytime now. It isn't the tit-for-tat fighting between the Sunni and Alawi–Shiite that is the big threat any more, it is criminal thugs operating a 'kidnap trade' which is only getting bigger and bigger. As joblessness meets lawlessness, money-hungry thugs have turned kidnapping into a lucrative business while other small criminals strip people down on the streets for mobile phones, jewellery, and money. Hollywood movie-like crimes such as hijacking of cars in public and anonymous phone calls demanding extortionate ransoms to get the victim back are becoming so common now. Of course, there are good people, but now there are also a lot of bad people.

People are now more afraid of the criminal gangs that are roaming the streets than they are afraid of the regime's thugs. There is nobody to arrest criminals and nobody to police the streets so, if you are a victim of crime, there are no law enforcers to make a complaint to. It is every man and woman for themselves.

I haven't seen most of my friends and family for ages but managed to see Reem and Emad to talk about Firas's death and Madmour's state of mind. Emad has been a calming presence in my life and we've had more chance to talk since his fiancée left – their engagement is called off for now because of the war. Although 'talking' consists of revolution-related stuff. He describes to me how the Free Syrian Army has already taken policing into their control in places like Baba Amr and are getting better organised.

'Every revolution has teething problems,' he said, confidently, 'And it may not be soon, but we *will* achieve our vision.'

And who knows? The new opposition council has a budget – with money coming in from rich Arab Gulf countries – and has been handing out medical and humanitarian supplies to the most needy.

Emad is now a FSA fighter, and I worry about his safety all the time.

My dear, stop worrying,' he said soothingly. 'Don't you know that what social media activists are doing is more dangerous? You going out to film the protests puts you more in danger than me.'

I couldn't argue back with that. It's very true. A camera's role is greater than a weapon. The activists know this, and the regime knows this. A camera is still the regime's biggest threat.

When someone with a camera is caught and arrested, they are tortured more than a FSA fighter. I have many friends who have lived to tell their experiences.

Still, the thought of something happening to someone so special tears me apart. Last week, Emad was in serious danger of being slaughtered in Homs. He and his fellow fighters had run to the scene of a suicide-bomb attack that had been allegedly carried out by Iranian Revolutionary Guards. He had been helping to remove the sixty bodies of women and children when the Shabiha had chased them with guns, even capturing two of their comrades and dragging them away.

What's really mind-boggling to me is how the I'm-so-secular Assad and the army generals are so opposed to religious fundamentalists but allow Iranian and Hezbollah extremists to operate in Syria. What kind of logic is that? I mentioned this to Emad during one of our talks.

'It's all about keeping them in power,' he said. 'The conspiracy theories and the propaganda. They don't give a damn about extremism and radicals, even the ones who have trained elsewhere and are just jostling real freedom fighters aside because they want to overthrow Assad for their own reasons.'

'Doesn't that worry Assad though?' I asked.

Emad laughed bitterly. 'If you ask me, Assad not only doesn't care about them, he actually is deliberately allowing them to run havoc. Hell, he's probably even supporting them just so he can sit back and say "I told you so".'

'That does make sense,' I said, thinking it over.

'He's hoping it will tear us apart,' said Emad, taking a sip of his drink and then shaking his head. 'There's so much infighting now and it's getting worse. The Sunnis and the hardcore Islamic groups are at each other's throats. Now it's not just Shiites fighting Sunnis, but moderate Sunnis fighting extreme Sunnis.'

'So much division,' I said, feeling a wave of hopelessness pass over me. 'Poor against the rich, rural against urban, Homs and Hama against Aleppo and Damascus . . .'

Emad took up my train of thought. 'Conservatives against secularists, Baathists against non-Baathists, Saudi Arabia against Iran, Russia against the USA . . . It goes on.'

Even now, back at home and writing in my diary, I still can't stop thinking about it.

I hate how the regime tries to continue to deflect the attention of the Syrian masses when it comes to Israel versus Palestine issues. How foolish do they still think we are? Dina used to tell us that the regime had always wanted to keep the mass populace dumb and uneducated so they'd be much easier to fill with propaganda. The truth is, Syrians now despise Russia and Iran more than they do Israel. Jumping on the Palestine bandwagon has long been a way to keep many naïve Syrians supportive of the Assad regime and channel their energies to that cause rather than their own.

It's absolutely sickening when you think how the Palestinians are just pawns in this. One just needs to see how Assad has really treated Palestinian refugees in Syria, who live like rats in their camps and ghettos, treated as the lowest of society, to realise he doesn't care about Palestinians. Keeping the public busy with anti-Israel rhetoric is no longer working.

Our blindfolds have been removed now and people's minds are awakened.

I let the scents of our courtyard jasmine fill my nose, taking a deep breath. *Boom.* A distant blast in the sky sent a massive ball of fire and a black mushroom cloud into the sky. I didn't even bother to spoil my sweet moment. Somewhere, far away, someone was ducking down, or someone had just taken his or her last breath. I decided that in light of the ongoing crisis and the fact that a bomb might just hurl our mangled bodies into eternity at any moment, it was time for me to leave for Damascus.

10 February, 2012

I've just put some vegetable soup on for later; I've got the nasty cold which is going around, but that is no problem, it will run its course. What *is* important is that we are all warm and safe and snuggled up in our beds. Thankfully, electricity has not gone in our area so we have fuel and water. I feel desperate here in Hama: scared, hungry, broke, awaiting death.

It is difficult enough to make ends meet with fuel and heating oil shortages, as well as the price increase of basic food and necessities. With the revolution, we have struggled even more. They say that our city of Hama still hasn't recovered economically from the previous revolt of 1982. The city, while it has developed slowly since, still has much fewer opportunities.

There is a job opening for a teaching assistant at a school in Damascus due to teachers leaving the country, and Father's Damascene best friend, Ammo Saleh, has put in a good word for me. Apparently they are desperate for someone whose English is at a good standard, and so they are prepared to overlook my qualifications and are willing to give me a trial. It has been decided that in order to save my basic wage, I could live in Ammo Saleh's home in Damascus while I work.

I am making the most of my last precious mornings with my grandmother. We have our morning tradition, where we sit around the kitchen table, eating pastries and sipping coffee and talking for hours. Of course, she teaches me, or has publications all stacked for me to read and discuss. Topics vary, from agriculture in Syria, to old Edward Said articles, to geography, to soap reviews, leaving her lessons from the *Seerah* – history of the Prophet Muhammad – and stories of the past prophets for the evenings.

We have so much fun too, listening to Fairouz – the iconic Lebanese singer for whom I was named – during the early mornings and singing to the other Arab icon Umm Kulthum's music at night. Teta's morning talks are always so full of wisdom. She recalls her memories, stories of her life at her father's farm, her family history, my grandfather's stories. As well as her intelligence, it's her memory that amazes me. My Teta is by far the most impressive woman I know, and we have plenty of amazingly accomplished women in both my mother and father's family, but nobody is as remarkable as she is. In exactly two months she will be seventy-nine. A seventy-nine-year-old and she is as sharp, active, fit, and as gorgeous and engaged in life as she has always been.

'*Azeezti*, my precious. You should make peace with your father before you leave to go to Damascus.'

My grandfather had been very much like my father – an angry but compassionate man by nature, my grandmother reminded me. She rubbed almond oil on the palm of her hands before patting her hands over my head, leaving my normally dry hair shiny and warm.

'It's funny, because your grandfather's father – your great grandfather – was a conservative who despised your grandfather for his activism and belief in an open democratic and secular Syria. He was very patriotic and believed in traditionalist ideas, and he and your grandfather never agreed on politics and religious ideas. But despite years of bickering, he still loved his son no less and always had his back, even when security police knocked on his door looking for your Jido. But they eventually made up for the missed years and enjoyed each other's company until his passing.'

'He loves you, *ya* Fairouz, with his whole heart and soul, and you children are his life. Even when it now feels like he has chosen a favourite, based on those who chose to follow his religious way, that is not so. He is just finding himself and has been sucked in by the Islamists. But you and your mother, despite being Christian, are the loves of his life.'

We both hugged with tears in our eyes while Teta mumbled something about distances and our eternal connection to each other.

Hama – the city referred to in the Old Testament as Hamath the Great – is not doing so great, and I am filled with guilt and sadness to leave it in such a way. But I must leave – for now.

Today is my last night here in Hama, the city where I was born, the city that raised me and built me. In the afternoon, my entire group of activist friends came to bid me goodbye. I was overwhelmed with the arrival of my friends-turned-family at my home, much to the objection of my father who was aghast at the mixing of sexes – for the first time in his life. Luckily, after an hour or so, he had been called out to go to Aleppo where there'd been two massive suicide bombs. Relief. We finally had the house and courtyard to ourselves and under the winter sky, we ate a warm meal of *dawood basha*, the Syrian version of meatballs, cooked in a tomato herb sauce and served with rice, and drank Miranda and bottles of al-Rayyan *arak*.

I couldn't imagine tomorrow without the enthusiastic voices and cheerful faces of those people around me. They have dedicated their youth to a cause, and have shown abundant love and concern for not only one another, but also towards their whole nation. Being a part of Syria's struggle for justice and liberation together is truly a sweet and inspiring honour.

When the party began, I felt that it was the beginning of the end of the happiest days of my life. I watched as Samer, Omar and Leila synchronized their *tablas*, and as Hassane, Lena, Mirvat, Qasim, Mary, Ziad, and the rest all joined hands and started *dabke* dancing to the upbeat Fares Karam music.

I watched as they laughed at Mirvat, the pretty blonde with blue eyes and a neat little figure, who couldn't keep up with the pace of the dance. She was dressed head-to-toe in leopard print – Arab girls tend to always overdo it with leopard print. On the other side, I watched Leila dressed in a masculine t-shirt, sitting beside the boys, shoulders arched straight and the movement of her fingers on the drums a mesmerising sight. Leila was perfect and articulate and even led the chanting at the protests with the loudspeaker and microphone, instructing and directing the crowds. She had led crowds of men at protests and created havoc for Assad's regime. And she was a she – a big accomplishment in the Arab world. She had done a lot for her age, for anyone that age in the East or the West. All I had done at fifteen was hit puberty.

Actually, each and every one of them is so unique and wonderful, and I was so happy that they'd thought of giving me a farewell party. The outpouring of love, care, laughter, and beauty made me realise how very blessed I am to have friends of such calibre, wit, and joy. As the evening drew to a close, and as hot tea was passed around, I could not hold back the tears. I tearfully told them all how sad I was to leave them behind as I stood at the top of the steps just before curfew time.

'I am thrilled, moved, and humbled. Next time we dance, we are going to dance on a free and liberated ground.'

These words made them erupt into singing our favourite song of the moment.

Jannah Jannah . . . Ya Watana. (Heaven, heaven . . . our nation)

I was greatly moved by the powerful, poetic, yet poignant words and wept like a baby who was leaving her mother. I gave each of my friends hugs with promises of returning to Hama very soon.

Emad, who had also made a very special effort to attend this party, came towards me. Black hair slicked back, mild green-blue eyes, strongly built and tanned, he exuded a raw magnetism. He has the face and body of a warrior, but a sweet, shy smile of a kitten. A sensual soul with the will of a lion, he is dangerously handsome.

He took me to the side, placed his strong arms on my shoulders, and gazed deep into my eyes as if to reassure me that we'd meet again. When he did that, I suddenly wanted us to relate in a physical way, not just emotionally.

I wanted him, but I knew Damascus was calling me. Some day, when it is the right time, I will let my love for him flourish.

Where will I be tomorrow? What will I see? Who will I be meeting? What shall I pack? All the questions that were going through my mind before I left with my brother to catch the morning bus yesterday. All these questions and the mystery of what my new life in Damascus would be like made this journey all the more intriguing.

We bumped over the rough and rocky desert highways for more than eight hours in a journey that would normally take less than three. We had to take back roads to avoid high-risk fighting areas. A look at this morning's Facebook feed showed updates from Homs showing very heavy shelling by loyalist forces in the Baba Amr district, mortars and bombs in Al-Khalidiya, and images of thousands of Homs residents hiding desperately in their cellars preparing for Assad forces who were about to attack with wrath.

I didn't know if the nervousness I felt was because of the daunting new life ahead of me, or if it was because I knew Assad's gangsters had filled areas around Hama and other cities to prevent people from fleeing and humanitarian aid from entering. I think it was a combination of both.

Soon we had lost Hama in the distance, and I could see only dusty desert roads ahead. Beside me to the right, through the creaky windows, I could see the scenery, which featured endless mountains, seemingly barren at first, but as I gazed longer and longer, I could see exotic birds, impressive trees, and mountain animals all amazingly camouflaged against the desert colours. At times, it looked like a beautiful Biblical scene, and at times, when the bus sped past huge trucks carrying commerce on the highway that joined Europe and Africa and got jammed in between overloaded lorries, it seemed like we were in hell.

I had almost nodded off when my face slammed into the window as the bus came to a screeching halt. I looked around at terrified faces as we heard yelling. As I tried to peer out of the window, there was a loud banging noise, which to my trained ears, sounded like guns being knocked against the door.

I looked to the bus driver, whose face was pale. After a moment, he pressed a button on his dashboard and the doors opened.

'Out of the way, fool.'

My heart sank. I knew then it was the Shabiha, whose name means ghosts in slang Arabic and who are Assad's plainclothes militia. They have plagued us Syrians for years. One of them, who looked to be the leader, pointed a Kalashnikov at the bus driver. 'No heroics and no one gets hurt, understand?'

The bus driver licked his lips and nodded, his hands shaking as they clutched the wheel. I sunk down into my seat, arranging my clothes to hide any semblance of my figure. The leader strolled down the aisle of the bus, poking his gun into people's bags and extracting items every so often to throw back to the men following him. I moved my bag slowly and silently underneath the seat in front so it was hidden from view.

The leader stopped by my row and glanced over at me. The old woman beside me was clutching onto her handbag, her knuckles pale, and staring straight ahead.

The leader laughed. 'What have you got in there that you clutch it so tightly?' He grabbed it from her and began rifling through, throwing her meagre possessions onto the floor. When he reached a small, dog-eared photograph, he stopped. 'Who's this?' he demanded, shoving the photograph in the old woman's face.

She didn't answer.

The thug grabbed her arms and shook her. It took everything in me not to reach over and push him away. But I couldn't draw attention to myself. I had to be invisible.

'I asked a question. Who is this?'

I could see the picture now – it was of a young man wearing military clothing and smiling broadly. He looked a bit like Emad, and it was clear he was a freedom fighter from his attire.

'My grandson,' the old woman said, eventually, reaching out for the photograph.

The thug barked out a laugh. 'Filth,' he said, and tore the photograph into tiny pieces. Still laughing, he spat on the old woman and moved on. I grabbed her hand and stroked it as a single tear trickled down her cheek.

When the leader was satisfied that no one had anything of interest, he went back to the driver.

'Tell these people to get off this bus, and then turn around and drive back to where you came from.'

The driver swallowed. 'Can't they stay on?'

The leader lifted his gun. 'Do it.'

We all gathered together our things, and I bent down to help the old woman retrieve her discarded items from the floor. Then we hurried off the bus and stood, watching, as the bus turned around and headed off into the dust, and the Shabiha thugs jumped into some jeeps and sped off in the other direction. We were in the middle of nowhere.

All we could do was walk. No one had any mobile phone signal, and so we walked, dragging our luggage. After about half an hour, we saw a village in the distance, and a ragged cheer went up. But when we reached it, it was deserted. At a rundown mosque just outside the village, the frail imam told us it was an hour's journey by donkey to the next populated village and suggested we find a taxi in the morning. It was nearing sunset and we didn't want to venture into the unknown alone.

But then, as we walked aimlessly, we saw clusters of black tents in the distance. Bedouins, masters of the desert. Their tents made of goat and sheep hair were easily visible from afar, erected in separate groups alongside their Toyota trucks filled with water tanks, goats and fat sheep, colourful and busy women, herds of camels, and children chasing after a ball.

As we got closer, we saw that they had lined up and were performing maghreb prayers, and we waited silently until they finished.

A rugged-looking Bedu approached us and invited us to the tents after seeing us limping with our luggage. The ever-hospitable folk received us well, offering us barley bread and fresh sweet milk.

To our delight, a big traditional brass pot was brought into the tent by one of the tribal elders. While sitting sipping coffee flavoured with cardamom in front of the fire pits on the tent's carpet, we warmed ourselves up, thanking these generous nomads over and over again.

The Bedouin – all of who are Sunni Muslims – instructed us that they'd be up early for morning prayers and would be breaking camp after dawn, but we were most welcome to stay with them. We learned that they'd been at the encampment for three days, and in true nomadic Bedouin form, were moving on about thirty kilometres to the west now that their animals had finished grazing the land.

I watched how the tough women prepared our evening meal using dried camel dung for cooking fuel. The older men in their loose and airy *jellabiye* robes took off their *kuffiyeh* headscarves and lay down on the floor cushions.

I decided to do the obvious thing and join the colourfully dressed women behind the decorative partition, the *gata*. While the other section looked homely and lovely, this one was overflowing with mess. Utensils filled the area, and there was hardly any place to move among the big-boned bustling women. They asked me where I was from. I told them our tribe's name and origin and they nodded their heads, continuing to bicker and fuss over the preparation of the food.

Before sleeping, the women filled up holes with goat hair in the tents to ensure no spiders or snakes could enter, and then they kindly lent us their thick woollen cloaks – *bishts*. I took one and immediately fell asleep.

After the sleepy morning prayers and a surprisingly filling breakfast, I watched the women swiftly pack up, the goats nibbling on the last bit of grass and the men loading the tanker trucks. The mean camel that had bothered me since I arrived showed me his square teeth. It was time to go.

I watched the women getting dressed in their vibrant attire in awe; these desert women were symbols of courage, endurance, and patience, and I had gained valuable perspectives on life from them to take away with me on my journey ahead. They were Bedouin in their purest form, unlike the sedentary ones we are so used to – the ones who have half-settled into towns, abandoned their nomadic lifestyle and integrated. These people truly lived on the edge of survival and experienced raw nature.

When the married women finished adorning themselves with heavy makeup and very heavy silver necklaces and jewellery, I fixed my camera lens and quickly captured photos of their beauty.

We paid a taxi driver a high price for the next part of our journey. The dryness made my lips yearn for moisture and my skin yearn for Nivea as we bumped over the rough desert track for hours, dust seeping in through the thin windows and choking our throats. As well as the heat, the cold air – winds from Asia – made the journey more uncomfortable.

Looking out of the window on the road to Damascus, I tried to remember the Biblical story of the Apostle Paul, whose dramatic conversion to Christianity occurred on his road to Damascus. Paul, whose name was Saul at the time, was on the way to Damascus, furious with Christians and all who associated with Jesus, and he was thirsty for their blood. It was on that road that a bright light from heaven shone on him and made him and his companions fall to the ground. The light was so powerful, it made him go blind for three days. Apparently, that is when Jesus rose from the dead and spoke to him.

His startling spiritual vision was far from my windowpane view, and so I was very glad when we stopped at Baghdad Cafe, where we had a place to wash, eat, and rest for a short while. We wandered in the souvenirs section, looking at the desert rocks and marine fossils on sale until the taxi driver called us back.

I knew we were close to reaching Damascus even without watching for the green road signs because of the miles of barren wild land – the description found in the Bible. I have not travelled to Damascus for a number of years and certainly never taken such a long and precarious journey in my life. It was nearly noon, and the sky was no longer brilliant blue. The only colours among the banal desert landscape were billboards of President Assad with patronising captions like '*Souria Allah hamiya*' – 'Syria, God protects her', and '*Ana ma' Souria*' – 'I am with

Syria' – a stark reminder that we were now entering a different playing field. This was no Hama or Homs. This was Damascus – home of the regime.

After avoiding much hassle from the numerous checkpoints upon arriving, I could finally breathe and I felt my nervousness disappear. And when we finally found our way to Ammo Saleh's apartment complex, I was even more relaxed. In true Syrian style, I was warmly welcomed with a grand dinner, skewer after skewer of succulent grilled kebabs and vegetables. Pride of place was given to a beautifully presented mountain of *mansaf*, the tender slow-cooked camel calf served on fragrant, fluffy rice.

Ammo Saleh's only remaining child in Damascus, her siblings now in America, showed me to the guest room, which was to be my new home.

Despite my tiredness, I was too eager to explore my new surroundings and neighbourhood, but I was strongly advised to get rest before doing anything. So I conceded, groaning inwardly, knowing that I really did need to rest, and besides, I could use the time to sit, absorb, and write about my journey and become acquainted with my new living quarters.

Sipping tea in a smoky Damascus cafe and trying to get used to the Damascus slang, I am waiting for Ammo Saleh's Eritrean housekeeper, Ella, to finish her supermarket errand so we can return home. It is the only cafe in Ammo Saleh's area that serves real coffee without the pretentiousness or price that goes with it. Having ventured into several 'boutique' cafes this morning, I was given disdainful looks from silky-haired baristas when I asked why they only had one type of bean and served only espresso-based drinks. Pretty latte art and fancy mugs don't make watered-down coffee any tastier.

I quickly figured out that Uncle Saleh lives in one of Damascus's nouveau riche areas, where Damascenes with money live and park their Mercedes in front of their high-rise buildings or villas. Nearby is the tree-lined, jasmine-scented Malki Avenue with its elegant balconied apartment blocks. The boulevards are filled with outlandish boutiques, expensive restaurants, and a shopping mall where Syria's upper class come to shop for French cheese and wine, gourmet chocolate and burgers, Heinz ketchup, the latest technology gadgets, and designer attire. This is very unlike the upscale residential areas we have in Hama; this one is more of a cocktail mix. There are expats here and people from all religions, social groups, and ethnic backgrounds. From Russia and Armenia, to Turkey and Uzbekistan, Iran and America.

'Welcome to the urbane and cosmopolitan world of Damascus,' Ammo Saleh said, laughing at me when I described my new shocking discoveries to him, having had a tour of the area.

From what I've seen so far, the upper classes (*al-akabir*) around me seem to have an obsession with the right schools for their children, social clubs, skin complexion, and dressing up.

People in this part of Damascus are image-conscious, and those who can afford it wear expensive clothing, perfumes, watches, and drive very flashy cars, and the elite women show off their family's wealth and status through physical beauty and adornment.

Ammo Saleh's normally haughty daughter, Mimi, must have noticed my bewilderment at the impeccably dressed women. She obviously felt pity on me and invited me to her bedroom. She was not the worldly snob I had assumed. After making me sit down on her bedroom couch, she looked me full in the face and said bluntly, 'I need to clean you up so people here won't know where you are really from.'

She then took out a huge drawer full of makeup and painted one side of my face, explaining why she was doing what she was doing, then told me to copy her on the other side of my face.

She spent thirty minutes teaching me how to contour my face through shading and highlighting.

'What do you mean I should "contour"?' I asked.

'Think of it this way,' she said while opening a liquid bottle which had a French-looking label on. 'Everything you highlight or lighten comes forward, and everything you contour or darken recedes.

'No, look, you've done your side of the face wrong.' She pulled the brush from my hands. 'Now you look like you have a streak of dirt on your face.'

I was really finding it difficult to grasp the concept, let alone the technique. I loved my soft features and slightly rounded face but didn't dare object.

'It's about creating dimension, which is why you contour and use this blusher and bronzer. As well as dimension, you must use it to bring colour and add depth to your face.'

She continued to explain to me how my face was a blank canvas and I must define all my facial bones in order to look more attractive.

Next, she gave me a handsome tailored silk blouse and matching pencil skirt, describing them as 'sophisticated'. Finally, I properly understood what the classical Arabic term *mudamshaq*, which derives from *Dimashq* – Damascus – actually meant. It also means to be Damascenised, which is to become urbanized and/or effete. And effete was what I was becoming, surrounded with all this extravagance. Mimi brought out a violet blazer for me and finished the look with silver jewellery.

'No, don't hide that belt buckle,' she said, scolding me.

I hadn't realised the belt buckle held so much value. It was just a letter of the alphabet to me, but as Mimi explained, the whole idea was to show off the letter.

'It's designer and worth a lot of money,' she said with bubbly enthusiasm.

I smiled politely, secretly thinking that the grotesque tan-coloured belt – despite being a thin one– really didn't suit the skirt.

I was distracted by my reflection in her large vanity mirror. My jet-black hair hung over my left shoulder. I had never worn proper makeup. It always looked wrong on me when I had smeared Mother's cosmetics on my face, although our products at home had been too low quality to ever work this much magic. After Mimi had finished my makeup, I was sprayed with some perfume and given a quick manicure. I got the shock of my life at my reflection when I was taken to her full-length Italian mirror. I was stunning, more stunning than I had ever seen myself.

Two hours after being waxed, prodded, sponged, pulled, brushed, sprayed, and dressed, I stood in front of the mirror with a tear trickling down my dewy face. I looked healthy and glowing, my turquoise eyes subtly shaded with eye shadow that made them stand out. Mimi had really brought out my cheekbones, delicate features, and full lips, and the entire outfit accentuated my curves and long legs.

When she told me to join her on her night out with friends, I took that as a sign of approval – even acceptance. She normally had a reserved and cold demeanour, and I expected more of the same from her upper-class friends, but upon arriving at a popular club, she enthusiastically introduced me to the group sitting at the wooden bar, which made me feel more at ease.

'You have lips that could drive any man to distraction,' Nadine said with an easy-going smile.

The tall blonde, Siwar, who stood beside her, examined me from head-to-toe before remarking, 'People pay money to buy contact lenses the colour of your eyes.'

I thanked them shyly. The other girls, all of whom were from urban Damascus, used the Western club's atmosphere to display the curves of their body in fluorescent Lycra clothes that left their cleavage and thighs exposed and very little else to the imagination. In contrast, non-Syrian women had barely any makeup on, their hair tied back casually, and were dressed in loose shirts with shorts or leggings and sensible shoes. No heavy makeup, no excessive jewellery, no ornamentation of any kind.

I noticed men taking second glances at me, trying to catch my attention, and even I knew enough about male body language to know they were very interested. I went to the women's restroom and had another shock. This restroom was amazingly spacious with its marble floor, onyx walls, and shiny hardware. I had never seen such a grand restroom in my entire life. I even hung around for a short while near the granite countertops that held objects such as makeup brushes, cosmetic cases, combs, hairspray, and makeup, admiring the women who had huddled around the mirrors and were applying makeup, retouching hair, perfuming, adjusting clothes, and talking about very personal things with each other. As the air filled with sweet scents from the hairspray that hissed from tall, fancy cans, I could not even believe I had been given privilege to enter such an indulgent and surreal world.

Mimi, now impressed with my sartorially induced status, even posed with me for selfies and danced with me the rest of the night. She seemed to be showing me off very proudly. I had mixed feelings of pride and shame about that. It seemed as though here in elite Damascus, they first notice your clothing then notice the person wearing it. People with money are respected and treated well. Even the well-dressed prostitutes or high-class escorts who cater to the elite are given respect. It's only the poorer classes – like me – that are looked down upon. During my first days in Damascus, I have wandered around the area in my shabby checked shirts, worn-out jeans and faded non-branded trainers, and I have been invisible to these people. Earlier, when Mimi dumped my old clothes unceremoniously in a bin outside, I was just too embarrassed to ask for them back. The sudden and dramatic change in the attitude of people here made me realise that the rich girl in a frilly designer dress is worth more than the girl in souk-bought sneakers.

Ammo Saleh and I talked comfortably for a long time today on the roof terrace. In front of us: a panoramic view of Damascus and the greenery of the heavenly oasis beyond. The call to *maghreb* (sunset) prayers echoed in the air.

'Your father,' he said, with a fond smile, 'was also shocked with this side of Damascus when he first arrived here as a teen.'

There was a peacefulness to Ammo Saleh's voice and personality, no doubt because life had been generous to him.

Sitting there with him, watching his contentedness, I was struck by a tremendous sadness for my father, who had stumbled so far the other way. I wondered if Baba had ever envied his old university friend's life. Surely Baba must have wished that, like Ammo Saleh, he'd have a comfortable life full of riches, fancy cars, exotic trips around the globe, fine food, and a prestigious status in society.

Ammo recalled how, decades ago, my father was amazed by what he experienced in the capital city, and that on the very first phone call he made back home to his father and family in Hama, he told them excitedly that 'Damascus was so brilliant, he could see money flowing out from the walls'.

To which my late grandfather replied, 'I see you've just discovered alcohol. You are drunk, go sort yourself out,' and hung up the phone.

For the next few weeks, my father would narrate the same story over and over, insisting it was true. Eventually my grandfather made a hasty call to Ammo Saleh, demanding to know if anyone had been slipping his son pills or if he was seeing jinn spirits.

Ammo Saleh laughed uncontrollably. 'It was then that your father marched me down to the street straight to a ATM cash machine and pointed at someone collecting money at a wall – *yaa'ni*, as in making a cash withdrawal – it was very embarrassing for him, but he wasn't humiliated.'

I pictured my father's bright-eyed intensity; he always had such a zeal for life, and even now, he had only taken up arms with the rebels because he hadn't been able to quench his thirst for living an interesting and fulfilling life.

As if he could read my mind, Ammo Saleh sighed. 'Your father, just like you, was inquisitive, and whether by nurture or nature, he was on a quest to learn everything.'

Damascus is a city of churches and mosques, souks and shopping malls. This place has soul as well. Here in Old Damascus, the sound of church bells mingles with the call to prayer. The oldest city in Christendom, Damascus is a living museum spanning thousands of years. The locals are still finding ancient ruins and thousand-year-old objects. This is a city that does not measure time by hours, days, months, and years, but by empires it has seen rise and crumble to ruin.

Sitting in a fine, fresh, green Damascus restaurant courtyard, under an orange tree, I watch people eat their lunch. Opposite me, a dozen frail old men in black and white *keffiye* scarves are drinking sweet tea and playing backgammon. I am writing and have called the smiley waiter to bring me a *nargileh* pipe and a cup of water.

Having spent the entire morning walking around the maze of narrow streets and old passageways, I got a true sense of a decrepit ancient city, and like I always do when I come across Roman ruins or very old places in Syria, I picture the lives and ways of my ancestors. Historic Pharaonic scripts show that this city was once known as Dameska. The Aramites, who spoke Syriac, were the original inhabitants of Damascus and during the second millennium BC, it was the main capital of the Aramaic kingdom, and known as Dar-Misiq – the irrigated house.

Syria is a place of exploration, but Damascus takes things to another level, and finding the unexpected has made me want to delve into the history of this great city. The Greeks, the Romans, and the Byzantines all left their mark on Damascus before the Umayyad Dynasty in 661AD conquered her.

Earlier this morning, after Jabir the Palestinian chef at the Saleh household fried eggs in olive oil for breakfast for me, the younger Eritrean maid was given instructions to take me on a tour of Old Damascus with the driver Ja'far. I had requested last night to go out and explore the souks and do some sightseeing, and there had been a worrying frown on Ammo Saleh's face.

'Are you sure? It's very claustrophobic, and there are pickpockets and dangerous people. You can go to the Grand Mall here instead if you need to shop for anything. I will give you my credit card.'

Despite his very kind offer, I was tired of seeing high-rise apartment blocks and cold, frozen, Botox-filled women swishing their expensive handbags. I yearned for some real, authentic, homemade Syrian food. As a Hamawi, I had a hankering for the bazaar, more for its smell than anything else. Syria's souks are an ethereal place to wander in.

When we finally arrived at the walled old city, after being stuck in the slow-moving and overwhelming morning rush-hour traffic on the four-lane Revolution Street (Shari' al-Thawra), I was pleasantly surprised by how this was an oasis of calm right in the middle of Damascus; a break from the frenzied pace of urban Syria. The quietness and peacefulness was only interrupted with the call to prayer from the spectacular Umayyad

Mosque. The noisy area is near the Shrine of Ruqayyah, which is inside the fancy Iranian-built Shiite mosque, where chador-clad Iranian women and pilgrims arriving on buses are always in a hurry to go to the Shiite shrines.

I noticed how Sunni Syrians welcomed the Shiite tourists arriving in buses, eagerly selling them Shiite memorabilia, religious books, and prayer objects, and making large amounts of money from them. They were very respectful of their large crowds, who were chanting and wailing, and allowed them to have large dedicated spaces to pray. Syrians really are business orientated.

Walking past the businesses, humming with the stream of movement towards the heart of the old city and finally arriving at the main entrance of the grand Umayyad Mosque, I took off my shoes in respect for the holy ground. The history there is unbelievable, and as I looked in awe at the architecture, I realised how the different parts of civilisation combined as the place expanded and changed throughout history. There must be very few places in the world where one can see Roman columns and Islamic arches with Byzantine-inspired mosaics side by side. It is a mixture of splendour; the mosque was a former temple of Jupiter for the Romans and a church for the Byzantines, and then a mosque for the Muslim empires.

The shrine and the head of Prophet Yahya to Muslims, and John the Baptist to Christians, is situated inside the great Umayyad Mosque. As the images of past horrors and beauty collided in my head, I hoped that my ancestors, both Christian and Muslim, had come to deeply spiritual places like this to revel in the peace, contemplation, and silence.

Yahya (John) was a humble and godly man and didn't care for worldly comfort or food. In fact, he survived on leaves and herbs, even locusts. He led an eccentric life and would go in the mountains to distance his soul from the world because he felt the world was too corrupt and needed purification. In caves, he would pray to God, where, sometimes, dangerous animals would wander in, but he didn't notice them, he was so absorbed in worship. Lions and bears would recognise him as the prophet who cared deeply for animals so they would leave him unharmed, bowing their heads in respect.

Both loved and feared, he was also quite the revolutionist who came into conflict with the wicked King Herod Antipas – the then ruler of Palestine. His resistance ended with his head being brought on a platter to the king.

It's incredible how supposedly right there in the middle of the historic Umayyad Mosque sits the severed sacred head of Yayha, Saint John the Baptist. I watched the Christian women inside the mosque wipe tears from their faces at the shrine. Our Muslim brothers and sisters have kept a sanctuary for him in their great mosque and left the shrine how it was for more than a thousand years. That means, for thirteen hundred years, people have been praying there just like I was doing; prayers for peace in the kingdom and prayers for people to understand each other.

This, for me, was my favourite part of Islam, where Christians have been tolerated, Jews have been welcomed, and where all Syrians have lived and worshipped side by side. We are so different, yet so similar. I sat for a while and meditated in the mosque, deep in my thoughts. I loved how the balance between domestic intimacy and religious formality gave the mosque a blend of historic and spiritual beauty – the Jesus minaret on one side and the gold-domed Shrine of John on the other; a symbol of the beginning of Jesus's ministry and the end of Jesus's ministry . . . both embraced, both honoured, both sanctified in the great centre of historic Islam, a truly beautiful place.

Another day, another slaughter, as more than a hundred martyrs have fallen today. Ten children, three women, three defected recruits. Forty-five were killed by artillery shelling in Homs, fifty-five in Idlib, two in Douma and Mesraba in the suburbs of Damascus, two in Deir Ezzor, and one in Aleppo. God knows how many injured.

'Keep a low profile when you are in Damascus,' my mother had warned. 'Remember, you are only there for a few months until things are calmer and safer for you to be here.'

When did I ever listen to my mother's instructions? A friend had given me the number of a Damascus-based activist who was part of a group of underground student activists in the old city, at the forefront of the protest movement in central Damascus. They were still small-scale, but nonetheless had the same goals as activists in the rest of Syria. I had sent a message to him on Viber and he had told me that hundreds of people had been arrested earlier today at the Hamidiyeh Souk in the heart of Damascus when security forces closed the two entrances and locked all activists in. He told me to come to their meeting place in the old city next Friday afternoon to become acquainted.

'We need lots of writers and photographers, and we need fixers to help the international journalists that are here in

Damascus but aren't capable of venturing out to other cities,' he said cautiously.

Just today, Marie Colvin, an American working for Britain's *Sunday Times,* was killed along with French photographer Remi Ochlik in Homs during the Syrian army's artillery bombardment on the Bab Amr neighbourhood. Syria is a dangerous place, not only for citizens, but also for journalists and members of the media who aren't as familiar with areas and routes. I found out from the housemaids today that Ammo Saleh and his daughter would be attending a pool party tomorrow at the grand hotel up in Bludan, a resort town in the mountains near Lebanon. This would give me the perfect opportunity to go unnoticed and visit activists in Damascus.

Today, students from Aleppo University held their biggest rally yet. Despite the raids, arrests, and the threats of expulsion, they kept protesting. It was when I came to Damascus that I realised what the implications and consequences of my own expulsion from university were. My application for a teaching assistant job that Ammo Saleh had lined up for me was instantly rejected. How could I have been so naïve? Of course they had files on me.

Instead, I had been summoned for questioning by the Idarat al-Amn al-'Amm – the General Security Directorate. I was picked up at the Sabe' Bahrat Square in midtown Damascus, near the Central Bank, and taken by security agents to Branch 255 – the Information Branch. There, amid an intimidating interior, the lieutenant who was investigating me handed me some paper and told me to start writing.

'We know you're very close friends with Dina, we know you're a Marxist, our eyes and ears are everywhere.' He flicked through my file and slammed it down.

'So, *al-muhim*, I need you to tell me of the organisations and groups and their activities.'

I remained impassive throughout and even convinced my interrogator that I had nothing to do with the revolution; I was a staunch Christian and my poem recital was just a one-off. He then offered me money to follow senior members and activists and report on them. I stayed quiet.

He clenched his teeth. Looking straight into my eyes, he said sharply, 'I'll have you back here next month. We'll talk about what you find out for us then.'

I have now started working for the hairdresser across the street, clearing up hair and making hot drinks for clients. I may have a dull job, but the situation in my hometown is more tragic. The slaughter of innocent Syrians *must* end. The hunger must end as well. When I was back there, I felt like I was contributing to the Syrian people's cause, but here, I am being sure to observe the laws. While I stay in touch with activists online and do as much as I can without gaining attention from my hosts and those around me, I feel hypocritical.

It is me who has said over and over to anyone and everyone, 'We will fall backwards if we do not demand our full human rights, and dignity, and a fair and honest government.' And now that I am so close to Assad's palace, I have become slightly fearful of his power and remained silent. I am as guilty as my grandparents in Maaloula who have avoided the revolution altogether; as selfish as the businessmen I see in Armani suits with a pen in their breast pocket that walk to their Mercedes in the morning; as self-absorbed as the high-class ladies at the salon who openly laugh when state television report on the deaths of the *musallahin* – or armed terrorist gangs as they call the activists – and who, while having their perms done, mock the *mukharribin* (troublemakers) and *Salafiyyin* (Salafists) in the countryside. *My* countryside.

'We live in fear of a massacre,' were the words written by Ms Corvin in her last article for the *Sunday Times*. She was absolutely right. As summary executions take place in Idlib, as more footage comes in from Baba Amr of the dead and injured, and as people get locked in their villages by security forces with nowhere to escape, the risk of death in the protesting cities becomes more certain. Oh, and now Syria is grappling with foreign fighters.

Oh God, they have to be stopped, and that is so hard with such easy ways to enter the country from neighbouring borders. You would think Assad, who claims to be against al-Qaeda and other groups, would stop any such creeps coming in, but no, he leaves the door wide open for the evildoers. And how can we forget about the high numbers of rape? It's an abomination.

It is time the men stand up, speak out, and listen. Syria is hands down one of the most beautiful countries in the world, and we Syrians deserve better. False rhetoric, like 'national dialogue', must also stop; the world must be told the real truth. My grandfather used to say, 'On the day I see a fairly elected person standing in government, I will know then that real change has been well seated.'

Why do Syrians have to be subjected to such an undemocratic system? It is so heart-breaking to know people are dying needlessly, but it is so good to know activists will never stop. We won't. The world needs freedom fighters, and Syria needs them the most. To hell with the countries that voted at the UN General Assembly to demand the Syrian regime end its bloody crackdown. We don't need international consensus to know the massacres need to stop. We certainly don't – and won't – negotiate with our murderous leader. Dismantling this merciless regime is a prerequisite. We won't compromise. Short-term gains become long-term ills.

23 February, 2012

I looked up at the thick grey clouds, wondering whether the snow would clear soon. In the distance, a MiG-29 fighter jet was preparing for take-off, probably on its way to bomb my hometown. I will get up and push through, even through the pain, and despite the daily hard work at my new job and the hardness of being away from my family and friends, who I miss more than words can ever say. But today we get up, and we wear our best clothes, and we speak of beautiful things; we speak of unbearable things, even, we reminisce, and we walk through life with hope.

Protests have been taking place outside the old hospital in the poor part of Mezzeh – extremely close to the heart of bourgeois Damascus. A lot of people have been killed in the past few days, which means the revolt is spreading and has reached parts of the capital. However, here in Damascus, police are only shooting in the air to frighten protesters away. Opposition to the regime is growing daily and spreading into cities that previously we thought would never be affected.

Despite cracks and lack of resources within the opposition, they are developing the activist network. After security forces annihilated Sunni neighbourhoods in Homs, Syrians all over have become angrier than ever. People now realise that lawlessness and chaos could reach the capital – even those that continue to support Assad. I have noticed how prices in cafes and restaurants here have trebled overnight, a telltale sign of rapid inflation and economic hardship. Tourists can no longer be seen, and expats in wealthy neighbourhoods can be seen packing up and leaving daily.

Having spoken with family outside of Damascus, I have heard the same thing over and over: the price of fuel has rocketed and there's a shortage of bread. A bag of flour can only be bought if you know someone related to the Assad family. Assad is sailing a sinking ship, and everyone knows this deep down.

1 March, 2012

In the soft glow of early twilight, the muezzin's call to the maghreb prayer can be heard from the Umayyad Mosque a few steps away from where I sit in the An-Noufara coffee house. It is a simple and delightful place that has been here for more than two hundred and fifty years and still attracts tourists from around the world because of its famous traditional *hakawati* (storyteller). After the call to prayer has ended, the storyteller begins his theatrical show.

Sitting on his elevated chair in his red hat and funny spectacles, his voice echoes throughout the cafe. With a wave of his sword, he starts to tell the crowd old Arab folk tales, showing off the power of the Arabic language. The heroic tale he is telling tonight is one I have heard in my home many times as a child. There are well-dressed *muhajabaat* – women with headscarves – sitting with other men openly, smoking water pipes and even flirting. The atmosphere is light-hearted and pleasant. I move over near to the basalt courtyard where the fountain has just lit up and wait for my new Damascene activist friends to arrive.

While I wait for Shadi, Mohammad, and Mohammad's wife, Hajer, I order myself some herbal tea and admire the paintings on the wall. Apart from the large portraits of President Bashar and his father, there are the most incredible paintings of Syria. I love the old paintings of ancient heritage sites in

Damascus. What a way to showcase our history and amazing cultural and artistic achievements. Umayyad royalty took inspiration from horseshoe arches built by Visigoths – people who came into power after the Roman Empire collapsed and stayed until right before the Umayyads came. The Visigoths designed these arches for their Christian churches built prior to the advent of Islam. It is well known that Muslims would always recycle materials, and reincorporated objects from old buildings and churches when they created new mosques. However, the horseshoe arch spread from the Arab world to al-Andalus (North Africa) and beyond, where Islamic architects recreated the arch and manipulated its design. All around me are delightful, intricate mosaics and complex architectural decorations by skilful artisans of the past and present. I sigh. What a huge reminder of the great, beautiful things humans can do; the antithesis of the barbaric inhumane things humans can also do.

It needs our *sabr* – patience. Resistance to oppression is not a crime. It is a social responsibility. This is what I told Ammo Saleh today before I left to go to the Friday protests in the centre of Damascus. When he realised there was no stopping me, he asked the older housemaid to accompany me, which she was only happy to do despite the risks. Ella is fast becoming one of my closest friends. This has surprised many of the neighbours and even Ammo Saleh and his daughter, who were surprised to see us joking, laughing, and enjoying each other's company. Arabs can be as racist as anyone. The words *abeed*, *abdi*, and slave are very common ways to talk about black people in the Arab world, and it's time to clean out closets.

I don't know what happened to my attitude today. I just decided I didn't want to remain in hiding and would visit every demonstration that took place in Damascus and take part in the 'illegal' protest activities with Damascene activists.

Since moving to Damascus, adjusting to the major lifestyle changes, and having to live and work among vain, self-absorbed, consumerist individuals, I started to recede deeper and deeper into myself, desperately trying to be someone I couldn't be. I was expected to be polite, politically correct, and fake. But I can no longer hide my real personality. I don't mind jeopardising my job and new friends if it means I get to be myself and show my real identity.

As soon as announcements were made via our social media group that protests would be breaking out in thirty-five points across the capital and its suburbs, I was ready and armed with my camera. Protests were taking place all over, including Mezzeh, Hajer al-Aswad, al-Aasali, Douma, Qadam, Qaboon, and Kfar Sousa. I attended the enormous protest outside the Zain al-Aabideen mosque in Midan, central Damascus. There were roars from people shouting 'God is great', and the usual freedom songs being sang by rebels-turned-DJs on the makeshift stage made from fruit crates.

I scrambled to the front of the crowd and grabbed the vocalist's microphone and in my loudest voice, screamed at the crowd, 'We shall not abandon Hama. We shall not abandon Homs. We shall not abandon Daraa!'

The hyped-up crowd began chanting this slogan loudly as they jumped up and down, waving their placards and Syrian flags.

Policemen surrounded the protest, tear-gassing a few activists who had got out of hand; they were spraying cars and shop traders' walls with paint, which was completely the wrong thing to do. Despite having their batons and guns at the ready, security forces in Damascus are tame compared to Hama. Police here are in combat mode: prepared for insurrection, but fearing for their own safety, and they are in no mood to get themselves hurt.

The non-violent marches here today were so well co-ordinated, well attended, well represented that they are a threat to President Assad. The organisers here are very strategic and secretive. Back in Hama, large protests require massive amounts of people and take much longer to organise. Here, they set up protests by gathering groups of fifty people from different streets and asking them to turn up at one point at a set time.

They are much more advanced with their posters and have printed out detailed pamphlets too, which they hand out to passing cars. 'Be authentic, and be well-behaved' were the instructions given by demo organisers. I was told to take lots of photographs and make video clips of the event, which were to be shared, live to the world, via social media.

Just a few weeks ago, there had been small-scale protests of around thirty people that were quickly shut down, and now there were hundreds. For Damascus to be protesting is a major breakthrough. The regime has cited Damascus and Aleppo's relatively undisturbed streets in the last year to reinforce to the world that most of Syria supports Assad.

While it is true many did – and do – support him, an increasing number are turning away from him, and his argument is becoming harder to sustain. People are rising up in middle-class districts as more and more horror stories come out from the rebellious cities. The regime cannot keep pretending to the world that the members of the revolution are al-Qaeda Islamists or agents provocateurs funded by the West. Even the naïve and gullible do not believe that foreign armed gangs and other sobriquets given to us have penetrated the area right around the presidential palace.

In fact, the regime has become so intimidated by the protesters in Damascus, that they push schoolkids and women on buses and drop them off to Ba'ath marches in Damascus, where they're then filmed by state television and used for propaganda. They even dare to alter the chants from anti-regime protests, twisting the words to praise Assad instead.

In my hometown of Hama and nearby Homs, my friends tell me that women are no longer seen in the demonstrations as it has become so dangerous to protest in rural Syria. Protest spots have become battlefield spots for Syrian troops and rebel soldiers.

Here today, hundreds of women, young and old, came out to protest. One of the women organisers suggested we should pick up the used tear gas canisters fired by security and then pluck roses and other flowers and place them inside. Holding ugly gas canisters filled with beautiful roses would send a clear message to the world – in case they needed convincing – that we are far from dangerous, armed thugs. Peaceful provocation makes more sense to me, and this is the exact image we need to portray to the world.

While marching towards the sprawling presidential palace, and very sure that the president himself could hear them, the women sung defiantly 'Hey and *yallah*, we do not kneel but to Allah.'

I sat waiting with my glass of Mountain Dew in Marmar Bar in Bab Touma for Shadi and the rest of the movement's members. It had been a while since I'd met with Hajer, who'd promised to introduce me to leading activists from Barzeh – the most defiant part of Damascus, and where opposition activists have already began to smuggle arms in, getting prepared for the worst.

This was the sleaziest bar I'd been in. But as it goes in Damascus, '*Kil shi mamnu*', '*bas kil shi ok*' – everything is illegal, but it's all good. The dampness in the air and the cloud of cigarette smoke that hung throughout the room made me feel as intoxicated as the 'singer' and his unfortunate band playing in the stuffy room with their carefully chosen frayed second-hand clothing, bad comb-overs, and out-dated jazz instruments. These reject Americans who move abroad for gigs in exotic countries to spew their untreated musical sewage for drunk businessmen and '*Ayrabs*' as they call us, are insulting to young people, who are familiar with the music industry. We know that these 'stars of the night' are unheard of in their native Western countries.

Suddenly, Shadi appeared, offering me a hearty '*Salam*' before taking me to the other side to introduce me to the leading activist of their group, Rayyan.

'You're the blogger from Hama then,' he said. The cross on my neck didn't go unnoticed by him, and he was immediately suspicious about me being a Christian.

'*Wa la yhimmak.* Don't worry, she's one of us,' Shadi offered out of courtesy.

Rayyan looked over at Shadi. 'You know we've been infiltrated before. I need to be careful.'

'You can trust me, I'm my own woman.' I tried to reassure Rayyan of my own independence with friendly, but direct, eye contact.
'*Tab 'an.* Of course,' he agreed with a smile.

I could understand why Rayyan, like so many others, felt immediately on the defensive, but things were moving in the right direction for me as the evening went on. At some point, a few men had entered the bar and greeted each other with four kisses on the cheek – a Syrian way of showing to everyone that they were from the Alawite sect. Rayyan and Shadi began to look around furtively, as if searching for a member of the Mukhabaarat to appear at any moment. After Rayyan was convinced that I wasn't one of the spies recruited by the regime, he invited me back to his home.

'If you are free, you are welcome to join my father's meeting this evening.'

Damascus is a city of tight-knit social groups and small close circles of friends and acquaintances who all know one another and belong to the same clubs and organisations. It helps to create pockets of order in a sea of chaotic diversity in the big city.

Rayyan's father greeted us with coffee at their home in the Qassa neighbourhood, which now also served as an underground meeting spot. The conversation was all politics, which is to say all revolution, and these men were masters of both. I watched the men huddle together, reviewing the videos of that morning's battle somewhere in Idlib on Rayyan's father's laptop.

These revolutionaries were not of the latte-sipping, cafe-based armchair activist variety like the ones in the West. They were serious game-changers – professionals, mostly, successful within the system, some with even high positions in the local government, politically astute, and progressive. And now they were seizing the chance to take over. When they were debating the merits and risks of the ongoing armed revolution, all agreed on the need for change and were fully aware of the risk to human lives.

With his jet-black hair and penetrating eyes, Rayyan's father, a diplomat, commanded everyone with his voice. 'The main reason we are not successful is because Syrian opposition has been fractured into very small groups.'

Everyone nodded.

I couldn't help myself. 'They also don't have proper communication with each other. They have the mentality "Even if we are a small group, let it be ours",' I blurted out.

Everyone nodded again. A maid entered the room with a tray of coffee and Rayyan's father motioned for me to be poured first. As I took my first sip, a powerful voice boomed behind us and I dropped the cup, coffee spilling everywhere. For a moment

I sat, frozen, as everyone leapt to their feet and stampeded to the back door. We were being raided.

Rayyan and his father remained in the lounge and watched, faces pale and drawn, as the men from the Mukhabaarat combed through the house with military precision. They couldn't find any evidence in any of the rooms, and I saw Rayyan and his father visibly relax.

Then they found the walkie-talkie. And all hell broke loose.

The men from the Mukhabaarat seized Rayyan and his father, shouting triumphantly, and dragged them by their legs down a set of stairs and out onto the street. They were then dumped into a military jeep like cattle and driven away to God knows where.

8 March, 2012

Well, Damascus ambulances and emergency rooms are nice . . . but they certainly weren't on my 'to do' list. I am feeling a lot better than I did yesterday when they first wheeled me in, after I had fainted, my broom in my hand, while sweeping hair at the salon.

I was hospitalised for dizziness, weakness, and dehydration. Doctors at Ammo Saleh's private hospital strongly advised time off from any laborious work.

Going to protests is very stressful and physically demanding. I have been working long hours and very closely with media news reporters and correspondents both on the ground here and around the world, sending them first-hand accounts and exclusive footage.

It is so important to remain non-biased and make sure the information I pass over is honest. In Baba Amr, which now has been taken over by the Free Syrian Army, I have noticed how Western media have been listing even the killed combatants as civilian deaths. There isn't a proper breakdown of the dead so that those caught up in the fighting and those who have chosen to fight (regardless of which side they are on) can be differentiated. There are also a lot of emotional bloggers and social media users who continue to exaggerate or fabricate events to the clueless media reporters, who are mostly unable to reach the fighting areas. It is so important that, as Syrians, we keep our news factual and follow the ethics of journalism so as to keep us all credible. Misinformation only hurts our cause.

I can understand why some Syrian civilians, out of frustration and desperation, would increase the figures of casualties, for instance, to make a grander dossier at the UN Human Rights Council or to grab the world's attention and sympathy, but I can't understand the analysts and journalists on Syrian official television who continue to deliberately deceive the masses daily by spreading false lies about the protesters. To embolden the government to carry out massacres, these 'analysts' in foreign countries spew out pro-regime propaganda by making up blatantly false events such as thefts and reports on false sectarian killings.

The 'analyst' I had been watching on the hospital's television was smirking while he narrated a series of false events. No doubt he was sitting in his Paris office with only a view of rain and fancy buildings outside, and most certainly *not* a view of what was happening in his 'homeland' of Syria.

As Syrians who are born and raised here, we are so in touch with what is happening in our country and what we've been going through. The information *we* are collecting is much more current and credible. A lot of Syrians in Canada, America, and the West have joined the pro-Assad activists online. Now social media has become another battleground for activists as each side tries to take control of information and news.

This morning, as I lay on the bed crying, feeling detached and listless, Ella came to visit me with the treasured, green almonds I had been craving. I don't know if I was more excited to crunch on the *loz ahkdar* or if I was excited to see her kind, warm face. Dipping my favourite green almonds in coarse salt and ravenously devouring the addictive spring treat, I felt happy again.

Things could always be more awful; it is very easy to be appreciative for what we have. By being thankful, I can cherish the better moments while accepting the bad. Besides, I have a million things to be grateful for. When I thought of other, much more seriously injured Syrians now in state hospital beds in the hands of evil medics, I was thankful to God. Just a few days ago, while I was working with some volunteers from the international Red Cross Committee – who had arrived with a convoy full of food, medicine, clothes, and blankets – I was told by one of the women there that Syrians were terrified of visiting the hospital, even for a normal illness. Not only are the hospitals being extremely careless by operating without anaesthetics, they are handcuffing patients to their beds then bringing in thugs to come to torture them.

'People come out of the hospital in a much worse state then they went in,' she told me. 'Patients are being starved as further punishment and nurses are tying the penises of men so they cannot urinate for days.'

Since when must everyone proclaim their religion over and over again? Since when? It most certainly is not – and never has been – the Syrian way. I am so sick of it. In fact, in our tradition it is considered rude. Any true Syrian has no need to ask. No need. So when Ammo Saleh's mean and entitled sister arrived yesterday from Toronto, it became sickening.

'So, this is your Muslim friend's daughter then?' she asked in a voice dripping with disdain.

France's Sarkozy is half-Jewish; Obama has Muslim blood and is a son of a black man from Kenya and a white woman from Kansas; India once had a Muslim president and a Sikh prime minister at the same time; Obama and Sarkozy's parents were immigrants; Angela Merkel and Sonia Gandhi are successful women in male-dominated politics. No matter your gender, background, or religion, you have a place in society and can even reach to the highest positions of power based on your competency.

I wouldn't dare try to explain those kind of democratic ideals to the likes of Aunty Georgette, who has come to Syria to 'sell her assets' in case the 'terrorists' manage to spread their 'mischief' to Damascus. She is the wife of an ex-diplomat who lives abroad, and I can't believe how cynical she is towards those that crave freedom and hope for just a little piece of her comfortable life.

As she sat down on Ammo Saleh's soft white leather couches in his ultra-modern living area, she slipped off her red-soled heels on the pale blue, faded Persian rug and started her rant about how Asma Assad was the most eloquent first lady and how the media had fabricated all those private e-mails that they'd leaked from her inbox.

Didn't she realise how conceited and ignorant she sounded? She seemed completely clueless about the butchering of Syrian people going on right now; about how corrupt and brutal the Assads are and how people are being killed based on their sect or ethnic background. Or was she, like the other people I had met in Ammo Saleh's friends circle, fully aware of the murderous ways of the regime but would rather remain in denial? A poor people's revolt would mean that they, God forbid, may have to come down a little on the social and economic ladder.

Since moving to Damascus, I have found that the idea of a pluralist society is abhorrent to elitists like Aunty Georgette, who praise and glorify the Assads and treat the rest of Syrian society as uneducated animals. They deem themselves as the 'chosen' ones, especially if they have dual passports and live in the West. In my opinion, they are the worst of the worst because they are reluctant to sacrifice their worldly comforts when their brothers and sisters around the country are getting sacrificed.

'As a Christian, I am sure you are pledging your loyalty to Assad and joining us this Thursday in Umayyad Square. Why don't you prepare a speech?' she said.

Ella's stern gaze warned me to remain quiet.

'You're a pretty face – you might be even given a reward for it if you appear on television.'

She was right. In fact, we'd heard of plenty of chestnut-haired girls and blue-eyed babies taken away from different districts to be paraded at the masquerades taking place to show 'support' for the regime. I've also heard that school pupils and civil servants who are increasingly resisting the compulsory call-up are being threatened that if they don't attend pro-Assad rallies, they'll lose places at schools and jobs.

The next planned pro-Assad rally is going to mark the one-year anniversary of the uprising, and for fear of enormous anti-regime protests, everyone, especially the Druze and Christians, were being encouraged to go to the pro-government counter rallies. *I am nobody's mule*, I wanted to tell her.

'Aren't the seven hundred Christians that have been killed good enough for her?' I muttered to Ella later in the kitchen.

Doesn't she know that as the violence escalates, more and more Christians are seeing the regime for what it truly is? Not far away from Damascus in Daraya, the church rang their bells to honour the three Muslims that were killed there by the regime. Hundreds of Christians even joined the funeral procession.

However, that didn't matter to the likes of blinded Aunty Georgette and many of my own family members, especially when they have forgotten basic tenets in their belief system.

The past year has been a difficult one for all Syrians, and I know there are genuine pro-regime supporters, but these foreign Syrians who treat Syria as a holiday home and have no idea about Middle Eastern affairs and geopolitics make me want to scream.

Even if the conspiracy theories about Zionists and the West teaming up to destroy Syria and Iran were true; even if one were to believe the bullshit about the rebels being foreign terrorists, there is no denying that Assad is a miserable failure at best and a war criminal at worst, and Syria needs to get rid of him. One cannot forget how even the most loyal Nazis realised Hitler only brought chaos to Germans and Germany. Even the most nationalist Serbs at long last admitted that betting on Milosovic was a bad proposition.

I find it hard to imagine a Syria where religions are divided. We used to be an example of religious tolerance; now we are the worst example ever.

Today, while peeling oranges and letting the peel drop aimlessly onto the gleaming white marble floor, I reflected on why I had come to Damascus. My journey on the road taken by St Paul was to bring me to a place where I could start a fresh new life and be shielded from the brutalities of war against women. I was supposed to become this empowered, independent adult. At that moment, however, I felt anything but.

I want my mother and my grandmother and I miss little comforts of home: the smell of fresh baking bread and incense, the taste of ripe fruits, crushed spices, and freshly killed meat. Local kids playing outside, carefree, the animal feed strewn on the streets, the intermingling smells of dung, charcoal fires, sandalwood, and musk. Familiar faces and smells.

I keep hoping of a reunion with Emad, but this revolution refuses to end. At times, I feel so estranged from him, as he only calls once in a while, and it feels that we'd need to become acquainted all over again. Then, when he *is* able to call, I can feel his presence in my heart again.

I know from speaking to my mother late last night that things are even tougher than before and that the homesickness I am feeling is for a home that no longer exists. Working at the salon is not getting easier. The tedious amount of cleaning, washing hair, taking off coats and hanging them in lockers, and helping women into luxurious robes while they moan that the hot drinks I've made are too cold, too warm, or too sweet is getting harder to bear as fear of war coming to Damascus builds up in everyone's minds.

This salon isn't like the ones I'd grown up visiting back home in Hama. This upmarket salon has a clinical feel to it. Each day actresses, ambassadors' wives, and other elite women visit us, and each client has their own personalised notes typed up on a computer database.

Contrastingly, at a traditional salon in Syria, women drop by with friends and talk and laugh among themselves or with the staff, make lewd jokes, gossip about celebrities or family members, and become comfortable enough to talk about their private love lives. At the salon I work at, not only are the staff not allowed to get personal with clients, they are instructed to be polite, helpful robots who nod at every whim.

Last week, when the salon's manager informed me very sternly to be extra courteous with the client I was with, I had wondered why . . . until one of the staff told me she was, in fact, a cousin of the president.

The temptation to add green dye into her hair mixture when the colourist isn't looking must be resisted, I said in a text message to Reem.

I observed the client, however, and knew it would be a poor decision on my part to fall prey to the whispers of Satan. I had to remember and remind myself about what I had read about karma. If more people understood the true meaning of karma, this world would be a much better place. Unfortunately, not many understand how the law of universe works. In life, you always get what you give. There are no two ways about it.

Kindness will bring kindness, light will bring light, and hate will bring hate. I am very fortunate to realise this at such a young age.

19 March, 2012

The secret to survival in a revolution is chocolate ice cream. I have been finishing tubs of it ever since becoming stuck indoors after twin suicide bombs rocked Damascus early on Saturday, killing twenty-nine and injuring more than a hundred. My head is aching again with the sound of violent gun battles raging so close by. Social media is on fire too as everyone knows rebels are now fighting the regime right here in the capital.

The noise and gunfire started after midnight from the direction of Arnous Square then reached Baghdad Street and then the wealthy part of Mezzeh.

'They are probably targeting the home of Assad's brother-in-law. He's the deputy chief-of-staff of the armed forces and he lives right there.' Ammo Saleh pointed towards where a huge glow of fire had erupted in the ritzy district.

Standing on the rooftop terrace and using my state-of-the-art camera lent to me by an Al Jazeera journalist I met last week, I am collecting great footage of rocket grenades being fired. Just a little while ago, warplanes were flying over the Barzeh neighbourhood. The regime went crazy, shelling the neighbourhood, and that made for some awesome cinematic photography.

Our catastrophes are now pictures. The pain in the images is just a picture to the world. 'Oh, how expressive!', 'Oh, how heart-breaking!' But nobody will do anything about it.

From the terrace, I can see that our neighbours have also all been staying indoors since the rebels rocked the capital. Aunty Georgette has hidden herself in the innermost room of the home while Ammo Saleh's daughter has locked herself up in her room, blasting Kanye West songs all day long. It has been a long couple of days, and even the housemaids and driver haven't risked leaving the safety of indoors. The regime has begun to isolate Damascus by using thirty-five checkpoints to control everyone's movement. Identity cards are being demanded, and the house raids that we'd experienced in Hama have now begun in Damascus.

Roads into the capital from nearby towns are now closed. Amid all the fighting, a spontaneous protest has suddenly started in Qaboun. Despite the heavy army presence, explosions and gunfire are visible to all and have shocked Damascene residents, who were, until now, simply acting as normal, deliberately ignoring the big fat pink elephant walking around the city, hoping that if they ignored it, it would go away.

Protests here have started to escalate massively since last Friday after Kofi Annan addressed the UN Security Council and encouraged them to assist the Syrians. Nearly every activist I spoke to or listened to in the chat rooms thought this was a signal that international military intervention would finally come.

'Everyone must make the effort to come out on Friday. Bring the women, bring the children, and bring your animals,' a

Homsi activist from The Syrian Revolution Coordination Union urged.

Cats, I have discovered, really do not seem to mind tear gas, and dogs like protests because they can run alongside the protesters.

Activists chose to call this first Friday of the revolution's anniversary 'The Friday for International Military Intervention'. I don't believe intervention is the best idea for Syria because Russia's presence here would make for a nice dose of World War Three. The last thing I want is for Syria to become a playground for other countries. It is bad enough to deal with the one mentally unstable lunatic regime we have, and along with the ever-increasing foreign militant groups, I dread to imagine what would happen if huge imperial powers and armies were to arrive.

There is one way to describe the mood of most people here and that is nervousness. I am pessimistic and confused, as are most Syrians, but we are clinging on to anything we can and hope to see the war out. The rebels who have entered Damascus are in the middle of the wealthiest area, very close to the presidential home. I wonder if Bashar and his wife are listening to the gunfire rumble from their bedroom window at night – the sound that could just be the sound of their reign coming to an end.

'I have a crisis!' yelled Aunty Georgette from her room early this morning.

When I frantically ran to her room, I didn't know whether to laugh or be angry with her.

'Wardrobe crisis,' she muttered in despair.

I'll give you a real crisis to worry about, I thought to myself. Starvation is looming in many of Syria's cities, including my own home city of Hama, and she is wailing in despair over having nothing fancy to wear.

'My God, I don't have the correct attire for tonight's charity gala.' She pointed at the overflowing wardrobe in front of her.

'*Wa la yhimmik.* Don't worry, you have time to go buy something,' I replied.

She obviously did not sense how preposterous I thought it was that the only crisis she could possibly think of right now was a wardrobe one, because she suddenly turned to me.

'Get ready, *yallah* . . . it's your day off today so you're coming with me.'

Before I had a chance to refuse, she had already run off in a frenzy, leaving me bemused.

Our understanding of the word 'crisis' was evidently very different. In fact, many idioms and expressions in the Ammo Saleh English-speaking household took getting used to. I still remember how one night, upon hearing Aunty Georgette shriek at Ammo Saleh's daughter Mimi to 'stop pulling my leg!', I had raced into the lounge, eyes wide open, only to find them laughing hysterically on either side of the room, nobody pulling anyone's leg, and then laughing even more at my dazed expression.

Despite many such embarrassing moments, I am happy to have them explain American English expressions to me. All this learning will become very useful for me when Syria is free and I can pursue a job educating non-English-speaking children at a school back in my hometown.

After instructing the driver to head to Shukri Al Quwatli Street, Aunty Georgette began to go into her chatty mode, as always. Damascus traffic coming into the centre was buzzing with cars and mopeds as people milled around street stalls and as traffic police tried to control both the pedestrian and vehicle movement. As we approached the luxury shopping centre in the prestigious Upper Sharaf west known as The Boulevard, right next to the Four Seasons Hotel, the venue of the evening charity gala, I couldn't help but spot the two daintiest and cutest Ayyubid-era domes in the midst of it all. In his traditional attire, the tamarind juice seller seated with his brass urn opposite the monuments sang an old Syrian song.

More than just a *turba* (tomb), the bigger dome was once a madrasa that specialised in teaching the *fiqh* (jurisprudence) of the Shafi'i and Hanafi sects, the old man told me.

'The smaller *qubba* (dome) that is adjacent to Farrukhshah's dome was built over fifty years later for his son, Al-Malik al-Amjad Bahramshah.' He pointed at the identical but smaller structure.

Despite being fairly unadorned, the design was still eye-catching. This style of tombs was inspired by Aleppo, with the domes being covered in plaster instead of exposed brick as was common during the Mesopotamian times.

There was no escaping history here, and while there are certainly no aromatic spices or traditional products being sold in the modern shopping complex that had incorporated the ancient tombs and madrasa, even the array of Western designer stores and international chain restaurants and cafes could not take away the sentimental feelings felt in this seven-thousand-year-old city, which held the bodies of some of the greatest characters in history.

Indeed, while the men in Saladin al-Ayyubi's family are famous for outstanding gallantry on the battlefield, the Ayyubid dynasty were also celebrated patrons of literature. Farrukhshah, who lay under the higher tomb, was one of Saladin's most trusted confederates and also *na'ib* (vicegerent) of Damascus, and was said to have had a great fondness for the poetry of al-Mutanabbi and was himself an accomplished poet. This talent was passed down to his son Bahramshah, prince of Baalbek

(Lebanon), who was considered to be the best poet and author from the entire Ayyubid dynasty.

I remember my grandmother forever remembering how my grandfather's penchant for poetry was the quality that attracted her in the first place. In fact, Jido was a great admirer of the work of the Ayyubids.

Throughout history, verse has been such an important part of Syrian culture. Jido himself was part of an underground poets' and writers' union in Hama, where poets have had to fight censorship, torture, and exile.

When the revolution began in 2011, Hamawis were among the first to break out in verse and use poetry as a tool to galvanise people to political action. Verses that were first penned in our poetic city of Hama were – and still are – used by demonstrators throughout the country as subversive chants against the regime.

Most notable of all are the lyrics composed by Ibrahim Qashoush, a folk singer, songwriter, and poet from Hama, whom I myself stood next to many times during protests. He had turned folkloric Aradha tunes into protest songs, incorporating his own lyrics to the old wedding and celebratory melodies.

The lively father-of-three and fireman, whose hobby was to write poetry, used to compose lines about love or harsh economic situations before the revolution began in March last year, but when the revolution started, he turned his pen to support freedom fighters.

At nearly every protest Syria-wide, crowds were singing his popular lyrics:

Hey, Bashar, hey liar. Damn you and your speech, freedom is right at the door. So come on, Bashar, leave.

I remember the feelings of complete joy when I first saw videos on social media of his words being chanted in London and Sydney during solidarity protests. His words moved us all.

In fact, I remember how on one Friday summer's night in Al-Asi Square, among huge crowds of protesters, he'd roared like a lion, his voice soaring over thousands of people. I'd watched him in awe, not knowing this would be the last time we'd sing and dance to his political songs.

Four days later, my father had come home to tell us that the man who brought Hama to life in demonstrations daily had been found dumped in our local river, with his Adam's apple and vocal chords removed from his neck.

The security agents that had sliced his neck open had intended to send a message to those who dared to raise their voices and write their thoughts. Such is the power of the verse in Syria.

Watching videos of his dead body and his head lolling from side to side was enough to scare me from writing anything online for a week. But activist friends of mine inspired by him were quick to go on the web and pen their own words. When one of them recited his spoken poetry at a demo from the rooftop of a mosque, Assad's militia climbed up and dragged him down, and beat his hands so badly that his fingers still hurt when he writes.

Art in all forms, including prose, is important to this uprising because art provides a fresh perspective on our suffering and the emotions we feel. It reveals the inner lives and minds of the Syrian people while spreading messages of courage and freedom. The tools of artists, their paintbrushes and pens, are filled with creative power – more powerful than Assad's artillery.

Speaking of which, the sound of falling shells pounding on the city's outskirts has become the soundtrack of the daily lives of upper-class Damascenes, who, even during the confusion and crisis, continue to maintain their sophisticated lifestyles. So, when we heard shells falling only about three miles away, Aunty Georgette, who was just about to enter a jewellery boutique in The Boulevard shopping complex, gripped my hand and said, 'Let's just pretend that never happened, *habeebti*.'

I realised from her uneasy reaction that despite her pro-Assad, elitist views, she was also deeply afraid of the repercussions of war and the instability that came with it – which was understandable and excusable to a certain degree. Despite my utter contempt of her views on the conflict and her continuous defending of the regime, this shopping trip surprisingly bonded us in a way that I never thought would be possible.

I had begun to appreciate her sense of humour and whimsy as she took me through every single one of the doors of the gallery of luxury shops built with Kuwaiti money – as part of a mission she laughingly called 'Operation Trendy Aunty'. Going shopping with Aunty Georgette is what one can call an enlightening experience because her mind wanders as she considers the texture and quality of each material and studies the hidden meaning behind each piece.

While browsing in a luxury jewellery store, she suddenly called my name.

'*Ta'aali shoofi.* Come here and see this.' She pointed me towards a glass display case that showcased stunning pieces of gold, unique, handcrafted jewellery. Delighted, she held up a huge sparkling necklace for me to see.

'I want to give this to you,' she said earnestly.

'*Amti*, no.' I shook my head.

She batted away my arms and with a covetous sigh said, 'You have the perfect long neck for this piece . . . *Essmaooni.* Listen to me, see how this big statement necklace makes your hair shine, and your eyes pop?'

'What do you mean, pop?' I asked, shocked. 'Like a balloon?'

'No, not like a balloon, silly girl, but it will elevate everything from a white crew-neck t-shirt to a sleek evening gown,' she said as the playful fringe of the enormous necklace spilled through her nail-polished fingers.

Like every Arab woman across the Middle East, I have a weakness for jewellery. In fact, most Arab households traditionally invest in jewellery for their womenfolk, especially gold, to ward against a rainy day.

I was in awe and knew I would never own such a big piece of jewellery in my life, let alone such an expensive piece. This exquisite necklace featured cascading strands of gold chains accented by faceted turquoise beads attached to an adjustable twenty-four-carat gold-dipped brass choker.

The semi-precious stones were not ordinary. They were turquoise, which as an Arab has traditional and mythical significance to our culture. Turquoise owes its name to a misunderstanding about it originating in Turkey. The name 'turquoise' was derived from the French term for Turkish – *Turquois* – because while it was not mined in Turkey, the stone came to Europe en route from Turkey, and Venetian traders often purchased the gemstone from Turkish merchants and bazaars.

For many thousands of years, the use of turquoise has been associated with all the ancient civilisations, revered as a stone for both healing and protection against the evil eye.

Despite always being very sceptical about using the stone as a talisman, I appreciated it as a symbol of Arab tradition and most of all because the meaning of my name, Fairouz, translated as turquoise in English.

'These turquoise stones here are a soft shade of blue because they are Persian turquoise,' the storeowner, Ali, told us. 'It complements your green-blue eyes very much, and your light olive complexion fully enhances the turquoise's audacious colour.' His younger assistant then walked over to help seal the deal. 'See, the blue in turquoise symbolises the heavens, and the green symbolises the earth – no two stones are ever the same.' He looked admiringly at the necklace.

'Yes, we'll take that please,' Aunty Georgette said briskly. She ignored my resistance, turning her attention towards a pair of huge antique-effect gold earrings instead.

The next few hours were spent getting ready for the gala at an upscale makeup artist's salon. Having our makeup done by the very talented gay makeup artist was a treat, and it also confirmed my thoughts that there is a very healthy gay scene in Damascus. Homosexuality is illegal in Syria, but I always knew there was a clandestine gay scene in Hama. Here, however, men are very open with their homosexuality and are even accepted by society. This is another complete revelation to me.

In the evening, Aunty Georgette in her magnificent ruby silk gown and I in my short black dress, adorned with my new jewellery, headed to the Four Seasons Hotel where we were cordially received by the host of the gala luncheon, a powerful diplomat. From the lobby, we were taken up to the Al-Halabi restaurant where we were again received with ceremony and conducted to the seating area. I took advantage of the usual confectionary and thick, muddy Turkish coffee as Aunty Georgette introduced me to her friends and made small talk with them.

The oriental interior comprised a wondrous hand-carved and painted Damascene ceiling, walls that were richly ornamented with arabesque paintings and coloured glass, impressive chandeliers that hung low, and wrought-iron screens and antiques that filled the dining room. The hotel dominated the Damascus skyline, and we enjoyed the views overlooking the Barada and the National Museum.

The restaurant specialised in Aleppian cuisine, hence the name Al-Halabi, meaning 'the Aleppian', and because Aleppo cuisine originally derived from Turkey, their food has a spicy, zesty, Turkish-Armenian twist to it.

The food was divine. When the servers bought out lamb with a sweet and sour cherry sauce, I couldn't wait to indulge. I could not believe I was part of such an out-of-this-world experience. There I was, a peasant mixing with royalty in the midst of all the top cadres – socialites, signatories, ambassadors, diplomats, actors, and people from the ruling family; the very people whom I detested and whom I considered the enemy. In all my finery, I sat in the enemy camp where we sipped the excellent honey-wine and participated in the conversational volleyball that attends all such social events, discussing the food, weather, and sports, while searching for some area of common interest but being careful of never mentioning politics or the current crisis.

'Who is this *asal* (honey) with you?' a socialite and newspaper columnist friend of Aunty Georgette asked her towards the end of the dinner.

I tried not to make eye contact with her. I recognised her easily, as she belonged to the direct media entourage of the regime.

Towards the end of dinner, as the tables filled with desserts including fried oriental pancakes with *kishta* and honey, I nibbled on my *kunafa* filled with pistachio and rose jam topped with luscious cream as the tall host of the gala in his shiny suit, fancy Italian shoes, and pen strategically in his top breast pocket began to give a speech, his face ashy, his blue eyes melancholy.

His speech was filled with discourse about Arabism, Syrianism, nationalism, and other such isms.

'We will fight for the survival of the Arab nation,' he screeched. 'We will show the *khawna* (traitors) and the *muta'miriyyn* (conspirators) what we Arabs are made of.'

I clenched my jaw. Using nationalist terminology and nationalism ideology is just an excuse to stay in power for these pro-Assad Syrians. These men in suits have abandoned liberalist and secular ideologies and replaced them with extreme forms of supremacist nationalism. The rest of the event was a blur. I sat clutching my wine glass, the huge necklace strangling me with guilt.

1 *April*, 2012

Today is Palm Sunday – or *Shaa'nini* in Arabic – one of the most festive and well-attended Christian celebrations. As Easter approaches, as bakeries proudly display the symbolic sweet treats of the season, we hope that Syrians will witness the resurrection of their country.

Like coloured chocolate eggs and marzipan bunnies, *ma'amoul* – delicious traditional Middle Eastern cookies – are ubiquitous in Syrian homes during the Easter holiday.

Here in Damascus, they are as pretty, but were bakery-bought by Ammo Saleh, making me yearn for my grandmother's homemade cookies even more. *Ma'amoul*, which literally means stuffed, can be made with a variety of fillings. At home, Mother would stuff them with pistachio and cinnamon, and on Eid, my Muslim grandmother would stuff them with dates. Despite them being time-consuming to make, we would stay up all night so that when everyone awoke, the home would be filled with their sweet aroma. We'd bake at least ten batches, some to serve to our guests over the Easter period, some to distribute to our neighbours and friends, and some to store in tins for ourselves to nibble on for the next months. Isn't it amazing how just the smell of a cookie can conjure up a wide array of memories?

I remember the Palm Sundays spent in my mother's parent's home in Maaloula, where it was an exciting time for all the children in the village. It was traditional for parents and adults to present the children with brand-new clothes for the festival, because it was the start of warmer summer weather.

My aunt would give us all curly hair-dos, which didn't even last until the end of the procession. Led by our priest, we would all go around the block and then march back to the church. Children in their new adorable ensembles would carry decorated candles and would revel in all the attention given to them.

Hama, or Damascus . . . Easter magic is felt everywhere.

Just before sunset, Shadi, Hajer, Mohammad, and I drove up the Mount Qassioun until we reached the top, where there is a long stretch of coffee shops and plenty of places to park and enjoy the spectacular view of Damascus. I was mesmerised by the beauty and tinged by sadness as well.

Sitting with my new friends on the mountain where Qabil (Cain) killed Habil (Abel), we smoked apple-flavoured *nargileh* and ate delicious *ka'ak* while watching the sunset and the illuminated roads filling with evening traffic. In the distance, we could see the home of the Assads – the heavily fortified presidential palace that is on the other side of Mount Qassioun. We also spotted a newly constructed military base on the mountain and contemplated the thought of them launching rockets into the city from up above. This is the sad reality for our fellow countrymen in Homs. Their neighbourhoods are still under bombardment of heavy shelling, mortars are falling like rain on them, and they are being blown up to pieces by snipers from up above.

Speaking to my mother on Skype last night, I was told that, according to my father and brother, who have been fighting with the Free Syrian Army in Khalidiya, the regime forces have been storming many civilian homes in the Homsi neighbourhoods of Al-waar and Al-qsoor. The regime is deliberately targeting the safest area for refugees – these neighbourhoods are filled with people sleeping in the streets and alleyways, and all the schools in the area are full with displaced refugees who have fled from shelling in their own areas. Now they have to run again, but where to? The dead are being bombed in their graves, and the ones alive are dying in their sleep as the regime, in its last-ditch attempt to 'cleanse' Homs, spills all of its rockets on them.

Oh, those brave fighters for freedom, those wounded activists, and those scarred children live every day inside my broken heart and my mind. I sat on the mountain that many say the prophets Abraham and Muhammad once stood on and prayed to God to give us peace, understanding, and victory. Then I cried inside because I felt so useless.

Easter had to be cancelled in Homs after churches were bombed for the first time in centuries. For Assad's Shabiha, mosques and churches are fair targets, and whether Easter or Eid, they'll continue to mark the occasions with more killings.

My brother Yahya tagged me in a viral Facebook photo of a banner with an Easter greeting in Hama. It read: 'To my Christian brother: I will protect your cross with my blood. Happy Easter.' It warmed my heart.

On Syrian state TV earlier, a priest was trying to explain to his faithful flock the astonishing similarities between Jesus and Bashar al-Assad. What a jerk.

In Damascus, we held a peaceful stand-in at the second oldest church in Midan. Silent prayers were said and the atmosphere was solemn. We greeted each other with the customary '*Al Massih qam*' – Jesus is risen – to which the other person responded '*Haqqan qam*' – He has truly risen.

After the muted celebrations, I decided to abandon going to join loved ones for the Easter feast and headed to the old part of the city instead to join an NGO who was helping to distribute bread to the needy.

With the cost of necessities rapidly escalating daily, millions of Syrians are facing poverty. The cost of living and food prices are on the rise, and gas and electricity are running short. With the latest influx of people fleeing Homs, the capital is rattled. The value of the Syrian pound has fallen and nobody is trading it because its price is decreasing every hour.

Aunty Georgette, Ammo Saleh's daughter, and many of their relatives and friends who can afford to are taking flights out of Syria, although almost all airlines are now fully booked for the next few months. People who were once comfortable now face destitution as the net worth of every Syrian has fallen by about eighty percent since the beginning of the revolution. More than half the country is living on two dollars a day or less. Hunger is spreading.

The exodus has begun.

On the day that death visited our family, I had woken up feeling like myself again. The pain had gone from my body.

It happened two weeks ago on a balmy spring day. To celebrate my good health, after my shift at the salon, I decided to go on a walking adventure. I strolled past wild irises and lost myself in the midday crowds in the Kurdish neighbourhood of Rukn al-Din then headed towards Souk Al Hamidiyeh. Near the entrance of the souk, I exchanged gossip and the latest news with silver-haired, one-legged Kamal, who, as usual, was at his favoured spot on the side of the road with his goods spread out on a blanket.

'*Na'iman*,' I said, congratulating him on his fresh haircut.

He did his tremendous and dramatic laugh.

'*Kayfal haal ya Ustad*? How are you?' I asked.

As usual, he poured me a cup of strong black tea and told me about his latest encounter with his maiden lover – a jinn called Mawaddah. The young lady spirit who apparently stood waiting in his room every night wailing from heartbreak.

'*Tikram, Ustaad*, but I've got to go.'

I'd tried to get away before he had a chance to tell me about the jinn's offspring, who sometimes took cat form and followed him around fondly and sometimes caused nuisance by mixing up his neatly organised pots and pans.

He suddenly grabbed my arm in a suffocating squeeze. '*Diri balek*! Be careful!'

I could tell he was forewarning me about something, but I wasn't ready to hear any of his fortune-telling. After all, he had a reputation for being a charlatan, who had acquired a bit of celebrity status for his attainments in spiritual and natural magic, and for holding conversations, face-to-face, with jinn. An eccentric character with a ragged turban, his handsome features had improved with age. Some claim he was once involved in satanic magic, *es-Sehr*, and practised enchantments by the aid of good jinn. He had repented after attending the *Halaqaat* of Sheikh Karim Rajeh, the imam of al-Hassan Mosque in Damascus, but had still maintained contact with the spiritual world. Others claim he is merely *majnoon*, crazy, but I enjoyed his quirkiness and light-hearted chatter.

As evening fell, I decided to head to the Al-Hijaz Cafe in Old Damascus, close to the Hijaz Railway built by the Ottomans at the beginning of the twentieth century. I smoked a *nargileh* pipe there and, as usual, mingled with intellectuals, politicians, artists, and poets and listened to tales of voyagers and orientalists who often visited the place. Then, when night fell, I took a taxi back to Mezzeh.

A warm breeze blew in from the open window, and I filled my lungs with a deep breath of fresh air when I entered the living room.

Ammo Saleh sat waiting for me. He turned the television off and closed his eyes for a moment. 'Fairouz, I need you to come and sit down. There is no easy way to tell you this . . .'

At that moment, my heart suddenly filled with intense dread. I reached for his hand and searched his eyes for strength. I knew I would need it. When he told me, no one could make me stop screaming, not even Ammo Saleh himself, who reassured me that he would treat me like his own forever.

My body shook with uncontrollable sobs as he lifted me up and took me to my bed. I stayed in bed for a few days screaming for *him* – at times it felt even the walls were wailing with me.

Well, there is no nice way to deliver bullshit. My father died while protecting the people in Al Rastan from the Assad militia. Part of me is falling apart, and part of me still doesn't believe it.

I am forever indebted to you, my father, in so many ways. To even stand in your shadow was a gift like no other, but to stand by your side was a great honour. To share many a podium, well, that was a source of great pride. I love you immensely and surely now, to be sheltered by so many memories, gives me great comfort in my grief.

You were one of my greatest champions, dear, dear father. My gratitude knows no bounds. Syria has lost a great son, a remarkably accomplished, brilliant, dedicated man, and an intellectual. And many of us have lost a great friend. We will never forget you. You were a remarkable man. Thank you . . . thank you, thank you.

The Syrian revolution is an orphaned revolution. We only have God.

Video footage of my father, labelled the smiling martyr, is widespread.

When he fell to the ground, he pointed to the sky with his index finger and began testifying to God. There were many witnesses who videoed the incredibly huge smile on his face as he lay dead.

He had led the *eisha*, or night prayer, with his wonderful voice and finished it off with an emotional supplication. Since the revolution, he had started to learn and memorise the Quran and spent long hours in prayer. Faith had become his strength. He would ask God for Shahadah or martyrdom in the path of God and his country repeatedly. Other rebels would enjoy praying behind him, saying they felt more *khushoo'* – concentration – when praying behind his voice. He would pray the special prayer of Qunoot, begging God to help Syria in every compulsory prayer. He would pray, 'O Lord, take from my blood until you are pleased.'

The story of his martyrdom is that his rebel convoy had stopped at the frontlines in the larger Homs area. He had decided to guard the base at night and had begun to dig for *khanadeeq* – ditches in the ground for the rebels to hide and shoot the enemy from. It was a cold and pitch-black night, with only limited sight on the frontline. My father heard via radio that Assad's troops were surrounding a group of rebels and civilians in a nearby village. He didn't hesitate but prepared for battle immediately and left camp without his sleeping comrades. When he arrived at the deadly scene, he stormed forward, set his gun to automatic, and sprayed left to right, and almost immediately took a fatal shot just below his heart.

His courage resulted in Assad's soldiers running away, thinking more rebel fighters were coming behind him. It wasn't just their armed foot soldiers, but also their tanks, their entire arsenal, retreated.

Father single-handedly fended off the entire enemy force and made them disappear, saving the lives of a whole village.

That morning at the *fajr* – dawn prayers – his fellow fighters looked around for him, as they looked forward to him leading the prayers. There was an anxious silence. A few hours later, an Egyptian-Emirati fighter arrived, informing them that a memoriser of the Quran with a beautiful voice had just been martyred. At once, his comrades realised it was my father. Some of his closest friends, who loved him immensely, tried to make excuses, hoping that it wasn't him.

But it was he. He'd passed on as a hero.

In hindsight, and growing up and maturing with the experience of the conflict, I can understand why and how my distressed father suddenly turned to religion and found God. Under terrible oppression, and in times of war and suffering, I have seen people turn to religion for solace and comfort. The beard on his face wasn't a sign of his allegiance to a terrorist organisation; it was a sign of his newly found piety in the same way he had started to pray five times a day.

People find faith during war in the hope that a greater power will relieve them of the pain. It is a natural reaction, which someone can only experience if they live through what we are living through. I have friends who have become more devout Muslims and school friends who have started to wear a hijab because they fear dying soon and are worried they might die in a state of sin. Some are simply preparing for the afterlife and want to collect as many good deeds as possible before their likely death. Almost all my Muslim friends have turned to the Quran to help with the mental agony and as a Christian, I have adopted Biblical sayings as I find them to be very relatable to my current situation.

From a Christian perspective, the Bible recalls how Jesus said, 'Come unto me, all of you who labour and are forced to bear burdens, and I shall give you rest.' There is so much sweetness in the precept; such solace in the promise; so much hope in that reminder.

Some people turn to alcohol – case in point, my mother. Some people, like my father did, find salvation in religious organisations. It doesn't make either of them criminals. In this war, we are all trying to cope. Religion wasn't the reason my father participated in the revolution. Religion wasn't his cause. His reason for going out there was because he was highly educated but unemployed due to the favouritism enjoyed by Alawites in all job sectors and the ostentatious corruption of the Assad regime.

From the very beginning, the role of the 'armed resistance', otherwise known as the Free Syrian Army, in Homs and other cities has been to safeguard the demonstrators and to support and defend the work of activists. Having spent the first months of the revolution in the countryside, I have seen first-hand how this cooperation has allowed us to protest peacefully and safely while also providing the world with information on the crimes committed by the regime. I have never seen Free Syrian Army members like my father or youngest brother carry out executions or go out on the offensive with the intention of war. It has always been to protect our lives.

The more patronising foreign correspondents I speak to, the more I feel the need to stress that this revolution is for all Syrians, and that the majority of the revolutionists aren't extremists battling to make a Sunni state; rather, the majority of Sunnis just want a fair chance at life and want equal opportunities for all. And besides, neither the regime supporters nor the opposition come from one sect or one religion. Still, they patronise Syrians by assuming our differences are beyond comprehension.

Today's Friday protest was named 'A Revolution for All Syrians'. Every week on Facebook, a poll is made to choose the name, and activists around the world chose this one over a more militant name. Peace activists hailed this as a victory against extremism. Eight hundred and twenty protests in total took place all over Syria today. For everyone else who came out with renewed vigour, it was due to the new United Nations-backed ceasefire that people thought would bring an end to the bloodshed and allow them to protest freely.

The road ahead of me is going to be rough. I strive to live a positive life: one that is peaceful and sees beauty in the world. There is an ugliness that has found me, but I will not let it define me. The Syrian regime roadblocks on the Damascus highway to Hama are returning fleeing families back to where they come from, and this means I can't be there to console my family.

When I just want to crawl in a hole and come back when this revolution is over, I remind myself of what my mother and grandmother in Hama are going through. I want to stretch my arms out and hug them both. This is so hard on them. On all of us. My family is the world to me, and seeing them suffering is like suffering yourself – worse, even, because you can't do anything about it, not even be there to console them. May they find strength in each other's company, and may my mother find wisdom in her heart to cope with this where it now counts the most.

Whichever religion Syrians follow, doctrine matters less and God matters more. I remember my grandmother telling me of the merits of the *qiyam al-layl*, which means standing in the night. In Islamic terminology, the term refers to the voluntary night prayer, which my grandmother would always pray in times of distress or mourning.

'Allah already loves you, it's okay, just get some sleep,' I remember telling her on one occasion.

She replied, with eyes wide, 'How can I? When it is during the last third of the night that our lord descends to the nearest heaven and calls out to us "Is there anyone to call upon Me so that I shall respond to him?"'

So sweet an invitation, so promising were the words, even an atheist would forgive her for turning to God's very personal exhortation.

'Call upon Me,' He says. He doesn't ask mankind to come via prophets or pious people, nor any kind of intercessors while calling Him. He knows what is in their hearts.

Is there anyone that needs to be heard? He is ready to listen. He invites us with the sweetest tune of friendship.

It has been just over a week since flames and smoke rose from burnt cars after two bombs exploded near a major intersection next to the southern district of al-Qazzaz here in Damascus.

A friend wondered how 'with all the checkpoints and searches, and the lack of movement in Damascus, anyone could sneak two five-hundred-kilogram bombs in'.

Another friend remarked that 'activists had put together complete evidence that proved that the bombings were an inside-job by the regime'.

I didn't want to hear the regime's side of the story, nor the activist's speculations regarding the explosions; I wanted to hear from the international community and the United Nations.

We trusted the United Nations observers to succeed in their peace mission and had high hopes that it would be much more successful than that of the Arab League. But, unfortunately, the same outcome seems to be happening. As violence in Syria spreads, the death toll is on the rise every day and all we hear is that families in the countryside are being trapped inside their homes in the middle of dangerous sieges.

Most cities have started to resemble battlefields from ancient civil wars, and it is the regime that gains the most from the violent disorder. From what I see, we are moving backwards and not to the future

Syria is for *all*: Alawite, Christian, Armenian, Kurdish, Druze, Shiite, Sunni, even the Cookie Monster. Stooping to racist bigotry is an insult to the martyrs who are dying savagely. The regime has robbed Alawites of their identity by playing on their historical fear of the Sunnis, leading many of them to join the evil Shabiha, who carry out most of the regime's butchery. Many Sunnis and Christians who oppose the actions of the Shabiha now have deep hatred in their hearts towards Alawites as a whole. This instilment of fear and hatred between sects is not conducive to the cause; it is counterproductive and plays right into the hands of the regime.

It is a pity how we have come to this stage. The Assads are using the same low-level tactics as their father did forty years ago, all to keep Syrians under the foot of Bashar al-Assad.

My father did not die for this; my fellow activists did not get arrested and tortured for this sectarian conflict. They all sacrificed their lives because they wanted the same things: respect, reform, dignity, and freedom.

The Assad's tactics don't end there. They are specifically trying to get rid of moderate 'voices of reason' in the opposition. It is only the non-violent, intellectual activists who are being detained. Just like Egypt's Mubarak did, this regime is releasing crazy dangerous criminals, al-Qaeda terrorists, and rapists from prisons and detaining scores of peaceful opposition activists instead. Media have not even picked up on this, because the horrific damages and deaths taking place overshadow it. This elimination process of activists who are willing to negotiate and who are interested in a transition to a new political system is systematic, and everyone I know is on high alert.

Going through the grieving process, I am told that I am simply passing each of the typical cognitive responses. I have already passed denial and am now feeling anger. I kick rocks on the road, scream, curse loudly. Then I want to go and hug that one person that I love so much – Emad. I am not sure if the pain will ever end or that, if it does end, I'll make it through gracefully.

An hour ago, on the busy Al-Thawra Street in central Damascus, I raised my middle finger in defiance at the hundreds of Iranian Revolutionary Guards stationed at the post office there who continuously harass the locals. Then I remembered my honourable father and all the other martyrs and how I did not want to sully them by stooping to the level of this legalised mafia.

'We are better than you!' I shouted with exuberance. 'You can kill the revolutionist, but you can't kill the revolution.'

12 June, 2012

Encircled by green gardens, the city of Damascus is still known by its epithet *al-fayha* – the fragrant – because of its profusion of gardens and orchards. As I crunch on the fresh strawberries and figs – which are also symbolic of the announcement of summer – I breathe in the heavenly sweet scents of orange blossom mingled with jasmine and roses among the brilliantly coloured flowers in the botanical garden just outside the wall in the old city.

The garden –and its cafe, a donation from the Swiss – is one of my favourite spots to sit to write and heal my senses. Many times after work, I retreat to the garden's quaint cafe, which serves the best Nutella shawarmas, and enjoy this small botanical oasis.

These simple pleasures are a far cry from the middle-class Christian neighbourhood of Qassa and the Alawite suburb of Barzeh; neon signs on urban stores and restaurants shine bright as ever. People there seem to be living far from ascetically, and consumerism is still thriving despite the struggles of many in the city.

In the evenings, the Syrian bourgeoisie and wealthy Gulf tourists come out to play, their tables generously covered in fresh vegetables, breads, and meat while prostitutes in niqab with their busts showing hang around to catch their attention. In the distance, a Justin Bieber song plays, a donkey brays, and a man with his many wives sits at a courtyard restaurant tucking into a rice and meat feast.

A socialist country has become a capitalist one under Bashar's rule, with the latest models of Porsches and BMWs racing all around while people across Syria fall deeper into poverty. Urban growth, concentration of wealth, status, and power, and the middle classes wanting to live a more cosmopolitan and Western way of life has made them move out of the old city and into class-homogenous residential quarters. The disparity between rich and poor has increased in Damascene society, and yet the regime that claims to follow the socialist ideology of the Baathists has consistently denied the significance of class divisions.

Class is an active significant factor in the Syrian revolution, and the alienation and anger felt by the mainly young unemployed Sunni underclass who live so near to the affluent, pro-regime middle and upper-class neighbourhoods has triggered many protests. Equally, for the affluent, class is also a factor as to why they choose not to join the revolution. There are so many of them who secretly detest the regime but are afraid that they'd fall off the social ladder if they spoke up.

Ammo Saleh's Syrian-Circassian neighbours are prime example. They'd packed up their whole lives and, like so many Circassians, are leaving en masse to their original homeland in Russia. Despite being Sunni, they've been treated well by the regime and have enjoyed great prosperity. While many Syrians struggle to eat, they have been complaining about caviar being unavailable.

However, according to them, their relative – Muhammad Said – died when the Circassian community in the Golan who, despite being neutral, were caught up in the conflict. Many of the villagers escaped to Damascus after burying their dead and stayed with Circassian families here. And even some of the poorer families are now seeking to return to the Caucasus.

This does not mean there are no Circassians involved in the revolution. There are many activists who are followers of the popular Islamic scholar of Circassian descent: Jawdat Saeed who belongs to the school of the famous Islamic thinkers, Algerian-born and Paris-educated professor Malek Bennabi, and Punjabi philosopher and poet, educated in England and Germany, Sir Muhammad Iqbal.

Shaykh Jawdat Saeed, known as the Syrian Ghandi, a peace advocate, pleaded for a non-violent revolution after the Syrian revolution became an armed conflict. At the beginning, he was encouraging Syrians and Circassians to join the peaceful protests, but he himself was forced to flee to Istanbul when his village of Bir Ajam was badly hit, completely destroying his home.

I look to the table near me. A man speaks loudly with a distinctive old Beirut accent, filled with heavy consonants and nasalised vowels. Raven-black hair pulled back in a well-oiled ponytail, tight white polyester pants and a v-necked shirt that shows his very hairy chest, he looks at everyone through dark glasses. Marvelling at him is his Filipino prostitute. I pity her. Filipino maids – a status symbol in Damascene society – in the rich neighbourhoods are one of the most desperate groups to get away from Syria but can't because they are undocumented, and their employers cruelly refuse to hand over their passports. They, just like the poor Syrians, are left to find their own way out.

15 June, 2012

I am in love with Damascus! The legendary Damascus – charming, enchanting, captivating, and it still is today. I don't believe I have been living in Damascus long enough to rightfully call myself a *Dimashqi*, but I like to think I've become pretty Damascenised.

This city continues to inspire me with her elegance, her rage, and above all, her capricious beauty.

I get lost for hours snapping photos and wandering through the elegant old and narrow streets, finding fascinating historic treasures, visiting churches, museums, and Ayyubid schools, and I can't help but feel I am following the footsteps of the great and glorious such as St Paul, Mary, and Muhammad. I am even out enjoying the heat during the six-hour daily power cuts – which mean no internet and no online activities – discovering new streets, drinking freely from the water taps that are all over the old city, which provide sweet fresh spring water to anyone passing by.

Dealing with my father's death, I have found that laughter is the very best medicine, and I have tried to stay upbeat and positive as he would have liked me to. People at the local church have also been kind to me.

Seeing the beauty in the world puts me ahead of the game already. That is a blessing in and of itself. Not everyone can see the beauty – there is so much ugliness in Syria right now that sometimes we forget to look for the good. I know this is going to be a difficult journey, and it seems so unfair that while other revolutions ended in regime overhaul, our situation gets worse, but we hang onto positive spirit and try to keep our morale high. We don't know how to run away . . .

As the sun goes down, I can see the Sufi whirling dervishes – the Mawlawi gather around a fire to chant rhythmically in unison, and I breathe into the scent of the *oud* that is coming from the mosque across. Watching them whirl like the wheels of Hama and spin in sheer joy, I envy their stillness and contentment even on the darkest of days.

22 June, 2012

'Start talking or we will strip you.' My interrogators had brought me to a cell full of women, all naked. Leering, the men told me that they would leave me here until it was my turn.

My turn for what? Pretty soon, I found out. Two ghouls from the Secret Intelligence came in. They had a plastic box with them, which was overflowing with lingerie and lipsticks.

'You have ten minutes to get ready,' they hissed at us.

The youngest girl among us let out a scream. The eldest woman, pregnant, took the box from them. She picked up a razor from the box and asked to go to the washroom opposite us to shave her hairy legs. Everyone else was motionless; the seconds we waited for the men ticked by with agonising slowness. Nobody said a word. We just stared at the disgusting lingerie: the crotchless knickers, the edible underwear, the grotesque garter belts – this wasn't anything like my mother's lingerie drawer. There were no sheer body stockings, no French girdles, and no charming baby dolls that celebrated a woman's body. But then, these weren't ordinary men; these were barbarians.

I tried to smear my face and chest with charcoal soot from the wall to make myself look ugly and dirty in hopes of discouraging them. One of the women looked at me disapprovingly as if to say *don't you know that they rape women and any woman will do? Virgins, widows, housewives – every living thing with a vagina.*

I hadn't even been feeling ugly lately; I felt attractive for once. A client at the salon had said I was at that rosy time of my life. As an adolescent, I was self-conscious about my small breasts – I remember asking my mother when they would start to bounce – but in the past months, and especially recently after enjoying rich food at Ammo Saleh's home, they had fattened and matured.

Clutching our breasts, we turned around when the door opened and the men came in. This time their uniforms were replaced with hairy legs. I started to cry. Now we were all crying. The vultures went to the youngest girl first, their hungry eyes raking over her body.

'You go out to protest like a whore. You give us your virginity, your honour,' the taller of the two said, smirking, then grabbed her buttocks while the other pulled her hair and spat on her.

In the small bathroom across, there was a scream from the pregnant woman followed by hot blood hitting the floor audibly in splats, seeping out under the door.

I don't know what overcame me, but I leapt up and kicked the door open before the men could. The mother-to-be had sliced her wrists with the razor blade and was slashing herself more with it, and screaming as she did so. I grabbed the blade from her hands but she fell to the side and squeezed her eyes shut while reciting the Shahadah.

'There is no god but Allah, and Muhammad is His messenger.' She kept repeating it, weaker and weaker, as death slowly took her.

One of the men chortled in a wheezy voice. 'She thinks she'll escape by death. She didn't know corpses are even more delicious.'

For the next few hours, the men ripped open the women's bodies, but for some reason ignored mine. I felt lucky and horrified all at once. Blood dropped down their thighs. Fresh virgin blood, dried blood, deep wounds from the whips carved all over them . . . like the strokes of an abstract painter.

After nightfall, an officer came in and escorted me to another room. I realised soon that it was the original interrogation room I had been brought into when I first came to Damascus. Only this time, there wasn't one man in uniform; there were two.

As my eyes met his, I was confused.

'Ammo Saleh, is that you?'

But as I stared at him, I felt my stomach lurch and nausea rise up inside me. For a second, I wondered how I would tell my father and what his reaction would be, but then I remembered that Baba was no more.

There was no trace of the friendly Ammo Saleh I had come to know – or thought I'd known – so well. His eyes were hollow as he stared at me, his face impassive.

'Fairouz, do you have any idea where your brother's battalion is right now?'

'No, I honestly don't,' I said, meekly, my stomach roiling.

'Can you tell me where your friend Shadi goes every morning at seven o'clock?'

'No, I can't . . . I mean I don't know,' I replied.

And on and on his questions went.

I felt as if the air had been sucker-punched from my lungs. Surely this was a dream. This wasn't the man I idolised – the man I saw as a second father. At times, I had even wished he *was* my father.

The stern note in Ammo Saleh's voice shocked me into fresh despair. I was sitting in front of the man that had, with all his goodness, opened his home to me – a luxurious one at that. Well, it was bound to be luxurious, I suppose, as his intelligence job was far more lucrative in pay; sadly, it was people like me who were a meal ticket to his life of luxury.

They made me kneel on the floor and asked me question after question about the opposition. When they sensed my reluctance, they attached cables to my body and ran electricity through me for ten seconds. I screamed again and again, crying out for my father and for Ammo Saleh to have mercy, but every time I gave an unsatisfactory answer, the electricity would start again.

They kept me for three days. I was placed in a room where I could hear the screams of other detainees being tortured using 'the chair' method, and I was told that I, too, would be placed in a spine-breaking chair hung upside down if I didn't co-operate.

On the third day, Sergeant Saleh – as I had come to think of him now – came in, telling the men that they must let me go to stay at a fellow activist's house to find out their secret hiding places and record the meetings of the organisation.

Sensing my unwavering resistance to being turned into an informer, they brought in torturers one last time.

I can scarcely bring myself to write about what followed, but I feel I must record it somehow. I was subjected to the most infamous tool of torture in Syria: the *dulab* (tyre). As I struggled, weakly through exhaustion and lack of food, I was stuffed inside a tyre until my limbs cramped. Then I was rolled in it and the men took delight in beating me. I have no more words to describe the pain, so I will simply say that even now, when I think of it, I weep.

When they finally let me go, I headed straight here to safety and warmth, to my friend Hajer's home. But safe for how long?

19 July, 2013

No, the date is not a mistake. It has been a year since that last entry, when I thought things could get no worse. I could almost laugh now at how wrong I was. My relief at being reunited with my diary is immense. I am so grateful to my dear friend who retrieved it and kept it safe all this time. When she placed it back in my hands today, I wept. It was like coming home.

One year ago today, I was snatched from my hiding place in Damascus and taken to Idlib central prison. If the journey there was terrible, it was nothing compared to the six months I spent in the dungeon. I'm not afraid to admit that as I sat, sobbing, in my mouldy cell, hungry, exhausted, and in pain, I wished that I would die so the torture and the rape would finally stop. So much happened in those six months, but also so little. It feels as though time stood still in there, with me trapped inside the hourglass, beating on the window, while outside the world continued, oblivious.

I had resigned myself to die in that place. I thought of Father often, and in the darkest hours, I thought I could see him in the gloom of my cell, smiling at me and reaching out a hand. But then the door would crash open and he would disappear, and I would be dragged to whatever fresh hell awaited me that day.

On the 25th January, 2013, a date etched in my mind for the rest of my life, armed rebels broke into the prison. When I first heard the explosions and gunfire nearby, I thought that death had finally arrived – and I was relieved that my ordeal would finally be over. I opened my arms, ready for it to take me.

Bang! The heavy thud of metal told me that the huge padlocks on the door were falling to the floor and that someone was breaking off the locks. Suddenly, death was not the only option. This was actually real; I could hear and see detainees running out of the prison grounds, and I knew that I had to go too.

I clambered up and ran out into the glorious daylight, ignoring the prison guards, who were shouting and shooting. The sound of the gunfights mixed with screams from all sides was deafening, but I knew I had to run for my life. The line between freedom and death has never been so thin.

I ran among scores of people trying to get out, bullets whizzing over my head. I edged ahead and finally came to a wall where I could no longer see the orange flames and black smoke spewing.

'Come over to this side, you are safe now.' It was a deep voice, and something in it made me trust it, against all the instincts I had. It was my only hope, and I followed it. Two strong hands suddenly grabbed me from behind, making me squeal. They were, as I later found out, the hands of one of the Chechen fighters who were known as the *Muhajiroon* – meaning 'immigrants'. They were, as I later found out, fighting alongside some of Syria's own rebels, and they'd even formed their own little units that were each given a Syrian minder who guided them around. As the very tall blonde men in hiker boots hauled us into armoured vehicles, nobody was celebrating. We were very much still inside, and bombs were going off in the distant compound. I knew it would be a while before I could step freely outside again.

The Chechen driver kept asking us to keep our heads down to avoid any possible random shots as he sped off. I couldn't take my eyes off the street and the surrounding buildings. Syria was an earthquake. Windows stripped out of their wooden frames, not a single wall was without holes. The permeating smell of humid burnt flesh filled the air. It was surreal.

When we reached the village of Yaqoubiya in the northeast of Idlib province, which was under control of opposition fighters, we were taken to a makeshift base and bought in front of a *mufti,* or Islamic judge. As the prison housed both political activists and real criminals, it was important to differentiate between the detainees before releasing all. Those that were established as real criminals were taken elsewhere to complete prison sentences, while political activists and protesters who had, like myself, been abducted from checkpoints, schools, universities, hospitals, rallies, or their homes and then been taken to torture in different prison branches around Syria were sent to safe houses.

A dozen of us females were sent together to a safe house in Idlib near to where the *Muhajiroon* fighters were settled. For six weeks, we stayed in their refuge because it was too dangerous for us to make our respective journeys home. I had been unable to make contact with my family and so we stayed in limbo, still grateful to the men who had rescued us from Assad's prisons. The men spoke to each other in Chechen, Tajik, Turkish, Moroccan Darija, French, Saudi dialect, Urdu, Pashto, and Libyan dialect. They'd bring us food and essentials until family members who they'd been able to get in contact with arrived to collect us.

One of the first things I noticed when I escaped prison was how the Assad regime had increased its bombing of civilians incessantly and unmercifully. The clashes had become so heavy between both the rebels and regime that highways had been completely closed off, and during the twenty-two months of fighting, the countryside had become a battleground, with only emaciated cats and dogs roaming the filthy streets freely. The increasing scale of the fighting meant that we were always locked up in the safe house with the old mother of one of the rebel fighters taking care of us.

Um Rashid would bring us dry bread and hot coffee each morning and rice and beans during the evening – far better than the rotten soup and insect-filled rice we had been fed while detained in jail. She would forever be lamenting her lost sons and husband – one of whom was buried in her courtyard under an olive tree, his grave marked with a dull brown stick. The other women and I were so grateful to her for opening her home to us, for keeping us warm with the little gas stove she had, for providing us with thick cushions and blankets to survive the harsh winter cold, and for accommodating our womanly needs. I remember a prison guard laughing in my face when I first begged him to bring me a sanitary towel for my monthly menses.

He laughed as he handed me the bloodied shirt of a young boy he'd just killed, telling me that the boy had died for me.

'Clean yourself with his shirt, you whore,' he said, laughing as he threw the stained shirt towards me. I had no other option.

There were twenty-nine women in total who had been rescued, plus a one-year-old child who was born in prison. The baby's mother had been raped so many times, she didn't know which prison guard was the father. We watched her take great care of the infant as though he was born out of love.

The dark and deep bags under our eyes tell of the horrors we've had to face and the things we've witnessed – the sadistic torture techniques that are not a new phenomenon in Syria. In fact, according to our old folk, Bashar's father, Hafez, had the Stasi come to train Syria's intelligence officers and they were taught the German tactics. In the same way the French government introduced extreme torture methods to Algerian prisoners in the 1950s, Syria's prisoners endured German practices of torture – the key one being to sodomise male prisoners with large objects such as guns and bottles.

Vivid are the sounds of male and females being tortured this way, and we ache and ache every day for the battered prisoners who are still trapped inside and dying slowly. The images of slow deaths will never leave me . . . men being skinned and burnt after having oil spilled onto them, pliers being used to pull out eyeballs and nails and hair, the twisting of limbs until the bodies are broken and left to die. Conditions were filthy; some inmates had skin ulcers that were causing the meat on their body to fall off, with no medication or help provided. Infections spread due to blood and pus from detainee's wounds and as the cells were humid, they attracted poisonous bugs that could be seen eating meat off prisoner's bodies. The smell was disgusting and the conditions were squalid, making the torture even more unbearable to cope with.

When I was first transferred from detention in Damascus to the state security prison, after initial interrogation and the confiscation of my professional camera and lenses, they asked for names of other activists in our organisation, scanned my social media accounts, and beat me black and blue in what they called a welcome session.

Inside, prisoners from all governorates, all walks of life, all ages and religions were screaming – their voices echoing through the corridors. They took me to witness what they said would become of me if I didn't tell them personal details about my friends. I refused to comply and I was dragged by my hair to rooms where men lay dead on electric chairs, where stark-naked men and women hung by their hands from their ceiling, some of them being molested, some being whipped with electric cords. Then came the cell where prison guards pushed rats into women's vaginas. A lady screaming '*Ya Hussein!*' was hanging by a hijab from a metal pole, her hands and feet cuffed. She was asked where her father was and when she couldn't answer, they shot bullets through her breasts.

This is just some of what I saw, and even now, a year later, it is beyond my explanation and comprehension. As I try to close my eyes and prepare for sleep, I am afraid of the horrible nightmares that make me keep reliving those moments again.

I remember being awakened on my first night in the overcrowded prison cell, stark-naked, out of my momentary paralysis, and unconsciousness. A vulture was ripping off my clothes and tearing me to pieces.

As my sore backside lay on the hard, cold tiles, I felt my soul trickle out of my body just like the blood trickling down my legs.

For our family, prison and revolution are not distant concepts but intimate realities they have suffered since my grandfather's time. However, when I was captured and taken away, they feared the worst and thought I had been killed in some underground prison.

The harrowing hunt, anxious wait, and my family's efforts to locate me and obtain my release with the money they had collected ended when they learned that I had escaped prison and was staying in Idlib – glad tidings brought from my brother Yahya, who had been stationed nearby at a checkpoint during my fifth week there. They thanked God for making us some of the fortunate few.

Chants of '*Takbeer*' and the proclaiming of God's greatness welcomed me in my village as my heartbroken family embraced me.

The highly emotional scenes and nonstop crying and kissing did not soften my mood at all, and my voice remained too subdued to even express my inner pain and feelings for the first weeks back in Hama. Despite being a survivor, I was weak and fragile, physically thin, inhumanly pale, and mentally disturbed.

The prison guards worked very hard on breaking our identity and our spirit. Despite my best attempts to stay sane by trying to think of stories my grandmother had told me, picturing the people I had met in Damascus and dreaming of my childhood in the countryside, it wasn't enough. I was terrified of the dark, yet scared of the light, recalling the way the prison guards made the lights flicker continually in the cell. It was just another thing in the long list of psychological torture we endured.

My grandmother, mother, and women from my neighbourhood did all they could to stop me sinking into depression. The women of Syria do what they can and could to ease the panic and pain of the wounded girls. The sadistic way in which the girls' souls, not only their bodies, have been violated means it was up to the Syrian matriarchs to carefully approach and counsel the girls to alleviate their pain.

It is taking a long while to forget. Images of the scary pale faces and broken skeletons walking round and round the cell, waiting for death, still haunt me. I am ashamed that we are safe outside while they rot in dark holes with no sense of time or day. I remember being one of them, sitting there, wishing I could die. Their screams of rape, sodomy and torture are being ignored and forgotten as the geopolitical game continues.

I can't stop thinking about the ones left behind. I can't move forward or begin to live my life because the memories of those mass rape attacks and inmates' screams of pain haunt my ever hour, awake or asleep. I fear they will vanish not only under the ground but also in the minds of the human conscience when their stories need to be heard and reheard endlessly for generations to come.

For forty years, our elders in Hama kept the past a secret fearful of the brutal regime, which was very wrong of them to do. Tables have turned and times have changed and we need to make sure there is a time of reckoning and accountability.

The night is bathed in brilliant moonlight – amplified because of the electricity blackout in the neighbourhood – and as the moon peeks through my window, I take out the old photographs from my grandfather's writing desk. I sketch his youth in my mind, and this time I can picture his struggles and challenges – some of which I am going through now.

He was the defeatist man who had always intrigued and annoyed me because of his negative attitude to life. He was the man I never thought I could ever become, but when I was lying in that dingy dark prison cell, hopeless and demoralised, with all my soul and personality sucked out of me, I knew better at last.

I was him.

You know you are back in Hama when you wake up to the sounds of the street vendors signalling their presence with the cling-clanging of brass bowls; even their fruit and vegetables are bobbing along. As the old man passed my door, I decided on impulse to give him some custom. Probably the toughest boiled corn – *baleela* – I have ever eaten, but I still felt okay about it.

The local street vendors plodding the streets in the September sun are rejoicing in the bounty that the late summer has bought us: *janarek* – green plums – that they pull around in their carts and which we bought three kilos' worth for our entire compound. Dunking them in coarse salt, I felt like I was munching into normalcy at last.

Laughing and enjoying special moments in the courtyard once again with my loved ones and neighbours made me forget for a moment that I had come back to an apocalyptic Hama city, where stinking piles of junk and rubble fill the streets alongside malnourished child beggars burning in the heat. The indiscriminate bombing in the sky is constant, but unlike before, nobody flinches with fear. They've torn down our buildings, but don't they know that our childhood memories are still dancing inside these places?

It's been more than two years, and it's unbelievable how our lives have changed significantly. Syria was beautiful with some pain . . . now it's bloody and the pain is unbearable. Although I miss the smells of Damascus, the nightlife, mornings sipping Abo Shaker smoothies to work and evenings eating Abu Al-Abd shawarma on the grass with friends, living in rebel-held territory is just more freeing.

Returning has been a mixture of emotions. The general atmosphere in Hama is sickening, with the concentration of checkpoints, the rising barricades and sandbags, and explosive detectors everywhere in addition to the rubble and war-torn landscape. Buildings have been emptied. Friends have disappeared. I would love to let them know I am alive and well – that is, if they are alive too.

I managed to make contact with Reem, who now works as a teacher for children displaced from all around the country in a United Nations shelter in Kfar Souseh. We haven't been able to trace most of our other friends; all we can guess is that they have all fled to refugee camps with their families.

Sitting and watching rebel fighters take a break from fighting in the fields nearby, my mind tries to sort through all the recent chaos. There might be less food and electricity, but we are less at risk of getting arrested and taken away for torture. I'd rather be here where we are safe from the worry of arrest, but not from the missile that could land onto our house at any minute. Living in a rebel-held suburb makes it hard to cross over to the government-controlled sides of the city, as checkpoints are dangerous places. It is the noble Free Syrian Army rebels who are at the frontlines protecting us, while the rotten apples who claim to be rebel fighters remain in neighbourhoods stealing and causing chaos among us. I don't know why these thugs pretend to be part of the rebels. There are now more than a thousand armed opposition groups in Syria, so even for us, it is hard to figure out who is legitimate and who is part of a criminal gang. Men in my family are not only fighting criminals but also fighting Assad soldiers. Also, many believe that the regime has hired some thugs to act like the FSA and commit crimes.

Yet the most noticeable change in Syria, and the biggest threat to our democracy and revolution, is the arrival of Islamic extremists. There was a flicker of jihadists before I was abducted and sent to prison, but that flicker has become a flame now.

Not all foreigners who have flocked here have come for a Salafist adventure or with a jihadist agenda; according to the FSA fighters I know, many have come to defend and honour the women and children and protect their Arab or Muslim brothers and sisters. However, extremists are quickly recruiting them. Those of them who have joined radical groups have made this war dirtier and played right into the regime's clever and sophisticated game. Releasing Syria's radical Islamists from Sednaya Prison, knowing full well they'd form opposition groups and start recruiting soldiers, was one of many ways the regime has helped extremists flourish.

Yesterday, when my brother and his other rebel fighter friends were sitting outside the house in the shade of the frail trees, clutching their guns and discussing the stresses of war, Abu Hatem, the rugged Iraqi, began discussing how the shortage of weapons has meant rebels in some critical areas of Homs are now having to ask their rivals from jihadist groups like Al-Nusra Front to assist them in defending their towns.

These groups are getting all the arms and sponsorship from foreigners while the original revolutionists receive little or no aid. Notice how little the rich Islamist backers contribute to humanitarian aid in Syria; notice how Iran has contributed four billion dollars to the Syrian regime since the conflict began, but their money goes to create the humanitarian crisis, not help it.

With all the arms and ammunition coming into the country, extremist groups need soldiers, so they recruit and brainwash young innocent boys into becoming child soldiers. Luring teenagers to fight for extremist groups is becoming easier because the Free Syrian Army are poorly armed with assault rifles and a few RPGs and have been infiltrated by criminals sent by the regime. There are about ten localised jihadist groups other than Al-Nusra Front, but another one is catching up fast. Calling themselves Islamic State in Iraq and al-Sham (ISIS), they've been operating in the north of the country for roughly four months. ISIS has already killed key Free Syrian Army commanders and in some instances, like in Raqqa, has driven away complete brigades.

Fighting between the moderate rebels and ISIS has reached a critical stage in the north as ISIS now governs villages, towns, and even a governorate capital.

Unlike what Arab and international media are reporting, the whole of Syria is not being dominated by ISIS or al-Qaeda die-hards; they are mostly focusing in the northern half of the country while our rebels are here lightly defended and struggling to fight both Islamists and Assad and protect freed territories.

Nobody was interested in arming the moderate Free Syrian Army and now what do we have? We have a remarkable expansion in jihadist territorial spread and influence because such a prolonged war and chaotic country provides militants from around the world ample opportunity to slip inside.

Neither the West nor the East wanted to arm the Free Syrian rebels with weapons, whether it is because of 'hands-off' policy recommendations or for fear that weapons could have landed in the hands of al-Qaeda and Islamists. The FSA are now facing those very same extremists that the world was so worried about, and their aim isn't to overthrow Assad to save Syria, but to establish an Islamic state on Syrian land.

Syria is neither Qom nor Qatar, nor Najaf nor Nasrallah's playground, nor Houthi land nor Saudi Arabia. Syria is ours. Or, at least, it used to be.

I came so close to a real burnout during and since the Maaloula assault, which has affected a lot of my mother's side of the family. It is a special place in the heart of all Christian Syrians and has been a Christian haven for more than two thousand years. Now the village of my ancestors has been handicapped by extremists who have fired at churches, shelled monasteries, smashed down the statue of the Virgin Mary, kidnapped nuns, and detonated a car bomb at the checkpoint near the entrance to the village.

Towns and villages in Syria that have been home to Christians for hundreds of years are being steadily emptied by sectarian violence and targeted kidnappings.

It's bad enough that Christian ancestral provinces such as Deir Ezzor and Hasakah in the north have been emptied by the violence and suspicion facing minorities in Syria. But jihadist groups are milking the remaining Christians of their money, land, and property while some are being forced to convert to Islam. Also, Christians are not armed at all. Kurds are given assistance from Kurdistan, Muslims get support from Gulf States, and Alawites from the regime. This makes Syria's Christian community an easy target.

My mother's family rang us on Viber to give us an update.

'Christians were left to their fate initially because the Assad soldiers retreated,' my grandmother told us.

There are still so many militants, roaming the snow-covered mountains. My uncle described the horrifying moment the village was woken up by loud explosions and gunfire, causing both the Sunni Muslim inhabitants and Christians to huddle together and hide.

Maaloula translates as 'the entrance' in Aramaic, named so because of its dramatic location at the entrance to a rocky gorge. The higgledy-piggledy butter-yellow and pale blue houses are stacked on top of one another – coloured in this charming way to attest the pilgrimage of their inhabitants to Jerusalem. My mother's family have owned one of the oldest and most successful souvenir stores offering sweet, locally made red wine, honey, rosary beads, prayer books, and Christian artefacts for generations. However, due to the lack of pilgrims – vital to the economy – business has suffered.

Granted, Maaloula attracts tourists from around the globe, but even as a Syrian I value and appreciate this sacred place. Childhood days spent in such a peaceful place where it felt like time was suspended, and where evil seemed a million miles away, I would help my grandparents prepare and clean grapes in large basins to have them ready for juicing. I would play and learn, and no matter where life takes me, Maaloula will always have the same unique impact on my faith, spirituality, and personality.

Today is the date that Christian inhabitants and the many Christian tourists and pilgrims are supposed to fill the picturesque mountain village for the festival of the Holy Cross, but the streets are filled instead with armed soldiers and tanks and people like my family packing up their belongings to escape to Lebanon – the one country left for Christians in the Middle East.

Christianity is one of the key elements of the Arab world even before the emergence of Islam; Christians have contributed to Arab and Muslim civilisation – if Christianity goes, then moderate Islam is doomed too. The regime is arresting mostly moderate Muslims because they want to create an 'either extremists or Syrian government' dilemma for both the Syrians and Western governments, like they have been doing for years.

Faces from my childhood are being hit by mortar shells as I write, blog, tweet, text, and speak. People who have my surname are being held hostages in the honey-coloured cliffs of Maaloula . . . videos on the internet show how they've damaged the St Thecla convent among other important heritage sites.

With all its ancient buildings, the village is a UNESCO World Heritage Site, and as there are talks of Western strikes on the extremist groups, those evil men are very clever and want to capture control of the village because they know the West will avoid aerial bombardment in this historically valuable area. Like many before, they are using religion to cover up their evil mission.

We need to continue to fight the hate with love, no matter how difficult it is. It's important to remember that our Muslim brothers and sisters are part of a solution, not a problem, as the media would have us believe. The Lord protects His people. He will never leave us. Centuries of persecution could not wipe the Christians from the face of the earth. Lord have mercy.

10 October, 2013

I have several crystal prisms in my window and when the sun shines brightly, there are rainbows everywhere. Today is one of those days – but I hate it when it is sunny now. For when the sun comes out, we have to hide indoors. I prefer it to be cloudy so that the airplanes that drop bombs can't circle as freely in the sky.

Yesterday, the full horror of Assadi evil was on full display with the regime intentionally bombing a local school. Teachers and children tried running away from the explosion, but you could see them being blown to pieces. Bits of meat lay on the ground like it was nothing.

Why? Because the regime doesn't want us to enjoy even a little normalcy. They bombed the water supply line, causing floods on the streets and leaving us thirsty. Snipers also continually strike bakeries during rush hour in a systematic attempt to deny us of bread.

Our beloved *khubz*; there are religious and superstitious feelings attached to bread in the Arab world, and bread is considered to be holy, a divine gift from God by all Christian, Jews, and Muslims.

It is a staple of our life, and it is no wonder that Jesus, who was born in Bethlehem, which means house of bread – *beit* is house and *lechem* bread – in Aramaic and Hebrew, is remembered in the humble and common form of bread and wine. Jesus also later said, 'I am the bread of life.'

Bread means so much to us, and it is always the centre of our gatherings. My grandmother raised her children on the bread she made in her *tanoor* bread oven and the money she made selling baked goods. She would send invocation to God while kneading the dough, and then another before slapping bread into the clay oven. If ever even a crumb of bread falls in Syria, you will always see people swoop to pick it up and kiss it, putting it respectfully on a higher place like they do with the Quran.

Egyptians refer to bread as '*aish*', which means life itself. At the start of the Arab Spring, the rallying cries of 'bread, freedom, and social justice' began in Egypt.

Heroic bakers like my grandmother have made loaves of bread during this war for both our neighbours and the Free Syrian Army soldiers on the frontlines. Taking bread to the other areas is a suicide mission, and those who have smuggled food supplies such as rice, sugar, pasta, and cooking oil have faced severe punishments by the Syrian security forces.

It is well known that if you are caught handing out bread, you are more likely to be a target to snipers than if you are caught out protesting. The regime soldiers at the checkpoints have started to humiliate us by replacing the sandbags with bags of bread instead, laughing at our craving for bread. Due to the lack of wheat, the cost and availability of bread is so limited now that in the past few days when we had to take refuge in the basement with my uncle's family until the heavy bombardment and firing calmed down, we had just one piece of stale bread to share among the eight of us. On the last night, when my grandmother passed the last remaining pita bread around the circle, we each took one bite, and by the time it reached back to her, there was no piece of it left for her to eat.

Today is a morning of mourning, our local church has taken a hit and the scene is utter carnage. The marble statue of Mary is smashed, the pews splintered, the altar crushed, and prayer books burnt. We walked among the rubble looking for survivors, glass from the stained windows crunching under our feet; fury shook us, we knew everyone had been buried into the ground. The only thing I scooped into my arms and carried back home to bury in the soil in our yard was a toddler's foot, still in its slipper.

We also heard from one of the gossipy aunts in our family that my father's sister is now divorced and living in the camps outside town. Aunt Rima's gang rape happened in front of her twin six-year-old daughters Aisha and Salwa. Their uneducated father, Uncle Kazem did not know what to do, because although he knew she was a victim of Assad's men, an 'impure' woman who had lost her virtue was a dirty woman. Losing your feminine virtue is the biggest degradation for an Arab woman. It was so disgraceful, he gave her three divorces on the spot – *talaq talaq talaq* – and threw her out of the home in the cold.

As a victim of rape, this rips me apart. In prison, women would tell one another to kill each other so they would not have to face the stigma from their community. The Syrian regime are playing on a dirty string, because they fully well know the sensitivity of women in the Arab world, the rigid way sexuality is seen in Syria, and they are using our dignity to punish our families. Rape and sodomy disgraces and degrades us more than any other forms of torture.

19 October, 2013

Starving us and bombing us isn't working, so it's time to gas us. Chemical Bashar has committed a crime against humanity in Ghouta, and the incendiary weapon attacks continue.

These machinations to eliminate us are wicked and evil to the core, and there is no doubt that sarin was used and now napalm. Sarin and other nerve gases were used in this conflict long before this last school bombing case, but this time the Syrians had the sense to record as much footage as they could from the latest incident and send it viral. And there are some lunatics on the internet who are suggesting that the napalm bombing in Syria is a Zionist hoax. The napalm footage is clearly napalm and even harder to watch than the sarin victims; their flesh was peeling off. We have, of course, seen napalm used by the US in Iraq and our situation is equally dire.

To counter the conspiracy theorists, who generally have no personal connection to Syria and have never even lived here, our underground activist network has well informed and highly reliable sources dotted around the country who work extremely hard to keep the world up to date with current events.

Being on time, and creating a tidal wave while all using the same hashtag on social media, is crucial for making it work. The hashtag is kept quiet until it's time, for that reason. These things are based on understanding the algorithm of Twitter. It has been extremely successful with 'trending' previous crimes against humanity and is as important as ever. If we all stick to this way of working, then it will be much more successful.

There are many – even seemingly credible – experts and journalists who continue to try to tarnish the reputation of the glorious revolution of the Syrian people and whose aim is to polish the ugly face of the once glamorised and chic Assad, who has now been exposed as a psycho killer in the eyes of the world. As the regime gets more desperate, their propaganda increases, and so despite the brown marks on my legs – scabies at its worst and the injuries I sustained in prison as a result of severe punishment – I have begun to take my camera out again to fight the fabrications with my raw images.

I have acquired the unconscious habit of looking back ever since the start of the uprising, but having spent so much time in prison, I had no idea how dramatically the conflict had changed. Islamists got involved and it became a totally different war. Back then, when it was just small rebel groups and the *tansiqiat* (coordination groups), the atmosphere was tense, but drumbeats accompanied the crowd in dances and well-rehearsed songs were sung by crowds that waved the revolutionary flag, jumping up and down as they yelled passionate cries of 'Death to Bashar, death to the donkey!'

That has all changed now. Men in fluorescent yellow jackets, who worked as stewards managing the crowds, are long gone.

Videoing violent protests and occasional air strikes is one thing, but collecting shaky footage in the middle of a civil war is a completely different story. The camera is a distraction when you are trying to dodge shrapnel and snipers, but every Syrian has recognised the importance of filming a part of history. Even Syrian rebels are fighting with two hands; in one hand, it is a camera, and in the other, is the gun. They have a dual role to play: fight the enemy and document the events . . .

One look at my rebel brother Yahya's Facebook profile and you will see his profile photo, cell phone in one hand, AK47 in another, taking a selfie. Scroll down and endless photos of guys standing on tanks with ammunition posing with their big guns, making funny faces, peace signs, and adding filters to impress their friends and family. At the end of the day, *everyone* wants to look cool on social media.

On a serious note, this is probably the most filmed war in history. There are traumatic and disturbing things I see during this war that even my handheld camera can't capture the true essence of pain and horror of. Sometimes the camera is great at capturing the experience and freezing the moment. My great numbers of followers on various social media pages are ardent consumers of images of war; whether still or moving images, they are addicted to, and captivated by, the content I post despite the choppy edits and sometimes poor image quality.

Gruesome images of injuries get the most likes and shares and comments. My intention is to only capture the revolution's many faces of horror, devastation, danger, terror, fear, and even triumph. Utilising my handheld weapon – the camera – to tell my story, I let the audience decide on the narrative and judge for themselves.

Last week, a fellow activist, Nouf, and I hid behind a tank for six hours, waiting for soldiers to finish with their military operations near the al Ghab plain. When finally screams turned to silence, Nouf, with her cigarette dangling from her lips, motioned me into a narrow passageway. She is suffering from leishmaniasis, the sores on her gaunt face oozing even more in the sun. We squeezed past some old gas cylinders and rusting metal crates, ducked under a low arch wreathed with electrical wires, and arrived at an abandoned house in Al Jood Farm. There, in the sun and heat, was a chamber of horrors: the remains of mangled bodies scattered in the courtyard. Heaped bodies of some one hundred and fifty Free Syrian Army fighters, all badly preserved, birds and dogs pecking at them, their skin infested with insects.

The foul smell of corpses stuck to us even after we hurried away – after managing to take some photos from a distance. We informed a Free Syrian Army checkpoint nearby of our discovery. As always, almost all the corpses we saw were of young men and boys. They were always more committed and fought hardest. They even fight willingly when commanders order them to stay back, and go ahead and fight the enemy even though they are certain of death.

Our enemies did not cross our borders,
they crept through our weakness like ants.
- Nizar Qabbani

2 November, 2013

I knew it had been coming. Sheer fuckery and evil insanity. ISIS has officially taken over our area.

There is so much emotion that I find it hard to put what I'm feeling into any type of sentence that cuts to the heart of the matter. They seized control within the space of just a few hours – the time it took us to go the local hammam to scrub and come back. The black ISIS flag could be seen fluttering in the wind only a few hundred yards away from our home at the checkpoint that was previously manned by the Free Syrian rebels – one of whom is a family friend, now blown up to pieces.

After being indoors with my brother Adam, my grandmother, my mother, and my cousin–sister for the whole afternoon on that day, we desperately wanted to go outside and see all the commotion for ourselves. Activists were not yet uploading photos on Twitter and I really needed to find out what was going on.

'No! Stay inside with me until we know what is going on. It's also better if those men don't find out we are Christian, so stay inside until they have passed our area,' my mother told me.

However, some time later we began to hear loud chants of 'Allahu Akbar' and 'Dawla Islamiya' – Islamic State – which drew us all to the doors.

My mother pulled me back quickly, saying, 'Don't let them see you dressed in shorts!'

Sudden loud clattering sounds quickly brought me to the balcony doors again, but this time I opened it just a little so Mother wouldn't get angry. A convoy of tanks, SUVs, and armoured vehicles passed, all loaded up very high and carrying a group of militants who swooped into view. They had *kuffiyeh* scarves wrapped around their faces, guns on their shoulders, and were waving the Islamic State's distinctive black flag to mark their arrival. I know I should have been dead scared, but instead I was rather excited by the theatrical show.

During the parade, many people from the neighbourhood were rushing out and enthusiastically welcoming the invading forces. For the rest of the day, seeing the concern on her face, I remained at my mother's side.

Later, we found out that ISIS fighters had stormed the headquarters of the moderate Free Syrian Army not too far away and quickly set up roadblocks and taken over a radio station and other key buildings.

They were able to deploy their anti-aircraft weapons in a nearby field and take a few villages quietly because the Free Syrian Army had been exhausted the past few days from fighting with the other Islamist groups. The Free Syrian Army and the stauncher al-Qaeda-affiliated groups, namely Jabhat Nusra, have been skirmishing in different areas of Syria for a while, but the relationships among Assad's foes are at their most tense right now. Militants from the newly formed ISIS are taking advantage of the volatile ground situation in the absence of a strong government and the division between opposition groups.

To serve their main purpose of destroying the Syrian revolution and using Syrian land as part of their wider plans to create an extremist Islamic state, ISIS and similar extremist groups are primarily concerned about establishing bases for training and recruitment inside small countryside towns – like ours.

ISIS has already solidified its presence in Northern Syria and is spreading like wildfire all over. All this talk of their movement, but there is no talk of how they are able to spread their power without being attacked by the Assad regime, who has recently bombarded civilians heavily but blatantly ignored the very visible and well-known headquarters and camps of ISIS and its counterparts.

Is this avoidance of ISIS by the regime deliberate? Do they have a secret alliance with each other? It all seems so suspicious. While these terror groups are here, rebels are busy fighting *them*, and not the regime.

A short while ago, Belgian-Algerian soldiers from ISIS knocked on our front doors and entered our courtyards. They had brought with them bags of food and domestic gas cylinders, which children ran like lightning to grab. This was an attempt to win the hearts and minds of the locals through distribution of much-needed relief aid, which, as I just saw now on Twitter, is yet another a PR stunt by the group. They've tweeted a bunch of aid distribution photos and highly publicised their 'good deeds'. They are even gaining popularity on social media.

These new jihadists are alien to me.

They are probably sent from Assad's regime – puppets on strings. My gut instincts tell me that they are mercenaries in disguise, sent to taint this noble revolution and destroy the social fabric of Syria. How are civilians even accepting them so easily? I do not trust them and won't forgive them for pushing the Free Syrian Army out of the way. Our men have fought so hard to overrun the regime thugs; we have lost men and dealt with casualties and it wasn't so that these overdressed fanatics could come to eat the fruits of their success. I have no doubt they are just wolves in sheep's clothing.

26 November, 2013

When al-Qaeda's group in Syria, Jabhat al-Nusra, looks angelic compared to the even more radical ISIS, you know it's not good.

Many factions of the secular and moderate rebels have formed alliances with al-Qaeda's arm in Syria, because they believe they are the only ones still capable of countering ISIS. Jabhat al-Nusra, meaning The Support Front, is a Salafist group who also aim to implement Sharia law in Syria, should they gain power. Currently, they control about twelve Syrian towns. According to extended family in Homs and Idlib, they have established Sharia courts there and have gained the trust and respect of the locals because of their excellent electricity service and generous distribution of food. Activist friends in Aleppo from our network have praised al-Nusra for reopening bakeries there and supplying flour to the hungry public.

However, having watched their propaganda videos – made with impressive visual and audio skill and spewed out from their media group, al-Manara al-Baida, translating as The White Minaret – I am not impressed.

No secular revolutionist like myself wants to get involved with the jihadist infighting, but I guess we are forced to join al-Nusra on the battlefield to use as a counterbalance against ISIS. Men in our family who are part of Syria's secular and moderate Free Syrian Army describe how they can't afford to carry out solo operations anymore. My brother described al-Nusra's war arsenal as being world-class, thanks to its strong back-up from wealthy Arabs. The members of the organisation are best equipped and better organised compared to other rival groups and use their weapons and explosives with huge skill and ferociousness.

It is important to remember that Jabhat al-Nusra originally took orders from both ISIS – formerly known as al-Qaeda in Iraq and led by Abu Bakr al-Baghdadi – and al-Qaeda senior leadership, led by Ayman al-Zawahiri. However, both radical groups had a major quarrel earlier this year when Baghdadi asked al-Nusra commanders to pledge allegiance to him as emir. Jihadist websites and forums were on fire as each side battled with the other

'An ordinary emir can't be considered a caliph, and it's sinful to fight for the sake of manmade organisations,' one jihadi, referring to 'arrogant' Baghdadi, posted on a forum.

So, just a few months after Baghdadi joined the Syrian revolution and declared the annexation of Syria to the Islamic State of Iraq (ISI), al-Qaeda and the now rebranded Islamic State of Iraq and Syria (ISIS) split. But the dispute has since destabilised Jabhat al-Nusra as many of its fighters – mainly the very radical foreigners from Australia, Europe, Chechnya, Tunisia, Morocco, and Algeria – have left to join ISIS. Now that the group is left with majority Syrians, mainstream Syrians that had previous reservations about al-Qaeda and foreign fighters are joining them, replacing the foreign jihadists and helping them make up their numbers again.

Taking on ISIS with the help of another radical group is the only solution we are left with, otherwise we'll turn into another Raqqah where public executions are as common as roundabouts. As al-Nusra has been labelled a terrorist organisation by the West, we face great criticism from them. Yes, they're the first to criticise; however, when it comes to supporting us, the West just doesn't want to know. Co-operating with the enemy of our enemy doesn't mean it's easy to trust their new pragmatic approach and their promise to tone down its extremist ideology. We can only hope that their transformation to a more nationalist group that has acquired popular support is sincere. I'm not for it, but it is sadly the moderate opposition's last hope in the struggle against ISIS.

My conservative Muslim grandmother doesn't agree that we should take assistance from radicals.

'Don't think of them (al-Nusra) as nimble jihadists, my dear. At the end of the day, they and ISIS both have a radical Islamist endgame.'

'I know that, but Jabhat al-Nusra are using more diplomatic measures, and at least they're not aggressive towards Christians and other minorities,' I argued.

When Jabhat an-Nusra came to the northern city of Raqqah – population ten percent Christian – they closed down churches and suspended services but didn't harm anyone. Raqqah is full of Armenian Christians who migrated years ago after the Armenian genocide; we see Armenian-Syrians as an integral part of our social fabric. Now they've had to flee again with the arrival of ISIS, who've held public Bible burnings, kidnapped and expelled Christians, and bombed churches.

'Such extreme ideologies are doomed to fail as their evil eventually makes everyone resent them,' my grandmother said. 'It makes my head spin to think we are having to consider al-Qaeda (meaning al-Nusra) as a moderate movement. This is Hama, not Kandahar, and death is more honourable than accepting help from them.'

8 December, 2013

Today marks the one thousandth day since the start of the glorious Syrian revolution. But this is no victorious milestone here in a land of lost fathers and wandering orphans. Who would've thought that at the start, when the regime was killing about one hundred protesters every Friday, that its militia would end up killing more than thirty thousand innocent people?

The unmatched spirits of the Syrian people are fuelling this great revolution, which is also now a war of independence. Navigating the chronology of this long three-year conflict is immensely complex – but we aren't dejected by the task. Are Syrian rebels pro-FSA, pro-Islamists, pro-secularist, pro-West, pro-GGC? Often, when I sit down with friends or neighbours to discuss, there is more than one answer, maddeningly, contradictory, equally correct. People make decisions based on their political, emotional, and economical reasoning, and as this is very much real life, there are no perfect solutions to our struggles. There is a tendency to lump all the Syrian rebel groups into one mass, but the truth is, Syrian society is as culturally and politically confused as ever. I can only speak of my own emotional anguish and personal feelings.

While the vast majority of Syrians I know despise the hard-line Islamists, and are dreaming of a new transitional secular government that excludes the UN-certified war criminals in the

Assad regime, no easy path to that destination has thus far presented itself. In the meantime, revolutionary ideologies of the youth are on its last breath. The spray paint has reappeared on the walls of our city. Only this time, we are spraying anti-regime graffiti as well as anti-ISIS slogans, for they are both totalitarianists and both deny that our protest movement is legitimate.

Yesterday, when my peers and I were near the city centre distributing leaflets in an attempt to rally Syrian activists to act, an angry ISIS soldier yelled that we were 'misguided by the ways of Marx and Lenin' and that 'there is no such thing as *thawra* revolution, only jihad.'

From the other side, we are still taunted by Assad, who calls us 'agents for America and Israel.' Our peaceful civilian activism is gradually withering because of accusations of *fitnah* or chaos. There's no such thing as 'Islamic' socialism and 'Islamic' democracy in their view, and as a result, ISIS have been harassing participants in the public sphere. Currently, those who are demanding freedom, democracy, and a secular state are doing so in secret – under false names – and operating mainly online, just like they did under Assad's entrenched police state.

Many older people are pessimistic and have stopped taking part in protests because they don't think it will bring any changes. Our local farmer, Abu Fadal, commented on how the cycle of media activists taking footage of him in the protests amounted to nothing in the long term.

'They watch the footage but it ends there. Even after seeing our pain, the world turns the other way.'

So many have lost hope that the demonstrations will actually translate into positive change.

I think revolutions are a risky business and deep change inevitably requires patience. For me, there is no other option but to carry on our counter-revolution until life here in Hama and its outskirts is restored. We want to be able to play music without fear that our earphones will be confiscated – ISIS's idea of a radical political system affects all young people, from the religious bearded youngsters to the hippie students, and from the messy-haired bloggers to the high-heeled hijabis.

ISIS is now beginning to become more assertive and controlling and is not worrying about winning the goodwill of the general public like they did in the beginning. We must not allow them to solidify their rule here through intimidation. After being apprehended and threatened for wearing makeup, my motivation to wear it – and wear it loudly – has increased.

My bold, vivid lipstick is my psychological weapon – a way to cling onto some sense of normality and uphold identity. It is a very visible form of rebellion against the oppression and sexism. As the parasites ISIS worm their way into all aspects of our daily life, we walk out of our cages and demonstrate our attitude towards them and towards life by applying lipstick.

'What a gesture,' my cousin–sister remarked when I took out a compact mirror and reapplied the dark red lipstick to my lips in front of a fully armed ISIS patrol passing by.

I got that familiar charge of adrenaline as I watched a long-bearded maniac approach us angrily. Before we ran away, I smeared the lipstick onto Nesreen's lips too – and generously to make them appear huge. Historically, many women wore makeup in defiance of Hitler and saw it as a 'badge of courage', and for young women here, not only does wearing lipstick represent bravery, but the instant glamour and happiness that can be achieved on dark days filled with bombing raids is also a way of surviving and boosting morale. The symbol of this war has been bullets, but if I were asked to choose the symbol for the fine independent spirit, courage, and strength of the womenfolk that endures it all, I would choose lipstick.

I finally saw a handsome boy today. He came to our neighbourhood Christmas gathering and was eating a peach. He gave me a bite. Soft and sweet like his lips.

Hearing his voice after all this time startled me. I looked back in the crowd and there was Emad. He was no longer the same person – at least with regard to his appearance, which was completely altered. The hippie young revolutionist that I'd met bore little resemblance to the toughened soldier who faced me now. His hair was longer, his skin sunburnt, and it didn't look as if he cared much for grooming. He wore a camouflage jacket, faded hiking boots, and combat trousers and carried a machine gun. When he saw me, his gaze softened.

And what a beautiful night and setting for a reunion it was. As Christmas approaches, we are trying our best to celebrate as usual; as ever, our Muslim and Druze neighbours helped us to decorate the neighbourhood tree, only this time there were no gifts under the tree and instead of ornaments, we decided to decorate the tree by hanging photographs of the Syrian martyrs from our area.

We won't let the lack of resources and the devastation around us dampen our moods, and we're enjoying dancing merrily around the tree in the run-up to Christmas. We've come to a point in the war where the abnormal has become normal, and where we try extra hard to return to some semblance of our old lives. We don't want the streets to remain eerily empty on such an occasion, so we've decided to go ahead with the tradition anyway. There are no twinkly fairy lights, no candy and toy stores open, no frilly dresses and pressed pants for the children, who normally rule the streets during the festive period.

There will be no scrumptious Christmas dinner again this year, no *makloobe* and *wara enab* to eat, but we've shared little plates of chestnuts from nearby groves. My grandmother fired up a small coal stove and gas lamp and the air was filled with the rich and evocative scent of *kastana* – roasted chestnuts – and the joyful shrieks of hungry children. We are holding our usual nativity play, made creatively using rubble, and performing the local folkloric Aradha dance. The old Syrian dance is song, poetry, dance, and fancy costume all rolled up in one.

Only in Syria will you find Christmas trees made from bricks. In our courtyard, the neighbours' children have collected rubble and bricks from nearby bombed buildings and adorned it with colourful chocolate wrappers. Even the Muslim children are waiting for Santa, or, as we call him in Arabic, Baba Noel, to arrive to give them presents. Sadly, their parents struggle to even make sure they are fed and cared for. Most of the kids here are sick, the others bored to tears, and subsequently cranky and miserable. Rotten teeth, runny noses, and scabs can be seen on the once immaculately dressed children. More than three million children nationwide have been forced to leave their education and instead watch cartoons on repeat all day. A cartoon image being circulated on social media shows an Arab Father Christmas looking at a wish list where the only wishes from the Syrian people are 'Bread, bread, bread'.

'I can see the sadness in your eyes and your heart, Fairouz,' Emad whispered in my ear. We'd placed a photo of my father near the top of the tree.

He put his arm around me. 'Worry not, he is safe among the ancestors.'

I relaxed into his touch. He was still the same Emad to me, even if his appearance had changed. He still felt the same. When we were together, it felt like no time had passed; like we were standing still while the world spiralled out of control around us.

I looked up at Emad and he smiled at me. 'What are you thinking?' he asked, touching my face lightly with his finger.

'Just that I'm glad you're here. And that you're safe,' I said.

'I just wish—' he started, but I held my finger up. I knew what he was going to say. That he wished he could have done something when I was captured. That the thought of me being tortured was its own kind of torture to him. But I couldn't talk about it. Not today. Perhaps not ever.

I looked over at my dear church school friend Lana, who had lost all of her immediate family when a mortar hammered down in their living room, and quickly wiped away my selfish tears. And Emad didn't press the point.

There is no greater energy and good spirit then spending Christmas partying with fighters and heroes of our country who fight for peace and for happiness despite all the broken hearts.

Without them, I wouldn't even be here, with wine in my hand, surrounded by my surviving friends in their faded frocks, ending a year and starting another in my beloved hometown.

Gunfire and bombs have replaced the sound of Christmas fireworks and the jolly music is mixed with the occasional nervous silence. If anything, 2013 has taught me so much about contrasts and everything in between. I have experienced triumph and loss, happiness and sorrow, pleasure and pain, certainty and confusion. I have learned how to remain positive and see the good in bad situations.

This year has taught me that music kills deathly silence and happy celebrations kill painful memories. To the outside world, it may seem that the war has turned people against each other, but for me it has only helped confirm my faith in the goodness of humanity. Friends, family, neighbours, and even strangers have welcomed each other in their homes with open arms and stand as one body, one soul, and one human.

Syria, you are humanity, you are strength, and you are hope. You inspire the world. As we celebrate and grieve together, I am excited about what's next: what I haven't lived yet, the people I haven't met, the songs I haven't sung, the memories I haven't created, and the lessons I haven't learned.

7 *January*, 2014

While for many in the Western world Christmas has come and gone, we in Syria still have another Christmas to mark today. We have a sizable population of Orthodox Christians in Syria who use the Julian calendar, which runs thirteen days later than the Gregorian calendar.

There are several Christian denominations in Syria, who, they say, make up about ten percent of the Syrian population. However, I think this must have increased dramatically due to the influx of Christian Iraqi refugees settling here in the past ten years or so. Today, a diversity of priests, patriarchs, and bishops celebrated and attended worship services together.

Greek Catholics, Syrian Catholics, Armenian Catholics, Chaldean Catholics, Maronite Catholics, Latin Catholics, Greek Orthodox, Syrian Orthodox, and Armenian Orthodox make our country an oasis of diversity. Syria's Christians have lived peaceably alongside one another for centuries.

The current sectarian tension in some parts of Syria is an unwelcomed new phenomenon, promoted at first by the Syrian regime to maintain its own legitimacy and now by the likes of ISIS, to advance their own political agenda to the detriment of the historic communities.

To prove that neither the Assads nor ISIS can divide us, Syrians have responded by calling this Christmas 'Revolution Christmas'. This initiative, which has become viral online, also seeks to honour the Christian victims of this war and to implement the words of Italian Father Paolo, well known for his humanitarian work in Syria: 'Don't fear each other. Fear *for* each other.'

ISIS has grown overconfident and is now firmly in charge. The first nationwide Friday protests of 2014 have been against ISIS – and not the regime – to condemn the killing and torture of Dr Hussein al-Suleiman, a prominent Islamic rebel commander. He was on the way to meet with an ISIS delegation to settle a dispute that had arisen in the village of Maskaneh, rural Aleppo, when ISIS snatched him and defiled his corpse in the worst way possible. This incident is just the latest in a series of widely despised actions by ISIS, who kidnap and execute humanitarian workers and journalists regularly.

The kidnappings have deterred some, as ISIS now shows zero tolerance for political dissent. The injustice is mind-numbing as well as infuriating; in the city of Kafranbel, the creative capital of the revolution and home to the revolution's most witty cartoonists and banner-makers, they ransacked offices belonging to Kafranbel activists and destroyed their world-famous banners and cartoons and electronic equipment.

I am proud of my Christian brothers and sisters in the northern city of Qamishli, famous for holding the biggest demonstrations and sit-ins during the last night of the year.

'Happy New Year to our revolution,' they chanted defiantly as Assad jets fired on them.

Another winter morning in Hama had dawned and another truck carrying all the dead and burnt bodies of fighters who had died overnight was being unloaded across the street. I poured myself another glass of hot tea, and then went up to my room to work on an article I had been asked to write for an American magazine and check if my YouTube videos had finally finished uploading.

As I tried to channel my creative energy, my phone distracted me. Images of Emad kept flooding my mind and since our long conversation last night about how best to build a coalition against both ISIS and the Assad regime, I was looking forward to our call.

'*Ahlayn, ya Amira*. Hello, princess.'

Hearing the voice I dearly loved made me feel warm. 'Emad! *Kaifak intah*? How are you?' I said excitedly.

"*Mashi al-hal*,' he replied, indicating that he was okay. There was a moment's silence. '*Waynik inti*?' he asked gingerly.

I told him I was at home.

'I'm not far from you right now,' he replied. 'Want to take an evening walk with me?'

Emad had come to back up rebels in a nearby village who'd had barrel bombs packed with screws, scrap metal, old car parts, blades, and explosives dropped on their building by Assad's men.

'I look a mess,' he warned me.

It took me ages to get to our meeting point.

'Emad, wait!' I cried as I hurried down the road to catch up with him. He had been leaning against a wall, smoking a cigarette, and had begun to leave just as I'd turned the corner.

'I was beginning to think you weren't going to come to chase me after all.' His cheekiness melted my heart.

'This way is safe.' He took my arm. 'There's a really beautiful empty mansion just off to the right. Let's go.'

He had taken these routes so many times, it was as natural as breathing. Hands ready on his gun, his eyes continually scanned as we crawled due to snipers being almost everywhere.

We reached the magnificent home twenty minutes later. Flowerbeds and cars outside it had been crushed by the tanks that had rolled over them. An empty bottle of painkillers lay in the mud, used syringes filled the fountain; Assad's soldiers once used the mansion as a hospital for their wounded. At the edge of the main decorative French-style door lay shoes and slippers – what remained of the soldiers after they were shot dead then taken away, according to Emad.

With an entrance graced by Corinthian columns, this twenty-eight-room palace was built at a cost of millions for a

Syrian general whose American wife missed the glamour of California.

Before I had a chance to remove my black veil, I noticed a light switch on from one of the many balconies with a terracotta roof.

'Do you see the light?' I indicated with a jerk of my head.

'*Wa la yhimmik,* Fairouz. Don't worry about it. I checked out this place the other day.'

Suddenly, we heard the sound of footsteps clanging on the iron outdoor stairs followed by 'Hold on! I need to put on my veil.' My mind suddenly began racing with uncertainty.

'Daesh,' I whimpered. An ISIS family had obviously just taken over the abandoned home.

We had to think quickly.

'Go!' I whispered and handed my handbag to him.

'I'll be over that wall, don't worry!' Emad reassured me and jumped over.

I was suddenly face-to-face with a petite and pretty ISIS member and her baby son.

'I am looking for my friend Basma,' I asked meekly, trying to control my breathing. 'Is she here?'

'No, you have the wrong house and you should be ashamed, where is your *mahram*? Male chaperone?' she grunted.

The young woman's exquisite beauty had become corrupted with savagery, and now the evil in her eyes was terrifying. She was no more than twenty years old, and was obviously European; she spoke English perfectly. The social media campaigns have romanticised the idea of an Islamic state and she was here living that dream in a home that she could never have afforded in the West.

She complained upon seeing my nose ring; she, too, used to have one until the local mufti made her remove it as it was not in line with Islamic beliefs. And, was I married yet, by the way? Because if not, they had a French-Moroccan gentleman who was looking for a pretty young wife . . .

Such were the capricious and pervasive powers of ISIS; they'd made this beautiful young lady sacrifice her future to join the frontline. Not only do they have to obey Sharia law, on pain of death, but also passports must be surrendered. She was stuck for life.

'We have to create a buffer zone between the people and ISIS now,' Emad murmured on our way home. We knew we'd had a lucky escape.

As we walked home, my mind flitted to thoughts of what would have happened if we had been caught alone together. It wasn't unheard of for ISIS to bury knives in innocent men's throats and then hang their heads on railings for public display around town. The thought of that happening to Emad made me feel sick.

The trembling in my body began to ease as we neared my home. I was safe for the moment and felt even more so when Emad suddenly grabbed my waist and tickled me.

'I don't just love you any more, I'm *in* love with you.' He brushed away my tears with the soothing touch of his hand as we rushed inside an empty dilapidated building.

I caressed his face gently, and as my fingers gripped on to his, he gave me my first, truly passionate kiss. We kissed hard. I let out a dreamy sigh and silently soaked his uniform with broken-hearted tears.

28 January, 2014

After air strikes by warplanes resulted in many deaths and injuries at a nearby restaurant, one of Hama's oldest and most talented songmeisters began playing his *oud* at the exact same spot in the midst of carnage. The man, who had a special fondness for his donkey, played the dreamiest music while his animal friend sat motionless by his side. People began to gather around and sing together, all believing in the power of art and music and how much it can change. The exquisite, serene music evoked a sense of tranquil assurance while also sending a strong message to the evildoers.

'This city will never give up on life no matter what happens. We are unstoppable and unbreakable!' a man with half a leg shouted as people hugged each other.

During this harsh and hard winter, the community as a whole is displaying a certain resilience alongside adaptability – something we're becoming very accustomed to here. Snow, rain, and freezing temperatures together with the chronic shortage of diesel means we can't use our diesel stoves but have to cuddle together in thick clothes and blankets. However, everyday shortages are often the least of people's worries when you stay awake at night listening to fierce artillery shelling with the *pew pew pew* sound overhead, not knowing where it is coming from or how high or low it is, and with the knowledge that a single rocket launcher could end everything and that, whatever our hopes and dreams might be, death will have the last word, ending all personal stories.

The randomness of death in a war is surreal. Everything seems to be fine one minute – people are living, walking, eating, playing, talking, sleeping, and the next minute, an explosion and all those people are dead, or some girl's body is on fire, some guy's head has been opened by shrapnel, some child has just lost their eyesight. Even mundane tasks, like going to fetch humanitarian supplies from charity trucks, are experienced at a heightened level because they can be a matter of life and death.

A few days ago, when my brother and I decided to treat ourselves from the only place that does decent falafel anymore, an explosion on the way threw us into the air. As the earth shook beneath us, we stayed still, but then we got up, brushed ourselves off, and carried on our way because we focused on the smallest of satisfactions of daily life. The sheer miracle of being alive in a country that's focused on killing you makes you want to cherish every living moment.

'I wish to get married,' I said, suddenly.

'Who to?' my brother asked, his eyes dancing with delight.

'You know Emad, right?' I said shyly.

'You mean the famous Free Syrian Army commander?' He snorted. 'Stop wasting my time with your silly crushes. I actually thought you were serious there!'

'I am serious. Emad has asked me to marry him and I've said yes.'

I told my family that evening. After losing each other and then becoming reunited, we'd discovered our feelings for each other were more real for each other. When you're in a war, maybe it's the knowing you can die any time that makes you feel more deeply, or perhaps it just makes you value things more . . . Whatever it is, Emad's intention to ask for my hand early on was so that if either of us died as a married couple, at least we could live out our married life together in heaven.

Syria gets to be herself . . . like a charming, wicked woman with many faces. And everybody gets to choose his or her favourite face. My Syria is this: simple, with streets that are far from pretence and plastic surgeries, real and raw, the older she gets, the more stories she can tell. She's far from perfection, and closer to me.

There is magic in Hama. Walk its ancient narrow streets. Allow the typical Hama white and black stones from the Mamluk era to tell you tales, and when you reach the Great Mosque of Hama, listen to the *dhikr* – chanting songs praising the Prophet – coming from within its walls.

Certainly not as fancy as Damascus or Aleppo but every bit as picturesque, Hama is graced by the Orontes River, thousand-year-old houses, medieval architecture, and overhanging Ottoman balconies, and has always been more quiet and traffic-free than other large Syrian cities. This once tranquil city is, of course, most famous for its gigantic ancient water wheels, known as *noriahs*, whose sound has a cooling effect. The polluted but picturesque Orontes River – or in Arabic 'Al-Asi River' meaning 'The Rebellious River' – floats through the town, and the greenery and water can be enjoyed from the windows of the riverside restaurants and cafes that line it. About a kilometre out of town, through a covered passageway, the small stone footbridge that crosses the river takes you to the Umm Hassan Park, the hotspot for family picnics and romantic pastimes. But Hamawis are not Damascenes with their lamb with cherries and sophisticated cocktails. Syrian peasant cuisine is what we are more partial to. *Fuul* (fava beans) are eaten with olive oil, lemon juice, or thin yoghurt for breakfast or lunch and a filling meal to us consists of bread, *lebn* (yoghurt) and tea. *Batersh*, a supper speciality in Hama households and uncommon in the rest of Syria, consists of smoked eggplant with minced lamb and tomato sauce with tahini, yoghurt, garlic, salt and pepper then decorated with fried pine nuts.

Hama's yoghurt is famous, as are its sheep, and *lebn arabi* (yoghurt made from sheep's milk) compares to no other. Hama's tribes are masters of yoghurt, butter, cheese, milk, and ghee, and these staple foods have kept its large families nourished and healthy despite having very little or no money.

Tourists have visited Hama for the famous Crac des Chevaliers and the Azm Palace with its parquetry floors and elegant ceilings. Not too far from the palace is the eight-hundred-year-old Hammam al-Othmaniya. Every Hamawi has a love affair with traditional public baths, where we go to refresh our body and mind. Next door to the spotlessly clean and popular hammam is the Hama Artists' House, or Ateliers des Peintures, which occupies an ancient *khan* (caravanserai), or traveller's inn, that is transformed into makeshift studios and exhibition spaces for local artists, some of whose work is for sale.

When skipping through the old cobbled streets, even as children, we'd notice the damaged buildings pockmarked with shell holes - silent reminders of that terrible episode in 1982. Entire neighbourhoods were flattened, and little was done to restore Hama to its former splendour.

'Hama was once Syria's most beautiful city,' my father would tell us. 'It was one of the prettiest in all of the Middle East . . . but in 1982, that all changed.'

He would stop there. Just like everyone else, there would be no further details of 'the events'. Once, though, we were in the old part of the city and my father stopped in his tracks. He pointed at a typical derelict home and after a long silence, said how three of his young cousins who lived there had been rounded up and burnt alive because they prevented Hafez al-Assad's soldiers from taking their ill father. They then took the women of the house, who were never to be heard from again. Today is the thirty-second anniversary of the Hama massacre and once again our city is as if an earthquake has befallen it.

Lest we ever forget . . . and my father is now lying in his grave too. Hama is being flattened by TNT barrels, chemical gases, SCUD and cluster bombs, Yarmouk camp has become the devil's workshop – ISIS has burnt all of their Palestinian flags, and civilian neighbourhoods full of starving people are under siege as Syria descends into hell.

There are no more traditional delicacies or meals as people are now eating anything that comes from the ground. At first, we survived on fruit and vegetables, but now that the once abundant agriculture has died out, we forage for plants and grass. The past week we have been taking shrubs and cooking them in water using wood because the price of cooking gas cylinders has soared so high. After Christmas, there has been no food aid distribution and even before, the little humanitarian assistance that made its way to us was stolen to give to 'special people' or sold onto the black market. The poorest and most vulnerable of society, including the Palestinian refugees, can be seen skinning and eating stray cats. Some eat reptiles, cowhide, and soil. At first, we were suffering from indigestion, but now even our bodies have accepted the diet changes to ease the all-too-familiar hunger pangs. We sold almost everything we ever owned to Egyptian men who travelled here last year buying entire household items, furniture, appliances, and clothes for little money to sell back to Egyptian homeowners for profit.

'What's the point?' they told us. 'They'll soon bomb all of this anyway.'

Aided by our experience in making do, we face situations previously thought unendurable, including seeing people die in front of you and fighting for survival using little means. The daily grind has made us realise that we are braver than we ever thought possible, and stronger than we ever knew. Make-do and mend is what we typically do after the bombing raids and electricity cuts and on the long dark evenings; Grandma has taught the women here ingenious ways of making skirts and dresses out of curtains or tablecloths and winter coats from blankets.

Even though we are in a full-blown war, wedding preparations must go on. My aunt has really nice cream lace and satin curtains that everyone decided could be cut up and altered to make a nice wedding dress for me. A neighbour has offered us her kitchen curtain nets to make into a bridal veil, but it is to be given back afterwards. I know there aren't many young women here who are able to have such an elegant wedding dress and I feel so lucky too, considering the harsh circumstances. Even though I'll go to bed again tonight not knowing if we'll be awake for tomorrow's sunrise, at least I am at home, surrounded with my most precious people. This city is my city. Its wheels are dry and silent, warfare has damaged its green fields, and the river now smells strongly of sewage.

There isn't much left of the streets of Old Hama, but walking through the meditative, slow-moving city, its buildings always speak thousands of words to me, and I understand why even when I'm far, I'm always here.

It was about 10:45 p.m. when we found ourselves following a dark street in the direction of the Druze village of Sarouj.

Emad told me that he hadn't much wandered there, but that the sheep-herders living in the ancient cone-shaped beehives homes had long gone.

The occasional solitary light shone from the interior of military jets above, spilling onto trees nearby. My heart was pounding in a good way as we walked together, his arms snugly around my waist.

I filled my lungs with the crisp cold air and slowly exhaled with relief. After all of the months of living in fear for my life, I finally felt safe. I was finally about to start a new life and was brimming with gratitude that the love of my life and I were still alive.

'We'll always be together wont we?' I asked in a voice as plaintive as a child's.

'Forever,' he reassured me, his accent smooth and confident. 'Our time to shine is coming,' he added, gently touching my mouth with a kiss.

'*Bardaana*? Cold?' He paused outside an ancient mud house, but before I could answer, he pushed me against a wall and pressed my mouth with a fiery kiss before pulling back to take a look at me.

'My God, I am deeply, wholly and madly in love with you.' He brushed my hair with his hand, admiring me with wild eyes.

My body began to sizzle beneath Emad's touch. My body ached for him. Suddenly, his probing fingers heightened my excitement to new levels that took over my senses.

'Make love to me,' I told him. I needed him to make me feel unbroken and beautiful again.

He kicked open the door of the beehive hut, where a mountain of colourful thick blankets were stacked along with mattresses against a wall.

'Let's do it here – now! I want you . . .' A cry escaped from my throat. I looked at his glistening lips and eyes that danced and wondered why he had to be so sexy that at times I almost ached when I looked at him.

'Love me, love me, love me,' I begged him.

Our bodies were pressed together in a flash, hungry hands pressed against one another, my mouth opening to his.

I lay beneath him as he eased my pain bit by bit and made me whole again, and then I returned his love with ferocity until with one last groan, he pressed his lips on my forehead with midnight kisses.

As I lay there, Emad snoring gently beside me, I pondered on how perfect this had been – and how much a contrast to what

I had suffered in prison. There had been no tenderness there, just urgency and violence. But this . . . this had been love-making, and I had felt the love every second.

'Our Syria is colourful. ISIS, take your black flag and go!' So proclaimed a banner we made and carried at a sit-in outside the ISIS headquarters yesterday.

The systematic takeover occurs while most of our people are just watching, watching, watching, like they are in a daze, as the so-called ISIS hoist their insignia and flags and erect their camps everywhere. They've painted entire buildings black and scribbled their slogans and symbols everywhere. What is offending us the most is that they are replacing the green revolution flags with their black ones, because the flag we use as shrouds to bury martyrs who died for freedom, dignity, and a civil state – the flag that unites peaceful Syrian opposition – violates their fundamentalist laws.

Activists from liberated areas in Homs and Hama have come together to organise demonstrations in front of ISIS 'Sharia courts'. Activists, who want to continue meaningful civic work in ISIS-held areas where everything has ground to a halt, have had to go even more underground because, according to ISIS, human rights are haram.

Earlier today, when about twenty media activists and students gathered in an abandoned warehouse on the outskirts of Hama to publish stories and footage about the group's brutality on social media, extremists raided the building and ordered us to leave because free mixing of the genders was strictly forbidden.

I remember how a couple of years ago at the start of the revolution, when we opposition media activists would gather to organise demonstrations or to swap our daily videos, share stories, and chat on Facebook and Skype to activists in other cities, we could do so fairly easily as long as we made sure we hid our tracks. Each night, friends would gather and discuss the day's events, which activist had died and who had gone missing – back then we actually marked each and everyone's death – but now deaths and tragic incidents are so common, we can't keep up. Now, there is no longer music blaring or joy with friends; no late nights editing YouTube videos and smoking apple-flavoured *nargileh*; no sipping cold beer in tents to lighten the mood; and no sneaky cigarettes to lighten the load.

Paranoid ISIS, who fear spies and journalists, have blown up telephone masts, making communication extremely difficult. For me, I am especially angry because I can't speak to Emad, who has been deployed in Aleppo. To stay in touch with the rest of the world, we have managed to get satellite internet lines for now.

At first, ISIS were not too onerous – they were actually quite friendly – but they've started to increase restrictions on people.

'The benevolent *mujahedeen* are here to establish *amr-bil-ma'roof* (ordering good) and *nahi anil munkar* (forbidding sin),' they announced.

The Quran statement that 'there is no compulsion in religion' was graffitied on one of the major walls of Hama by activists. However, trying to explain real Islamic concepts to psychopaths is not a good idea unless you want to get whipped with a stick like my neighbour was for his impudence. Our local imams are being forcefully sacked from their positions and being replaced by foreign preachers, mostly North Africans and Western converts to Islam.

In a nearby village, the local imam, who had been vocal against ISIS's brutal campaign of intimidation against ordinary people and even spoke against them from his pulpit, describing them as 'hijackers of the Islamic faith', was beheaded inside his own mosque.

Not only do they try to barge into the front lines of military campaigns, but ISIS have also started to engage the population through other means. Social (*da'wah*) programmes primarily target the youth, brainwashing through distribution of ISIS newspapers and booklets, religious lessons and gatherings, family fun days where sweets, toys, and ice creams are handed out while spectators can enjoy tug of war and stand-up comedy; all is part of their new strategy to buy popular support.

ISIS soldiers can be seen holding up black dresses that cover every part of the women's face and body – money from the sale of these goes to the ISIS treasury, and every woman who doesn't own such a garment must buy one. The resentment among all – but especially women – is deepening as the enforcement of outlandish rules continues. Their draconian legal system is contrary to our Syrian religious and social traditions. Syrian women have never been covered up, especially not their faces, and are known to be strong and independent. Our elders – even the conservative ones – have always taught us that narrow-minded religious cults produce herd-like mentality, and it was only ever encouraged by Assad's autocratic regime.

ISIS makes no pretence about preserving minority rights, and this week they have targeted Christians and Sufi Muslims. They've exhumed and sabotaged Sufi tombs and shrines of sheikhs and ancient philosophers. They are crudely defacing churches and crosses, clearly a deliberate act to drive the Christians away.

They are destroying heritage and historic monuments that have survived for thousands of years in far worse conditions. These structures have withstood time, elements, and many wars. Now we have moronic barbarians wiping out our culture and our roots, and it is a rich and ancient one too. Some would say it's only rocks and statues, but to someone like me, it's a glimpse into another place and time. A world gone by, with a fascinating story unfolded with each discovery, teaching us about ourselves. I pray this ends soon, for the human suffering as well as historical preservation.

My brother, Adam, came home last night bruised but alive, *Alhamdulillah*. He is weary and has lacerations and stitches all over his good-looking face. He told us he was defending a woman friend from abusive behaviour and trash talk from an extremist in the queue for water. He'd spoken up, and the ISIS buffoon smashed a bottle in his face. And Adam struck him back, and knocked him out cold. All that gym time and years of champion sports, honour he has, and respect for women, and a passionate intolerance for abuse like the women in our household. We are just relieved and glad he is home safely.

He is sleeping and he will heal soon. Bless his heart. We can't forget, of course, our brother Yahya, who has been on the battlefield since the beginning, protecting us all. He is one hell of a man and so very strong. Remarkably, he has always triumphed, even in the most extremely harsh situations; he is a stellar fighter, and carries on despite his injury. A few weeks ago, he had fled a trench where he had been shooting from, but on the way he was hit and was brought home with raw cartilage in his knee exposed by a bullet wound.

Cyber activists like myself are a dime a dozen. It is the actual on-the-ground revolutionaries making the changes that we only verbally recycle on the web. I am so relieved and thankful for their safety.

'If he has your strength, Layla, he will be all right,' my grandmother assured my mother during her panic attack late last night.

Maternal laments are frequent here, and every mother's worry is that the baby they raised will die fulfilling his or her patriotic duty.

'Mama, you didn't have to worry, I'm a man now and I can handle danger,' Adam mumbled.

They were empty words from a foolish son who has no understanding of an anxious mother, who can handle almost anything but injury or harm to her children. Often, we are oblivious to her pain and sorrow, having lost her husband to the revolution and now having to deal with the fact one son is out on the battlefield and the other, who is at home, is constantly coming into altercations with ISIS fighters. My mother is in even greater anguish right now because of a new conscription law under which every family has to send one of their sons to be an ISIS fighter – an obligation that is increasingly difficult to avoid and is leading many families to try to leave ISIS-controlled territory, which is no easy task to do.

Years of basketball have given my sporty brother, Adam, good muscles and strong legs, and as a result, ISIS fighters have their eyes on him. The more he refuses to swear allegiance by making a pledge – or *bay'ah* – to the fanatics, the more chances there are of his defiance resulting in his death by execution.

Conscription is not limited to teenagers and adults; in fact, ISIS are actively recruiting young children to strengthen their force in the longer run. Last weekend, Dawood, Salman, and Harith – young ISIS 'cubs' who live across the street from us – came home from their lesson at the 'Sharia Camp for Lions'.

'I won the Quran competition today and I received this football,' Dawood boasted to all.

ISIS are luring them in with gifts and then brainwashing them slowly against even their parents, whom the children are now describing as apostates for condemning ISIS. It all starts off with an intensive Sharia course for forty days, and then a military course for the next forty, and afterwards the children are sent directly to the frontline, where, as they are immature and inexperienced, they die quickly. Some are recruited to be suicide bombers; others are just used to do manual jobs such as loading and cleaning weapons and carrying ammunition and medical supplies to the soldiers. There's no school for the withdrawn and traumatised children, no routine, and no prospects, and ISIS are taking advantage of what the Assad regime has deprived them of. As children grow, the residual effects of war fold into their lives. These young boys who were born into this war, suckling on their mothers' breasts, have grown up too much, too fast.

Syrian children are being raised in a gruesome bloody film-like world; they don't know love or compassion. The young boys who live opposite to us collected their father's hands and toes in a plastic cup when an Assad rocket landed on their living room not long ago. They had to witness a Shabeeh from Assad's army rape their aunt who was staying with them when they came to look for their uncle – a wanted rebel. I remember washing their tiny hands and faces covered with blood after they were carried out of the carnage. Syrian children are tortured, and their mothers are raped in front of them while they are left to live the memory. Our children have to go to sleep at night fearful of their own nightmares, visions of their dead parents lying beside them. When all you know is poverty and the militarisation of life, it is very easy for young minds to be poisoned. ISIS are not only creating a child army of human fodder, they are also giving these innocent children false hope of a better future, and it's heart-breaking to watch the new generation being taken advantage of in this way.

Deprived of economic hope and possibility, some adults are altering their moral structures to survive, be it through joining ISIS or other militant groups for a respectable wage that gives their families electricity, gas, food, and water. They do what they have to do to feed hungry mouths.

But even those desperate adults don't want their infants to sign up for training.

'We will enlighten your children and show them the true path,' ISIS promised.

However, every parent wants the best for their child. Even my father didn't want my brothers to fight in this war. 'We'll die so that your generation can live happily and freely,' he would say.

Everyone is optimistic that the children will go on to build the Syria that our ancestors have been dreaming about and never thought would ever happen. It may take a while for them to do that, but by the time they are old enough to have children of their own, I still trust we will have that Syria as a definite reality.

The Middle Eastern region's beloved almond tree is a well-known symbol of resurrection because it is the first tree to flower, adds much appreciated colour each spring, and is mentioned numerous times in the Old Testament and scriptures. The almond flowers are loving this spell of rain; as the sun moves higher in the sky, the days are becoming longer, and the quality of light brings with it a more luminous radiance. The light is causing the trees to pop out in resplendent colour. Our almond tree with the palest of pink blossoms is blooming, and it seems we have a new addition too – a curious small orange tabby cat has been sleeping under the tree. At first, we thought she was feral, but when I was cleaning the courtyard, she came right up and began nuzzling. In Syria, everything needs saving. Everybody wants love. Cats. Dogs. People. Children. The rain has replaced the snow, making everyone happy. And now Bortuqal the cat has a tree to lie under, and it seems I do too.

There's something to be learned from the land. It brings comfort when you see that a predictable cycle of life hasn't been too disturbed in the garden yet. Warfare has all but destroyed the vast fertile plain in Syria; the grain fields and the olive and pistachio orchards nearby are now reduced to nothingness and home to homeless Syrians in tents. It isn't only human habitat that has been destroyed. Normally the trees at this time of the year attract birds and butterflies, but in Syria, pigeons no longer perch on trees; they once blackened the sky like dark clouds, but now all the colourful flocks of birds are absent from the landscape. It was one of the first things I noticed when I looked up to the sky after months in captivity.

Good weather not only means good crops, it also means children playing outside in this dry wind, full of pebbles and dirt. Chronic exposure to war has resulted in troubling development of children. They are obsessed with violence and are depicting it when they play aggressive games.

'I will be Bashar and you can be a fighter,' little Ismaeel shouts inside our courtyard.

'No, I want to be Bashar!' six of his friends yell back.

They all want to be Bashar because Bashar is the strong one who has all the weapons to beat everyone, and therefore will win the game. Children's play is disturbing to witness; Ismaeel climbs on top of the wall and drops soft drink cans, pretending they are barrel bombs. His friend kneels while another child stamps on his head before shooting him in the head with his toy pistol.

The children were never disruptive like this but as the days go by, all they do is fight with one another. Mouyad, an older boy whom the little ones look up to, is back from the Sharia camp. ISIS deliberately gives new graduates a period where they can return home to rest because they know that the children will go back and discuss their heroic and exciting ventures with their friends. Mouyad is already inciting the naughty youngsters to join ISIS fighters. Mouyad, who once accompanied me on the school bus journey every morning, has now returned . . . but a total mental re-programming of his mind has taken place. These impressionable children who play with pretend guns in the back alleys are like fresh dough in ISIS's hands; they can and will shape them as they like, because nobody else seems to show them any care in this critical part of their developing years.

'Stop stealing my wood to make toy machine guns. I will tell Bashar to come to get you and lock you away!' Ismaeel's ill-tempered mother snaps from the balcony. Not understanding his inner frustrations, she and the other distraught mothers punish their out-of-control children instead of soothing them, making them sullen and sour and ten times naughtier. In this weary war, single mothers like Ismaeel's are struggling without a figurehead in their family. She is twenty-five years old but looks a decade older now. Assad's army tortured her husband after dragging him away from a protest and she heard about his body dumped in a pit a few days before she gave birth to her twins, now two years old.

'I'm just so tired,' she sighs through her chapped lips. 'And I can't afford to raise the children any more.' Her hair is greasy and uncombed, and her teeth are yellow with neglect. Her breasts seem deformed and there is a huge scratch on her cheek. Her bloodshot eyes tell it all. As the war enters its fourth year, the UN describes this as the worst humanitarian catastrophe since the Second World War, but only we know what it is really like to live in a society that has been transformed into a pit in hell.

6 April, 2014

It's Sunday, I finally have access to the internet, and once again while real rebel Syrian fighters are in the forefront liberating another Assad town, their archenemy ISIS are busy making glossy action-thriller-style videos and actively recruiting fighters online. In comparison to the Syrian revolutionists' non-professional shaky and grainy videos, ISIS manage to whip out professionally edited media that is witty, sharper, clearer, and saturated in colour. Their emphasis on resolution, editing, lighting, composition, and their pre-and-post-production planning shows that there is a deeply dedicated and advanced team that not only has a high level of media skills, but also that the propaganda itself follows a distinctly Western design aimed at contemporary English-speaking youth worldwide.

The group considers social media its most vital means to attract more foreign fighters and make announcements, as well as spread terror in the hearts of the rest of the 'apostate' world.

There are approximately eighty thousand social media accounts that offer advice, money, and even logistical support for travel. The people behind these accounts do most of their marketing, including publishing statements, debating ISIS views, sharing up-to-the-minute news, and keeping everyone entertained with thematic jihadist videos and jihadist anthems.

However, what annoys me most is that the ISIS mouthpieces and fans online are extremely naïve and uneducated in Islam.

Baghdadi 'fanboys' sprout their narrow-minded and uncultivated opinions mainly on Twitter and sadly are being taken seriously. Western journalists quote them and interact with them, even though they are just kids who have no weight, no life experience, and are unable to answer basic Sharia-related questions.

Most shocking of all is that adults worldwide are willing to take Islam from unknown strangers –some of them who have just reached puberty.

Real Islamic scholars, both past and present, have had years of travel experience and have learned mastery from even greater pioneers before they even reached the pulpit of a mosque to give lectures and became credible enough to give Islamic rulings and opinions. I should know because Syria is full of scholars, some alive and some lying in their tombs. Today, we have rambling online scholars who are self-appointed and use YouTube as their pulpit to call on their blind followers. These internet sheikhs with their authoritarian state attempt to reinvent the wheel of Islamic law to suit their own agenda and don't allow room for differences in *fiqh* (Islamic jurisprudence). They have no prominent *shuyookh*, scholars of the Muslim world, supporting them, not even a handful.

When they announced their caliphate and considered all other millions of Muslims deviants, this confirmed how shallow they were in Islamic knowledge. Groups like the Taliban, who had the backing of several prominent scholars, never announced the *khilafah,* and neither did the *Wahhabi* movement or the *Mahdi* movement of Sudan because all of these movements knew that *khilafah* is the representative of the entire Ummah, Muslim populace. ISIS, who claim to be Sunni, have killed many respected Sunni Salafi, Sufi, Shafi'i and Maliki scholars.

It's very simple: if they don't like you, and if you don't adopt their cult, they kill you. Syria's Sunni Muslims have always been diverse, and there's always been room for all Sunni sects and different viewpoints. Here you can always find followers and very competent scholars of all four *madhabs* (sects) in appreciable numbers. Relationships between the Syrian *ulama* scholars have always been great and they are known to analyse and study a lot together.

It's impossible to penetrate the destructive, extreme mind-set once an ISIS follower is brainwashed. Instead, my friends and I mock and laugh at these hateful *kukus* with long beards. Despite everything, I always can find humour all around me. In fact, I rarely go to sleep without watching or reading funny things . . . it's a saving grace, and we Syrians, oh we have never lost our sense of humour. We are resilient like that. As they say, *al-mudhik al-mubki* (that which makes you laugh and cry).

'Knock knock,' I said.

'Who's there?' my cousin–sister Nesreen asked.

'You're all *murtadeen* (apostates), open the door or I'll chop your head off.' I said.

'But who are you?' she asked again.

'A random teenager in the West,' I replied and we laughed ourselves to sleep. While we share funny jokes about ISIS and detest their men, women, and in particular Western women online, are being lured to the 'land of caliphate' on social media platforms where the jihadist Twitter users promise them adventure and romance. The mainstream media and the West thinks they are only here as wannabe jihadi brides, but they are not as vulnerable as they seem. While there are many flocking here to meet their ideal guy, I have bumped into some ISIS women that are as equally savage as the men. They tell us that they are here to play a part in the upbringing of a new generation of *mujahedeen* and have started their own religious order run by women for women, where they terrorise local women into submission. They spy on women by patrolling the streets, pretending to be housewives, and then report behaviour back to their leaders.

We met three European ISIS women coming to inspect the local internet cafe a few days ago to ensure the computers were restricting access to certain websites. They asked the storeowner to segregate the cafe so women could have a section. They also used computers to make video calls to their families back in Europe. Shaima was from the Swedish city of Malmo and was of Moroccan origin while her friend Filsan was from Norway. She was of Somali and Yemeni descent - on her mother's side she belonged to the Reer Xamar tribe from Mogadishu. They were cheerful. Then there was the blonde from Poland who converted to Islam in Milton Keynes.

Ironically, it was the white Muslim that was most strict in her ways. She could be overheard encouraging girls on the other side of the screen to come to Syria to offer their sexual services and fulfil the needs of the fighters. *Jihad al-nikah* – or sexual holy war, as they refer to it – is the bizarre idea that women who want to participate in jihad can do so by satisfying fighters with their bodies when they return from battles. This is nothing more than prostitution, except the silly girls don't even get paid.

'*La bass a'lik?*'

'Mother, I'll be getting married, with the will of Allah,' Shaima replied.

'Really? You broke up with the Pakistani one?'

'Yes, he was convinced you were doing black magic on us.'

'*Kif walou.* No big deal,' she said, not denying it.

Her mother was clearly trying to conceal her anger at the choice of her daughter's new husband, a forty-year-old Algerian who, she argued, their relatives who prayed at the Finsbury Park Mosque in London knew of.

'Is there anything you need from here?'

'Yes, brother Hakim will be returning soon after his last mission here, *Bi idnillah*, with Allah's permission, if you could prepare a small bag for me.'

'Sure, what do you need?'

'Yves Saint Laurent Opium Perfume, Estee Lauder double wear foundation in shade fresco, and important, some cotton pyjamas – the ones they sell in the markets here are poor quality.'

Unlike the other two who seemed weak and impressionable, Irena is more confident in her interpretation of religious laws. She is social media savvy and runs a number of social media accounts.

'How can you allow the atheists to murder and maim our Muslim brethren in every corner of the world?' It is obvious her speciality is radicalising Western converts like herself, but she is also responsible for an online marketing campaign aiming to lure girls and women from North Africa.

She married an Australian convert, with some aboriginal roots, who had initially converted to Sufi-Islam at a mosque in the suburb of Lakemba, in Sydney – until he could not contain his anger against Western and Arab dictators who were corrupt and did nothing to help the like of the Palestinians.

'Shame on you all, especially our imams, who are scared of the establishment and so comfortable with their Western life,' he writes on his Facebook page.

They were both furious and turned their backs on preachers in the West who never supplicate for the Syrians at the end of prayers, let alone call for action in support of Muslim resistance. They had a hatred of elites and establishments, as did a small group of ISIS sympathisers in nearby Bankstown, who welcomed them and other Australians who were alienated from their mosques and Islamic centres for being too radical.

Ironically, these Western Muslims believe that the original religion has been corrupted by Western modes of thinking, and it is their calling to return Islam to its purest form. Irena is a strong advocate of *jihad al-nikah.* 'Women need to agree to pleasure marriages because it helps the brothers fight better against the *kuffar,* the disbelievers.'

I didn't press her on the logic of such a statement, nor its veracity, as I didn't want to cause attention to myself. Until now, they think I am a Muslim because of the mandatory veil I wear. Irena, who by her own admission used to be a former wild child and party girl, has helped set up what we locals see as a brothel in an unoccupied hospital, where beds could instead be used to house the poor but which is now a place for ISIS fighters to have fun with women.

Such indecency and haram activity from the so-called haram police and there are still people on social media crying out 'ISIS are not Muslims' and 'How is this even Islam?'

Well, you don't say so? Please come up with something more original – surely anyone with a brain cell has realised that ISIS with its wife-swapping and sex parties is not Islamic by now. In fact, anyone who has studied Islam up to a basic level can quickly refer to Qur'anic proof to show how Baghdadi is a fake caliph and see through the group's deception. As for these gullible small-minded, spoilt, egoistic, selfish kids who want to use our Syrian land to resolve their identity crisis in the West, we will deal with you insects, just like how the Taliban is dealing with ISIS rats in Afghanistan. No mercy shown, not even to ISIS sympathisers. There are no excuses for anyone who supports or sympathises with these *kukus.* That boat sailed long ago. It cannot become clearer. ISIS is anti-humanity, anti-morality, and anti-Islam.

They knew she was Kurdish right away because of her name. 'Your name is *ajeeb*. Weird,' said the masked ISIS fighter as he examined Helan's identity card. That's when she realised she was in trouble.

She nodded her head politely. A strand of her silky red hair escaped from the hijab she had worn to escape ISIS attention. Her body curves filled out her black *abaya*; Helan's majestic beauty was talked about far and wide among the Kurds in our city. At that moment, though, her clear skin turned purple with shock.

'If you want to continue breathing, do as we say,' a voice told her in perfect English.

'Please can I go?' Helan mumbled in Arabic.

An ISIS goon translated for the Westerner, who had no grasp of the Arabic language.

'Fuck you.' He slapped her into submission. 'If you resist or make it difficult for me to search you, I'm going to chop your fingers off for identification.'

My cousin–sister Nesreen and I remained still on the balcony, shaded by a broken refrigerator, as we didn't want to prompt an ISIS member to come to look for us – there were five of them in the blackened jeep. The determination in the eyes of the men was enough to scare us to silence.

We watched as the Westerner – an American from his accent – marched Helan to her home, just a few rows away from us. Islamic State fighters were storming into homes in different villages and abducting Kurdish civilians this past week in retaliation for a huge Kurdish-led offensive on its territory in other parts of Syria.

But surely not Helan's family. Her father and brothers had actively fought alongside different FSA factions against the regime. They were the kindest and hospitable people we knew. No, this could not be happening.

It happened as soon as the hefty American ISIS fighter banged on their door. The ground shook throughout the street.

The rumble of armoured Land Cruisers armed with KPV-14.5 heavy machine guns in the hot midday air caught the ISIS fighters off guard. Simultaneously, someone from inside Helan's home threw a smoke grenade in front of the three ghouls outside.

Through the smoke, we could see the American holding Helan by her neck at the entrance of her home. Her vivid red hair was visible through it all. Then the first shots were fired and tore away at bricks. From the opposite side came the splutter of a heavy machine gun, then from above a hail of light machine gun and rifle bullets from Helan's family.

Suddenly, we heard someone open our balcony door. Nesreen and I froze.

'*Hala banaat.* It's me, Madmour.'

My grandmother had let FSA fighters into our home as a strong street fight was now taking place between the inhabitants of Helan's home, the FSA rebels, and ISIS fighters. The firing went on, shells flew past us, hitting cars and piercing walls.

The FSA ambush had frightened the Westerner, who cowardly clung on to Helan and readied his rifle to shoot her neck. If he was to die, he wanted to take her with him. A single shot rang out from the opposite direction, and his accomplice collapsed on the cobblestone. Helan didn't flinch, because she knew not to annoy the man holding her hostage.

Suddenly, a woman with a Kalashnikov emerged out of the home, a red and-white-checked *kuffiyeh* over her head. She sprayed their vehicle with continuous fire until one of her bullets found their mark. Within seconds, we could hear the tires squeaking and grinding over her body as the ISIS motor rolled over her.

Kurdish women from within the home came outside hand in hand, armed and ready to die with dignity. Hearing their battle cry, the jeep abandoned the American and sped away. ISIS believes if a woman, a lowly creature, kills them, there is neither heaven nor seventy-two virgins for them – they won't achieve martyrdom. This hideous rule they created for themselves has encouraged many Kurdish women to join the fight against ISIS.

An all-female Kurdish military branch of the Kurdish People's Protection Units (YPG) was recently formed to defend people from attacks by IS militants in Rojava, Northern Syria –

or Western Kurdistan as Kurds see it. The women are ISIS's nightmare. The American ISIS fighter, terrified, raised his rifle, fired, and struck one of the women square in the eye. The women stood defiantly. Our hearts were racing. If ISIS doubted the strength of the FSA, they were wrong. We know that the Free Syrian Army was declared dead by many at the end of 2013, but 2014 was a comeback year. They were stronger and more united than ever.

Madmour decided to make the most of his position. He fired a shot from where we lay still. The direction was perfect, but it fell about ten yards short. The lean American turned around to see where it had come from. Madmour crouched down then jumped out and fired again, but missed. Time was ticking; bullets were flying from all sides. The casualties in the lower houses of our street must have been heavy as blood was streaming down in pools. It was only a matter of time before ISIS returned with back-up.

Madmour got up one last time; his rifle was not fully loaded, and only two rounds were left in the clip. From forty yards away, he fired, striking the American in the back. The bullet ripped through his neck, shredding his spinal cord. Madmour swiftly jumped over and ran down to rescue Helan, who had collapsed in the middle of it all. He picked her up as if she were a feather and draped her over his shoulder, placing her in the FSA Land Cruisers where the rest of her family were climbing. It was a relief I couldn't describe. Madmour had saved Helan and saved the day.

We blog, we exist. I have been unable to express my personal grief on paper or computer screen properly and consistently the past year and especially the past few months, and that, along with the six-hour daily power cuts, are not helping the blogging cause.

I am exhausted, enraged, yet calmed and pained all at once.

I have been too preoccupied with the revolution's relief work, helping NGOs instead of political and revolutionary organisational work, which was once the main priority. The humanitarian work is as dangerous as ever as we deal with volunteer shortages and a lack of resources.

The closure of most NGOs has put pressure on the other NGOs that are still active. Volunteers and people travel far to NGO offices even though most of the time, when they reach there, there aren't enough aid parcels or medication.

It is also harder than before to be updated on the rapidly unfolding events all around Syria nowadays. This then makes it harder to collate news and blog about it. Maybe I've just grown cynical of reading about the most recent massacre on the news, the recent death of so-and-so on the Twitter feed, and the steadily flowing miserable updates about which town is under siege. In general, I hate being a bearer of misery; hate being the first one to announce which friend has been wounded, which one has just been taken to an Assad dungeon, and which one is missing.

Yesterday, when rebels withdrew from Homs in a symbolic victory for the regime, an NGO called us to go to collect and wash the corpses of those executed in Homs the night before. When we arrived in the once 'capital of the revolution', it was a doomsday scene: no food, no bread, children crying, and families tentatively walking the war-ravaged streets where they used to live, picking through piles of furniture and photo frames.

We don't know how, until now, rebels with their light weaponry had managed to have control of Homs. Assad with his elite 4th division guards, airplanes, Hezbollah insurgents, Iranian financial backing, Russian military supplies and socio-political support, and Chinese political backing could not manage to forcefully take Homs. The rebels voluntarily opted to retreat for the sake of the innocent people, who were besieged and needed access to aid. Having met with the Christian community of Homs, who had fled to mountain villages like Mashta El Heleu and now returned, it is clear they had not fled their city because rebels were massacring Christians, but because of the regime's vengeance on their district. The regime during the three-year siege has bombed Christian orphanages and historical churches like the Homs Syriac Orthodox Um al-Zennar Church causing people of all religions to flee; it has not been because of terrorists trying to religiously cleanse Syria as some academics and regime-sponsored journalists have been trying desperately to claim.

The withdrawal of the rebels from Old Homs city is disastrous strategically for the opposition. It proves how the fight between the rebels and Assad is uneven. It underscores why now, more than ever, the Free Syrian Army needs weapons that will give it a fighting chance against the military's firepower.

19 May, 2014

As spring turns into summer, more ISIS families have filled our countryside. They set up a special institute about ten miles away designed to 'prepare sisters for the battlefields for jihad', according to its mission statement online. Nesreen and I were sent text messages from Shaima inviting us to enrol, complete with heart emoticons.

In al-Qaeda's wars in Afghanistan and Iraq, fighters kept their womenfolk far from danger. This is also the case with the hundreds of other Islamist and armed groups fighting in Syria currently. My brother told us how a group of students who travelled from Dammaj in Yemen, who had previously fought in Afghanistan in the eighties, left ISIS immediately when they saw their handling of women. According to them, when in Kandahar and under constant bombardment from American warplanes, Afghan warlords took all the women and children as slaves once the mujahideen were killed.

Most of the women are missing even now. Dragging women along to battlefields became something heavily frowned upon by all Muslim Scholars. One fighter described how under the rule of Mullah Umar, when a group of Arab foreign fighters were killed, he enforced a rule that despite being in serious danger, no mujahid was allowed to leave the area until every last foreign female was safely carried out of Kandahar. 'Until the last drop of blood in my body, I'll remain to protect them,' Mullah Omar had said.

But in Syria, ISIS aims to install a purist Islamic state – complete with home-cooked meals from their wives. They want to build lives in this land and not just fight a war. As such, bringing women over is key to building their new society. They don't care that the women are in serious danger of being kidnapped, traded, and raped by Assad's militia and other thugs. Nesreen and I, to stay on their good side, accepted Shaima's invitation to be taken to one of their main gatherings for both men and women. Some of the most prominent ISIS fighters and executioners were to give lectures there. I was nervous as grandmother had taught me little of the Quran by heart and I didn't know how to perform Salah. What if they tested me?

Luckily, the turnout was huge. The study group was a diverse collection of extremists from the four corners of the earth, including from as far away as South Africa and Indonesia. Despite the efforts of the Turkish border soldiers, there were plenty of people who made it through easily, among them British Pakistanis from Manchester and Luton, Lebanese and Afghans from the city of Aarhus, Tunisians, Malaysians, Moroccans from Spain, Bosnians who had fought the Serbs, Arabs from Cardiff, Yemenis from Liverpool and Sudanese and Nigerians. They came from many places but were united under what they believed to be pure Salafism.

These are not average pro-Saudi Salafists but a new generation, seething with anger and an unshakeable belief that they alone have found the path of righteousness.

They want to destroy the Saudi royal family, annihilate the Muslim Brotherhood, get rid of Western powers, implement their version of Sharia on all, and kill religious sects whom they think are misguided – according to them, even the Taliban are overly spiritual because they pray excessively.

'What about Anwar Al-Awlaki's view about collecting money for weapons? He was on the *haqq*, the true path,' a bright-eyed teenager from Rotterdam, who was well connected with militants in San'aa, said during a discussion about raising money in mosques under the pretence of charity and then using it to fund weapons.

Baghdadis men soon shut him up. Even Anwar Al-Awlaki was not pure enough. A group from Birmingham boasted about how they'd raised money for ISIS through charity stalls and door-to-door fundraising during Ramadan right under the noses of the *kuffar*.

It is obvious, though, that there are struggles among themselves. The Somalis and South Asians are especially distrustful of converts because they are wary of spies. However, they make an effort to get along because all of them share the same end goal in the land of Shaam.

During the long day of theological disputes and lectures – barely any prayers – they set up a projector. Flashing images of Muslims being persecuted around the world were on display: Guantanamo Bay, Abu Ghraib prison, Assad's dungeons, humiliated Muslims in Iraq and beyond.

Then popped up latest videos of beheadings carried out against Westerners. James Foley, the journalist, an aid worker, a nurse. Triumph in their eyes. I was angry inside because they were using the persecution of fellow human beings to justify their merciless actions. It is a vicious never-ending cycle. It is impossible to be sure whether their outlook has stemmed from Western foreign policy or a vendetta because of the alienation they feel in the West, resulting in their need for belonging – or both.

22 May, 2014

One, one, one: Assad and ISIS are one. We spray-painted that early this morning after a night full of fierce mortar shelling targeted the Free Syrian Army bases and residential neighbourhoods.

As expected, at midnight, ISIS also began to target rebels with rocket launchers just as the rebels started to kick off a new offensive against Assad's men. I know there are a lot of conspiracy theories floating in the air; things like ISIS are an Iranian-American project and are here to annihilate Sunni areas, however, there is one thing we can be sure of right now and it is that Assad and ISIS have conspired against the revolution. ISIS and Assad are working in tandem daily to consume the weak and scorch the land. ISIS has killed more anti-Assad Muslim fighters in Syria than they have killed Assad's army.

Assad already has a history of training and collaborating with ISIS (when it was called ISI) against the Americans in Iraq, something even his ally – Iraqi Prime Minister Nuri al-Maliki – accused him of. According to proof from the Syrian National Coalition, many ISIS field commanders are former military or intelligence officers in Assad's army who are now directly coordinating military operations with Assad's forces, giving them vital intelligence about rebel fighters and facilitating the recapture of rebel-held territories.

At first, the extremists from ISIS launched a charm campaign to win support among many opposition fighters and even formed alliances with tribal and militant groups. However, after they deceived people into joining them under the pretence of fighting the Syrian regime, people began to quickly realise they are, in effect, fighting Assad's fight. Local rebel brigades were all but obliterated; entire units destroyed or chased out of areas they had liberated from Assad. At the end of 2013, when many Syrian cities were being barrel-bombed heavily, we began to notice how ISIS was never targeted by Assad's air force, despite their conspicuous and large camps, easily visible huge, black-painted buildings and convoys clearly marked with their flags. Instead, it was the smaller and less visible outposts of the Free Syrian Army and civilian neighbourhoods that came under heavy attacks, which lasted months. Rebels became suspicious, and so raids were carried out on ISIS camps, which confirmed the alleged ties. Syrian army ID cards, Iranian-stamped passports, and weapons and ammunition from the Syrian regime were found at ISIS headquarters. Many times, we've witnessed ISIS pretending to fight Assad sporadically – or at least caught them lying about it on cyberspace – but the regime does not even pretend to strike them at all. Instead they pretend to be spectators when in fact they are essential players. This phenomenon is clearly demonstrated even now, as the regime continuously bombs rebel checkpoints.

Outsiders tend to think that moderate rebel groups and extremist groups are mixed in with each other. This is, however, not the case. They have their own distinct territory and have their own clear checkpoints marked by huge signs. Until now,

ISIS has no physical confrontation between Assad, but instead focuses it's 'jihad' on fellow Muslims. The rebels can't match these madmen, who are armed to the teeth. However, these foreigners aren't the same as the ones we've seen here before – most of them kept their heads down and did as instructed from Syrian commanders. ISIS is full of heartless heavy-handed men who remind us very much of the Hezbollah soldiers that once ran riot here. These foreign men who have absolutely no connection to Syria do as they please; they can give death sentences without provoking tribal warfare, and unlike locally based brigades who are part and parcel of our community, they don't face angry backlash from the locals if they get a decision wrong.

The Free Syrian Army have always been held accountable by the public – most of the soldiers fight in areas where they have extended family and relatives, but with ISIS, there is no room for scrutiny. We sit back and watch them masquerading as the new saviours of Syria.

These foreigners who have different ambitions than the rebel Syrian fighters remain the fastest growing and most operationally active group. At the same time, a stagnation of fighters joining the Free Syrian Army has limited the growth of the fractured revolution and resulted in the loss of more than a third of the revolution's liberated territories to ISIS.

The entire world is complicit in allowing terrorist foreigners to infiltrate Syria. Syrians asked for help; the world stalled while young people from around the world gathered together and answered. We can say with confidence that these unwanted terrorist guests have taken over and made the rebels and revolutionaries irrelevant. Most Syrians see all the mad foreigners who come here with no sincere interest in the Syrian cause and the Assad regime as different sides of the same blood-soaked coin.

Whether Baghdadi or Khamenei, Putin or Nasrallah, Zawahiri or otherwise, all foreign fighters who are aiding and abetting criminals of the worst kind have something in common: they deny Syrians the right to exist.

'I'm Hodan, the sister from Birmingham.'

Emad glided through the crumbling building in stealth mode, his powerful muscles rippling, as we made our way into an apartment full of mostly Chechen ISIS escapees lying in wait for help from smugglers. There she was, the young Somali girl. Tall and slender, her body swathed in soft *jalabiya* folds, she came forward to greet us. '*Sis, subhanAllah*. Praise God, we didn't think you would make it.'

'Nice to meet you, I'm Fairouz from Twitter and this is Emad, my fiancé.'

Emad had already shaken hands with Hodan's husband, a Chechen who'd been handpicked for her by her ISIS recruiters. He kept his gaze down because my face was uncovered but mumbled a gentle *salam*. He was a thin figure; a wisp of strawberry blonde hair fell over burnt freckles, a Soviet gun on his arm, and he wore socks with sandals.

He sat in one of the armchairs and she perched on the arm. I couldn't take my eyes off her. Her skin was radiant, spectacular. The war had not spoilt it, and her natural lips were full and plump. There was an awkward exchange of words between Emad and Hodan's husband, Abu Huraira al Shishani. Then

Hodan began to speak fast in her strange accent, nasal and difficult to understand at times.

She began from the beginning, leaving nothing out of the timeline. '*Wallahi*, at first we felt elated and happy here, you know? It felt like I had finally come home.'

ISIS had welcomed the group from Birmingham warmly, but they were soon sent to training programmes where they began to see how the heads of ISIS operated.

'They literally worship Abu Bakr al-Baghdadi and make up religious laws on the spot.'

'Tell them about the horrible treatment,' the Chechen says to her in broken English. Hodan is gregarious and Abu Huraira is shy— but somehow the odd couple made an effective team.

'Oh yes, they have no respect for the average person. They are the most arrogant bunch ever – we were treated with no love at all.'

According to Hodan, they were just human fodder and could never have an opinion.

'Once, a brother, he wanted to get married cos he was getting older, and you know he thought that coming to the *dawlah* (state) would mean getting hitched, but every time he asked the commander, he was told that it was better Islamically if he was to continue being a guard rather than get married.'

Many jihadis think that marriage is part of the package when they arrive, but it is in fact only the chosen ones who enjoy the women. Youngsters are sold fairy tales only to come here to find out they've bought into a nightmare. Hodan, however, was married off because they feared she was a troublemaker.

'I went on hunger strike – many others did too. It's common, a lot of people want to escape but they can't, so they try to die or get ill instead.'

She describes how marrying Abu Huraira was a blessing in disguise. One of the first things he taught her was that what ISIS was doing was not in accordance to the Quran and Sunnah.

'We fought jihad in the *Kavkaz* – Caucasus – but we'd never seen such foolishness ever.' He shook his head. 'We thought that we would be living like the *sahaba*, the companions of the Prophet Muhammad, but when I saw their ways, I realised this is not authentic pure Islam, this is pure satanic evil.'

He was regretful but kept it hidden. He knew the fate of the many Uzbek and Afghans who had tried to escape; he'd taught his new wife how to pretend to be enthusiastic and eventually they won the trust of their keepers and managed to escape – here.

Emad, with support from other Free Syrian soldiers, helped the couple make the journey safely towards the Turkish border, where they stayed in a smugglers' tent. Five nights ago, they attempted to cross the border, but the Turkish army caught them. Abu Hurairah was handed back to ISIS, while Hodan was allowed into Turkey, where her brothers waited to take her back to England. They told their relatives in Birmingham that she'd been a TEFL teacher abroad.

On the journey back, as a warning sign to others who wanted to flee ISIS camps, ISIS torched her husband's body. He lay on the ground not far from the border with warning notes stuck to him. 'This is your fate if you try to escape.'

His head lay beside his chest.

28 May, 2014

When Hezbollah thugs first invaded the Syrian revolution, they would do the same as these ISIS freaks are doing now, which is to create more division between Sunni and Shiites. Not far away in al-Salamiya city, also in the Hama province, where the majority are from the Ismaili Shiite sect, ISIS has driven out Shiites and Alawites. The Shiites of the town were known to come out with great passion in anti-regime demos but are now going through the sectarian cleansing that Sunnis face under Assad's men. The regime and ISIS keeps trying to stir sectarianism and to convince the world that this is a sectarian civil war, which is the opposite of the truth. The recent attacks by extremists against Shiites will result in backlash against Sunnis, even though the attackers are not Syrian. It was the same when the repugnant Shabiha and Alawite soldiers massacred entire villages of Sunnis, and innocent Shiite locals had to take the heat.

Innocents who die in Shiite or Sunni villages are all poor without any money to flee. They are just victims of a bigger game played by Islamists and Imperialists. They die while rich Alawites and rich Sunnis enjoy life in Dubai with the millions of dollars given to them by relatives of Assad for their loyalty.

Where are the so-called 'Friends of Syria' who promised us support? Why is it that Assad's extensive allies and foreign mercenaries support him in all possible ways? Perhaps it is in the interest of other autocratic governments to elongate our struggle for freedom so that their own countries don't revolt.

Just as much as the monster that is ISIS needs to get put down, we need to ensure we deal with and remain focused and outraged at the regime that caused its creation. Media networks around the world seem to enjoy the more sensationalist tales from the ISIS camp, which, to Assad's relief, distracts from his crimes – which are a million times more brutal and barbaric than that of ISIS. As Assadist jets repeatedly bombard neighbourhoods and rebel hideouts, while leaving ISIS well alone (best of buddies), you've got to ask why. And if you answer the why, we can collectively deal with the what. Therein lies the answers and how we can unite against all forms of tyranny. Be it from foreign terrorists or a mafia regime (peas of the same pod), we Syrians will not accept the fact we have two choices – or the lesser of the two evils.

We won't stay under the foot of Bashar al-Assad or live under ISIS anarchy. Assad always preached his famous slogan – 'me or terrorism' – but what makes him so sure that ordinary secularist Syrians who rose up against Assad extremists won't rise up against religious opportunist extremists?

20 June, 2014

The war carries on. Deadly and slow. Morale is low. My friends Bassam and Madmour came to visit us this evening. They bought with them large containers of food, labelled with the flag of Qatar – food that was previously stolen by the regime's soldiers. A relief for the women in our village, who were scouring the garbage for food the past few days, increasingly forgotten with each passing day, increasingly on their own, When the last aid truck came from somewhere in England, which was some weeks ago, Syrian mothers were pushing their infants on to the truck. 'Take him with you, please save them! Keep her for me.'

Their children look like they're from Ethiopia, bones poking through the skin, but at least we'll all survive the next week or so. Finally sacks of rice, some pasta, chickpeas, oil, sugar, canned soups, and beans and, most importantly for me, coffee.

The moment you're lying in bed, scrolling through Twitter, and you hear a fighter jet coming. The sound gets louder, you realise the plane is close and is low. Then it climbs up again and then comes straight back down. Little girls start screaming, babies burst out crying. These are the cruellest moments.

If you're sitting in the living room, one family member will say their shahada, pray to God; some like my mother will just clutch her cross with one hand and grab someone to hold with the other; some people are wide-eyed; others pay no attention; a sleeping person will wake up and sit up.

The bomb is bound to land any second but where? Is it our family this time? Then with a terrifying loud noise, it lands, the house trembles, and you feel the vibration go through you, but thank God, it is not us who are flattened. At least not this time.

We are stuck indoors as ISIS has banned women from leaving homes, except if they need to go to hospital to give birth. I haven't heard from Emad. The last time he called, we had only sporadic signals; the FSA are probably on the run again. The Free Syrian Army isn't what it once was. It has been so badly infiltrated now. Few good people remain here. I am still stunned when the names and faces of the world's most wanted men appear on our screens because they are right here, running our lives.

When I managed to get hold of a male chaperone to go to a main town, it felt like we were in an alternative universe. Heavily bearded men patrol the streets and keep a close eye on us. A doctor was caught treating a female patient alone in a hospital ward. The patrol ordered that he had to marry the teenager or receive lashes. The man had a wife and five children at home so he accepted the punishment instead. Shopkeepers are ordered to cover their female mannequins with full face veils. Syria is a dark, dark place.

7 July, 2014

On the brighter side, we have been eating better. With the arrival of Ramadan, ISIS have invited locals to join them for free meals. The food is diverse and substantial during this month. Chechen *khingalsh*, Somali *canjeero*, and Pakistani *paratha* are served up before morning prayer and at sunset, bowls of *harira*, Bangladeshi *beguni*, platters of Afghan kebabs and *pulao*, and plates of cous cous. The other night, we devoured *gullac*, a Turkish dessert made of rose water.

Last night, among the girls preparing the meals, I encountered Masuma, a young lady of Bangladeshi Sylheti origin who had spent a few months in Taiz, Yemen, before emigrating here. She was petite with olive skin, had deep brown eyes, and luxurious black hair, and wore a lot of makeup behind her face veil. She could have been a model or anything she wanted . But she was from Leytonstone in East London, a place that did not have any opportunities. She was delighted and impressed: a Syrian woman who spoke good English.

She peppered me with questions. What was Syria like before? What I had studied? Were there any good female tailors still around? We were able to become friends instantly as if we had known each other for a long time. She told me she was trying for a baby. Her naivety at times was worrying. She had met her husband on a Muslim matrimonial site and she had eloped from her family to live in his house in Rochdale. He had separated from his first wife and the mother of his four children because his South African-Indian wife had been a materialistic woman, who was in love with designer brands and trips to Dubai. 'He wanted someone on the *deen*, you know?'

She told me with pride that they had even met and even spent time with Abu Bakr al-Baghdadi. 'He is doing Allah's work and this is just the beginning.' She pointed at her husband on the other side of the partitioning and with unmistakable pride exclaimed how he had been involved in beheadings in Raqqah.

'But I thought shaving the beard is illegal and why does he have a haram hair cut?' I asked. My brother has told me about ISIS publicly flogging his barber for grooming violations because he added fades to a customer's hair.

Masuma explained that he had just returned from a week in England and this was part of his cover. Jihadists in the West shave off their beards to blend in better as they plan to go operational. Zeeshan is extremely security conscious and very smart; gullible Masuma isn't. She told me he is now in charge of traffic police officers keeping intersections clear in the city and he also plans to open a business. After the meal, I watched them walk hand in hand, along with the other jihadists pushing prams with their spouses. Marital bliss at the cost of our freedom. Syria was once a place where young couples hung out and flirted in parks, but now it is a land of bachelors and widows.

22 July, 2014

An ISIS soldier, high on hallucinatory drugs and obsessed with sex, has been stalking us. He entered our home, stole and demolished its contents; all the while, my grandmother screamed in his face with a show of bravery. She was not one to bow to these tyrants. Instead, she defended the house with her righteous courage. The soldier fired random shots on our street, intending for her to witness his power. But she sat mightily on her antique chair at the entrance of our house for three days and refused to negotiate.

She announced her presence like a palm tree, and never asked nor accepted help from any of the neighbours – not that there are many men left. She was full of resilience and was fearless.

Last Friday, as she went to pick up the broom to sweep the courtyard, a gunshot shook the air and a bullet pierced through her heart. As my grandmother lay on the ground, she whispered, 'It's beautiful where I am going, I can already see it.' And then there was silence for a short while.

'I bear witness that there is no God but Allah and Muhammad is the messenger of Allah.' Those were the last words she spoke before it seemed that her soul left her body, ready to be received by the angels on the other side.

It all happened within a space of a few minutes in the morning sun. It was the most peaceful passing I have witnessed during this war. She wasn't shaking with pain, she wasn't panicking with fear, and it was as though she were embracing her final abode. This was her last moment on earth, and she was in control of her journey to the next. She passed easily, gently, and with a huge smile on her face.

While it was happening, we began crying. My mother wailed. The neighbourhood women folk began to read Al-Fatiha for her soul. She was a woman of great faith. I know she is finally at peace and relieved to return to God. My grandmother was a great dreamer of portentous dreams, and the last few months she would mention things she'd seen – 'I met your grandfather today, and he said he's building a palace for me.'

We all sensed in the last few months that she was moving into a much deeper and more mystical place, a place in her mind that she couldn't wait to go to. She was absolutely ready to leave.

I clutched her hands as they grew colder and blood left her fingers. Light shone from her beautiful face . . .

'I'm sorry, it should have been me,' I wept.

It's true. It began when the foreign fighter knocked on our door and asked to meet the head of the house. My grandmother welcomed him and asked, 'What can I do for you?'

He told her that he'd had his eyes on 'the pretty young girl' and wanted to ask for my hand in marriage. She refused his offer and refused each time he knocked on our door. It was better not to tell him that I was already engaged to a rebel fighter, we firmly said we were not interested.

ISIS fighters have recently begun to hang posters that 'call upon the people of this county to bring their unmarried girls' so that they can fulfil their 'duty in sex jihad for their warrior brothers', warning that if anyone does not adhere, they will receive the full force of 'Sharia law'.

The sexually sadistic men terrorised my grandmother for three days while I was sent off to hide in my neighbour's basement for safety. The soldier entered the house, pulled my mother's hair, stole our last belongings, and shot bullets through the wall as Grandmother warned him that 'Syrian girls are not for sale' and that their actions were completely against any kind of Islamic law.

And in the end, a so-called religious fighter killed a religiously devout old woman, who looked him in the eye with confidence, pride, and determination and said, 'I only fear God almighty.'

My neighbours were there to witness it. My beloved Teta rests in peace and in the power of her good deeds that motivate each of us to continue in her stead. We still haven't absorbed her loss. I can't believe I am actually writing it. I lost my whole world. My best friend. My life. My soul. My inspiration. The woman who nurtured me and guided me through devastation. My grandmother, who would give me the last piece of bread and starve for the rest of the night.

I can hear my grandmother's voice telling me not to be selfish. 'We Syrians have become selfish,' she'd say. 'We only care when it's our own blood, but what about the thousands of others who have died? Are they not our family too?'

It gives me great comfort in knowing that she will forever be here. She would refuse every opportunity to leave to go for the camps. It was never even an option.

'I will never leave our home. Never.'

I lost my father because of you, Bashar. I lost my grandmother because of you, ISIS.

August is still vague in my memory – I do not remember when things happened exactly, but I do remember *what* happened. For the first time in a couple of years, we were getting regular electricity and some services. It felt like a normal city again because ISIS started to fix roads, repair infrastructure, and resume services, but everything else was far from normal. We had escaped to our uncle's house in another town after fearing the 'moral police', or the *Hisbah,* as they call themselves. My brother Adam decided to go back to stay with friends in Damascus and managed to get there, but for two women living alone in a place that now demanded women to cover head-to-toe in black clothing and constantly be accompanied with a male relative, we were not in a safe place. Syria was no place for women anymore. Especially not Christian women.

It was initially my friend Bassam who suggested that we contact the smugglers advertising trips to Europe on Facebook.

'You're crazy,' I told him, even though deep down I knew lots of families who'd made it there safely. It was only when my mother encouraged the idea that the decision was made.

'*Roohi benti*. Go, my daughter,' she told me one cold night. 'Go with Bassam to Sweden.'

I peered over our blanket at her. '*Enti tahki jed?* Are you serious?'

Yes, she was.

In fact, many local families had been pooling their money together so that one teenager from their family could be smuggled to Sweden. This is because once a young person receives asylum in Sweden, they are entitled to sponsor their families through the reunification procedures and immigration officials assist with their paperwork and with the cost of the trip as well. This Scandinavian country offered us our last, best hope for a future on this earth with its permanent right of stay and full social services, including income and housing, to all Syrian refugees.

The exodus from Syria for us started with a phone call to a smuggler from the Viber app. At midday, one warm Tuesday, a bullet-riddled Toyota came to collect us.

I had just finished the last meal my mother had prepared for me. Ahmad, the tenant's youngest son, had seen the overloaded truck approach first. The dozen children outside were playing.

'Travelling?' He looked solemnly over at the scary men with machine guns in the truck making space for us.

'Yes,' I said.

Ahmad shrugged. He'd seen his father's guts cut out of him by an Assad government doctor, he'd scraped his cousin's body parts from the ceiling of their classroom, and he had recently enlisted in the rebel group Ajnad al-Sham.

We joined three other families to make the dash through the mountain passes that separate Syria and Turkey. Warned against carrying too many belongings that would slow us down, I carried only one small Nike rucksack filled with essentials, like my underwear, sanitary towels, two jumpers, a lipstick, a blanket, my camera, and diary.

With only the help of the torches on our smartphones, we navigated the checkpoints on the road out of Syria. I was nervous about being a Christian passing areas where ISIS were active. It was a short but dramatic journey along deserted paths and mountain plateaus. Our feet were sore and blistered. We didn't relax until we saw Turkish signposts. Most of the group collapsed with fever then.

Sipping on fresh Turkish lemonade and apple tea, gazing at the deep blue waters, for once, free from purplish body parts, sewage and blood, spirits soon lifted and we made it to the capital in buses.

Sat in a teahouse in an Istanbul ghetto, the idea of a direct boat ride to the southern coast of Italy troubled me deeply. I'd remembered my mother's last words, to me – '*Ala mahlek ya benti*. Carefully, my daughter.'

There'd been news of another sinking vessel, and I knew I could not afford to be careless as the others. Had I really thought this through? We looked at the man we were now to entrust our lives with: he was a Syrian Gypsy from a community known as the Dom – marginalised and shunned by society and associated with crime and immorality. And now, this once poor man was richer than and in control of the lives of Syrians in Istanbul, the same ones who were heavily prejudiced against the likes of him.

'*Kheir, shu malkom el yom*? Is everything okay? What happened to you today?' Bassam nudged me.

Until that point, I had been strong and fearless, and even maintained my calm as we navigated our way in trucks to the Turkish border. However, I wasn't ready to face the water like I was ready to face bullets in the mountain tracks. During the discussion, the smuggler suggested that there was another safer way, but that it would cost me another four thousand dollars to the additional three thousand I had paid already.

'We can buy you a ticket to an African country that doesn't need a visa, but it will have a stopover in Morocco from which you will take a flight to Stockholm instead,' he suggested.

'What if she gets caught in Morocco?' Bassam asked, a sudden tightness to his voice.

'Don't worry, we have insiders at the airport that will take care of her,' he reassured my friend. 'Well, you have your family gold Fairouz', Bassam turned to me. 'I want to see the jewellery you have,' said the smuggler, bashfully. I put my hand inside my bra where the gold was secured to make sure it was still all there. Bassam had Saran-Wrapped our money safely and he'd taken that out too. The smuggler held my mothers jewellery greedily in his hand, but his black eyes sought my huge gold necklace in the paper bag beneath. 'I'll take the ring and bangles as well as this'. 'I don't want to give you that', I said, my voice catching in my throat, my hand grabbing my priceless necklace. The smuggler sighed loudly. Hesitantly I handed it back to him. At this point, I felt like I lost everything.

My flight was booked and it was time to leave the derelict hostel the smugglers had been keeping us in.

'Go now, dear,' Bassam said, tears squeezing from his eyes. 'You are in control of your destiny – I know we'll be reunited again.'

Our hearts were heavy like stones in a rolling sea, and we cried and held onto each other for the longest time.

Haggard and smelly, I boarded a plane to Istanbul. The flight was smooth and non-eventful. After my arrival in Casablanca, I sat waiting in the airport transit area, clutching the cross in my pocket A Moroccan security guard recognised the anxiety that filled my eyes.

'I'm just waiting for my mother to come back from the prayer room,' I lied to him and relaxed back deeper into my seat.

Whatever, I had no cause for concern; I was on my way to a safer haven. After what seemed like years, a young lady in uniform approached me in the early hours of the morning, asking me to confirm my name. Yasmina then handed me a ticket to Sweden and asked me to follow her to the gate and put me onto the flight. She had dark, kohl-framed eyes and even darker hair, and with her tanned olive legs, she surely could get away with any sin. Sure enough, she breezed past security with ease, even blowing a kiss at one man, and put me straight onto the plane. I slept for hour after hour, I cannot remember how long I slept in total on the flight, but I drifted in and out of consciousness the whole journey. Suddenly, the pilot announced that we were starting our descent. It was the moment I had been longing for and I could not quite believe it. I was euphoric, I was finally free. I rehearsed what I was to say to authorities upon arrival in my mind and tried to keep my composure.

At Stockholm Airport, the routine interrogation was surprisingly easy, and the people were warm and graceful. I felt like a human being again.

When at the arrival centre in the Stockholm suburb of Märsta, waiting to have my fingerprints taken and for my asylum interview, I asked the Swedish Migration Board for one thing only. 'Wi-Fi password please.'

Logging into my WhatsApp for the first time since leaving Syria, a wave of unread messages notifications caused beeping noises on my smartphone. Syrians around me slumped on plastic chairs, some resting their heads on bruised suitcases, others arriving without a single belonging, looking towards me enviously. I had run water through my hair and applied lipstick. Everyone in the Märsta reception centre looked visibly shattered, and nobody said a word. For most of them, the journey to Sweden was a more long and painful one; they'd spent months crossing countries and oceans on foot and dinghies, risking and fearing for their lives every step of the way – 'the journey of death' as Syrians call it, and the smugglers 'the agents of death.' There were a few women from Idlib, Hama, and even Damascus, all with kids, who sat and shared stories about their harrowing odysseys across the Mediterranean Sea.

Like beads of a broken necklace, which have slipped from the thread and are lying scattered, Syrian families are scattered around Europe and the Middle East. In the beginning, everyone escaped to the wealthy Gulf countries, which were accommodating, but Sweden's reputation for generosity and their forward-thinking has given Syrians hope to start all over again.

I long for my grandmother's bread, and my father's coffee, and the smell of home, but the initial difficult adjustment period and the feeling of disorientation and isolation have passed. At the Lidl supermarket where I work, the customers speak mostly Arabic and Syriac, but I am now taking Swedish language lessons with the help of the local church to help with my integration into society. I have also dyed my hair blonde to help my cause.

'You don't even look Syrian! You look European.' Ignorant comments that secretly make us happy. Looking European means I'm not treated 'less than human'. Fair haired and light-eyed Syrians are often confused for Swedes. But look closer: you can tell from the burns and scars, or from the missing ear, that they're refugees.

I don't want us to be labelled as refugees. The word is strange and dehumanising. We ourselves call each other *muhajireen* – immigrants – instead of *laji'een* – refugees. We want to be positive and optimistic and rebuild our lives and redefine ourselves here. It is already difficult to see Syrians forced to work in the lowest-paid positions such as drivers or cleaners, because before the war, they had been Syria's artists, students, doctors, accountants, teachers, lawyers, business owners, architects, computer programmers, musicians, comparative literature scholars, and much more. Although we try desperately to forget, one often sits and ponder how we reached this point; from an Arab Spring to a Swedish winter.

A sweet sun is going down here in Sweden. In the palm of my hand is the string of rosary beads belonging to my late grandmother. My fingers touch the cold, smooth shapes with my palm turned downward, just like she would have. These weren't just her prayer beads, they were her worry beads; little did I know that they'd also become my essential accessory so soon.

One night when I was stacking shelves at the supermarket, an intercom buzzed for me. I wondered who it could be.

'They didn't give their name.' My co-worker shrugged at me.

There was only one way to find out. I headed towards the back and out of the security gates to greet my unexpected visitor. I gasped with my hands over my mouth and stared at her. It was Dina. A much-aged Dina, but with the same intelligent eyes and vivacious smile. My eyes began to cloud with tears, and my entire body shook. She was alive . . . my best friend was alive.

'You're here too?' I squealed with tears streaming down as she threw her arms around me.

She squeezed me tightly. 'After I read online that you'd been sent to prison, I thought I'd never see you again!'

'It's a miracle, I made it out,' I cried. We spent the whole night in a bar talking about revolution, the war, family, aid work, and everything in between.

She described the deaths of her late mother and father, and that when they fled Rastan, they had to step over the bodies of their loved ones to get out. What a way to say goodbye. I could see the pain etched in the fresh lines in her face. She was still beautiful, but there was an edge to the beauty that had never been there before – almost like a dark shadow.

Luckily, Sweden understands the kind of help we need, and she is seeing a counsellor.

At one point, we flicked through our old friends' Facebook accounts checking for updates.

'Did you hear about Madmour? He made it to Germany for his eye operation. And his wife had a baby boy there yesterday.'

'What?! Madmour married? When? How?' I asked, amazed.

'Oh yes! And she's super-hot, look!'

'He married Helan!' I was laughing with tears.

She scrolled to the next photo, showing the first child born to them, a red-haired boy, whom they called Firas.

Four years later, I am often filled with pangs of regret filling my stomach – even though I shouldn't, but I do. However, I wonder how Syrian liberals like myself thought that the best way to modernise and democratise Syrian society was possible by revolution. And even as the barricades went up on the streets of

Cairo and Tunis, we believed that Damascus and Hama would be spared such bedlam. How wrong we were. Alas, whatever the good intentions were, there did not emerge from this revolt a nice, cuddly, liberal-democratic state with reforms and a free and fair UN-supervised election with full rights and equality for all. 'Chief among those responsible are Syrian liberal progressive forces – a group of which we count ourselves a part in,' I said to Dina.

'So, we're to blame for the state of affairs?' Dina jeered as she raised her eyebrows.

'I can't say we dug our own graves, but we held the diggers, no?'

Dina was hostile. This was a sensitive subject to bring up with her.

Indeed, the regime's reaction was needless and genocidal.

'We all agreed to sit down and talk to them from the beginning and liberals offered to help Assad launch reforms.' Dina crossed her arms in disgust.

It was true, of course; nobody fired a shot first, and it was Syria's forces that monopolised death and created the worst humanitarian disaster on earth today. However, even she eventually agreed that we'd gravely misread the ability or desire of the regime to reform the Syrian state. We did have a hand in this.

Even when I smile and laugh now, I feel guilty. I'll laugh and then I will immediately remember that young Down's

Syndrome boy who was tied to a lamp post, covered in meat, and then fed to the dogs, or that moment I held a dead protester's limbs in my hand, unable to put them back together.

I close my eyes and see these images, snapshots of a surreal world I wish did not exist, but does – a horrifying planet I left behind to come to a world where the only people who approach you in uniform are outdoor cafe staff who provide blankets and serve you steaming hot chocolate, where the lakes are free of purplish human remains, and where pet dogs are better fed then our children. This contrast disturbs me, and I do not yet know how to deal with that.

'Anyway, what happened between you two lovebirds?' Dina brought some beers to the table.

'Emad?'

What hadn't happened? I dropped my head, the weight of painful memories dragging my spirits. My stomach began to churn with pain as I relived that night I'd got a call from his brigade leader, Abu Jandal. When Assad's army bombed a building in Idlib next to where Emad was stationed, people rushed to find ammunition on the ground, and Emad had been injured while doing so. Abu Jandal informed me in his earnest tone that he had been sent to hospital in Turkey to recover. As I spoke to him, battle raged all around; I could hear the familiar thud of artillery shells landing on buildings filled with exhausted soldiers. I didn't want Emad to go back to that.

I felt a sickening revulsion ripping through my gut but relief soon overcame me as I realised that I had a chance to search for him in Turkey and convince him to join me. He was the one who had given me promises of a brighter tomorrow.

Dina put her arms around me and rocked me in her arms to console me. 'I know it hurts, sweetheart. Broken hearts need time to mend. There is life after Emad.'

'That's easy for you to say,' I sobbed. 'You were in Europe long before us. We bonded through our struggles.'

'I say you come over to my place to stay tomorrow,' Dina suggested. 'I can cook *mujadarah* as good as my mother now.'

'You girls better pay attention while I cook,' her mother had said. 'One of these days I'll no longer be around, and then what? You'll never get this food again.'

If only we could go back in time to taste one of Amti Diana's savoury concoctions. When she left us, so too did our dinner parties. Knowing she no longer had to be brave, Dina finally let the tears come.

We began this revolution for liberty and dignity, but I see no liberty or dignity in our stories. This was a fight for self-determination and freedom against terrorism and the forces of dominance for the sake of resistance. And yet I see no freedom and self-determination, nor resistance anymore, in our stories. I see horror. I see despair. I see hypocrisy. And I see brutality.

Words like contempt and disgust fall short in describing how we feel about the active participation of Russia, Iran and ISIS and all the other regime supporting gangs in the murder of hundreds of thousands of Syrians.

Last week, I received a message from my brother that made my blood run cold. My mother, my beautiful, wonderful mother, has been kidnapped and sold for just twenty-seven euros to a Tunisian ISIS fighter from Copenhagen. There is nothing I can do here. At least we know she is alive, but sometimes I feel life is little consolation when you are in the pit of hell.

In our village, Christians were given three choices by ISIS: either convert to Islam, leave, or get killed. My Christian friend told me on Twitter that many Christian families we knew converted to Islam because they were poor and could not afford to leave.

Is the world oblivious to the fact Assad has the means and weaponry to target ISIS without foreign help? Don't they know he already has a healthy amount of plane and missile donations from his foreign allies? Alas, ISIS is fighting his fight. Assad was unable to reach the leaders of the revolution, unable to reach every activist or armed rebel, but ISIS could. Assad was unable to fully penetrate the people's revolution into a terrorist manifestation so he could portray himself to the world as the lesser of two evils, but ISIS could. Assad did this calmly and deliberately.

From the very start of our uprising, he painted a false picture for the world: we activists were all part of a great foreign plot, we were all funded by *Wahhabis*, we all wanted to turn Syria into a radical Islamic state. Then the excellent strategist that he is, he planned and plotted, and waited for it to become a reality. During the first days of the revolution back in 2011, the words that were on people's tongues were democracy, freedom and dignity, and there he was talking about Al-Qaeda and Afghanistan, completely alien concepts to us as a liberal nation. So very familiar to us now.

With ISIS's expansion in my homeland, it was with a heavy heart I went to work yesterday. It was still early and Fairouz was singing Marmar Zamani from my iPod in my ears. I was stacking shelves when I felt him behind me. I can't even describe how I knew it was him; it was as if the air around me changed – became more electric. I didn't turn around, but clutched the shelves as my knees trembled.

'How?' I asked, as I felt his arms slide around my waist.

'Your crazy friend Dina,' he said, and he spun me around to face him.

I drank him in.

'Your leg,' I gasped, looking at the empty space where his beautiful muscular leg had once been.

'A casualty of war,' he murmured, kissing my hair and my neck.

I wept then, both with joy and grief, for being reunited with Emad, for his loss, for my mother's fate, for my grandmother, for my father, and just a little bit for myself.

'I'm here now. We'll get through it,' Emad whispered, wiping away my tears.

I believe him.

Last night in Emad's arms I dreamt that I went to Syria. I know they say you can't smell in dreams, but I disagree. All I could smell was apple *nargileh* and cardamom, henna and galingale, and aniseed.

And jasmine. It was heavenly.

Lipsticks & Bullets

Notes

Notes

21277219R00225

Printed in Great Britain
by Amazon